ELEPHANTS ON ROLLER SKATES

IDEAS THAT RUN AWAY FROM US ABOUT TRUTH, POLITICS AND THE WAY WE LIVE

ELEPHANTS ON ROLLER SKATES

IDEAS THAT RUN AWAY FROM US ABOUT TRUTH, POLITICS AND THE WAY WE LIVE

PETER SHELDRAKE

Travelling North

Front cover image by Dorling Kindersley
Dorling Kindersley RF, Getty Images

Portrait of the author by Linda Kent

For Linda

Contents

Table of Contents

1. Introduction

In 1908, a young academic at the University of Cambridge published a short guide for the academic politician, a satire that, as is sometimes the case, contains more truth than you might have expected.[1] Francis Cornford had observed his learned colleagues at work, and noted that there were some key strategies they used, especially to stop any changes taking place in their comfortable ivory tower. Two of his favourites were the *Principle of the Wedge* and the *Principle of the Dangerous Precedent*. The Principle of the Wedge was that "you should not act justly now for fear of raising expectations that you may act more justly in the future" - something to which no wise person would want to make a commitment! Similarly, the Principle of Dangerous Precedent is that "you should not do now an admittedly right action for fear you, or your equally timid successors, should not have the courage to do right in some future case"[2]. In other words, every thing one does that has not been done before is either wrong, or if it is right sets a dangerous precedent, so clearly it is better to do nothing for the first time! What wonderful advice, to which we might add that both these principles are today summarised in terms of what is often called the *Slippery Slope*, which is that once one does something new, there is no way to stop that action leading to further actions, the process inevitably snowballing with consequences too horrible to consider!

I thought of the slippery slope some time ago while walking around the City of Melbourne. There I saw an arresting sign: a picture of a rhinoceros on a skateboard. The sign was there to remind pedestrians to watch out for trams, especially in the pedestrian precincts. Under the picture, the sign commented that anyone seeing a rhinoceros approaching on a skateboard would get out of the way! Well, a tram weighs as much as 30 rhinoceroses - so be careful!!

To my mind that sign also suggested another image, that of an elephant on roller skates[3]. I saw this, too, as a warning. For a long time, we have used the phrase 'the elephant in the room', to represent a big and critical issue of which everyone is aware and knows is affecting what is being done, but which no one is willing to articulate and discuss. Common sense tells us that we need to discuss the elephant in the room. Reveal this big but unspoken topic, and then we will be able to make progress on the issues that are facing us without being blocked by what is being left unsaid.

However, having identified an issue of this kind, there are many times when discussion continues without our noticing the elephant is no longer in the room. It has escaped, on roller skates, and is hurtling along down a slippery slope – dangerous and almost unstoppable – and we are dragged along, unable to let go!! An elephant on roller skates is an idea, a belief, or a philosophy, that we have stopped thinking about in a clear way. We have acknowledged the previously unspoken issue, and then believed it has been resolved. We have recognised there was an elephant in the room, but then allowed it to slip out of our minds so that, as a result, it is free to run away from us. The issue is still affecting us, not because we haven't acknowledged it, but because we have stopped paying attention to it. Without thinking further about the issue, we fail to realise that it is still shaping or constraining the way we live, pulling us in a particular direction. We do not seem to notice what is happening.

This book is about a number of elephants on roller skates. They are ideas that have surreptitiously got out of control, and at the same time slipped out of focus. We no longer see them clearly – we hardly see them at all – but they are still racing along, carrying us with them, often leaving a trail of chaos and destruction. It is not enough merely to recognise and admit that there is an elephant in the room, as if naming an issue were sufficient. Failing to pay attention, in time we will find we have to rein in an escaped elephant if we are to save ourselves from being taken to a conclusion we neither intended nor would have chosen.

In the chapters that follow, I have identified some of these fuzzy runaway ideas. They concern a range of areas of our lives. Some have to do with the nature of society, embracing such matters as the operations of the marketplace, or the ideology of libertarians. Some are more individual, covering such topics as keeping in touch with others, or telling the truth. In each case the topics I have explored come down to such very specific concepts as justice, truthfulness, respect, loyalty, liberty, and even habits. If some of these issues seem more important than others, well, all I can say is that elephants come in various sizes, from the very big down to quite small ones – but they all can drag us in unanticipated directions.

In writing about these ideas, I often touch on the work of philosophers: after all, their task is to explore questions about such matters as how we live together, what makes a good society, and so on. However, I am not a philosopher, so I write as 'a man on the street'. In referring to various philosophical analyses, I touch on works that I find hard to understand (and each time I reread them I realise there is so much more there than I had understood the first time around). If nothing else, I hope that my comments and references encourage you to read more: there is a rich body of philosophical debate for you to explore, and I am simply providing some sign posts for you to follow.

While this book addresses a number of topics that I believe may be running away from us, I do not claim it to be comprehensive, for I suspect there are a lot of fast moving elephants out there. Rather my purpose is to encourage you think, and join me in the task of spotting elephants on roller skates, and exploring ways to bring them back under control. At the end of the book I have written about some of the ways we can maintain our focus as 'elephant spotters'. I hope you will find suggestions that help you set about curtailing the stampede.

*****

There are a number of stories in this book that illustrate issues that I want to explore. Where the stories are about me, I have said as much.   Where they are about other people, I have changed names, details, and even settings to ensure confidentiality.

There seems to be a convention today to list everyone who might have contributed to a book or influenced thinking over the years. I prefer to take a rather more conservative approach, and only name those who have played a really important role. While many unnamed friends have been generous in discussing some of the topics I cover, I do want to acknowledge that I received invaluable editorial assistance from Douglas and Emily Cardwell, Hayes McNeill and Tom Mullen. Despite their best endeavours, I still have problems with superfluous commas and unnecessary dashes.

Many years ago I read a comment by Sir Isaac Newton, who was reported as saying "if I see a little further, it is by standing on the shoulders of giants". I haven't been able to stand on the shoulders of giants, but I have been able to learn from some extraordinary people. Three of those were people who played a part in my development. Edmund Leach taught me to think, and to rethink. Anselm Strauss taught me to care. Charles Handy showed me how to see things in a new light. In more recent times I have a huge debt to Stephen Carter, who I met at The Aspen Institute, and whose writing has been an inspiration. How fortunate to have learnt from such giants, thinkers who, in different ways, have all been guides, ahead of me but still showing a path worth following. However, they are absolved from any responsibility for what follows, as on this occasion the content is entirely my own doing.

There is one other enormous debt to acknowledge, and that is to my wife Linda: she is my source of inspiration, my firm critic, and my companion in adventures in the world of thinking – I love her deeply for all of that.

2. Trying to do the right thing

One the principles we confront early in our lives is the importance of "doing the right thing". We learn about it at home, when we are visiting relatives or when we are taken out for a meal. We learn about it in school, where we have to deal with formal school rules, and the equally important rules of the games we play. You quickly learn that doing the right thing is the way to be accepted, to belong and to keep your membership in a group.

As we get older, we start to recognise there are shades of grey in doing the right thing (no, not those fifty shades of grey!). In fact, soon after we start going to school, we learn that you don't "tell on your mates". If the teacher asks who was talking behind her back, we keep quiet. If we are asked point blank, we say, "I don't know". Doing the right thing by one group often means we don't do the right thing by another! This often means that we have to tell deliberate untruths, rather nicely called 'little white lies'. We *should* tell the truth, after all that is the right thing to do, but instead, we sometimes tell a little white lie because we think it is safer, kinder or easier to skip over being frank and honest, and so we gently bend the truth.

Sometimes telling a white lie is easy. A friend calls and invites you to go out for a drink: you are tired, but don't want to seem rude – this is the second time you have been invited out – so you respond, "Look, I'd love to, but I promised my mother I would go round there tonight, and help her do a bit of cleaning: it's getting harder for her now". It just trips off the tongue, and no one is hurt.

Actually, it isn't always easy. The next morning, your friend calls you at work. "I tried calling you at your Mum's place last night, and she said you weren't there. She seemed a bit confused". "Oh, yes, well Derek called and said he couldn't get his car started, so I had to go and help him, and bring him home". Phew – that was close. Of course, I am making it easy. Sometimes the story runs and runs, and the more complex it becomes, the more likely the whole edifice will fall apart. Well, that might seem like an elephant on a set of roller skates, but it isn't: I think it is more like a rabbit jumping about, keeping us on our toes. After all, you can always call a halt and say, "Look, I feel bad about the other night. I was just tired, and made up an excuse, and look at the trouble it has got me into. Let's make a new date right now, and you can tell me that I should have learnt my lesson!!"

There are some cases where doing the right thing can be a lot more complicated. We can find ourselves drawn into situations where a little white lie will not suffice, and we are part of a much bigger fabrication – no longer white, but a dark grey, if not actually a black lie. Such a situation arose a little while ago in one of the offices of a multinational company (as I mentioned in the Introduction, while these events did happen, I have changed some of the details: the industry, the context and the names of all those involved).

The essence of the story is quite simple. The company needed to send a large batch of drugs to France, as part of a new marketing initiative. When the drugs were delivered, the local office was asked pay various import and customs charges. Back in the US dispatch office, Frank realised he had cost the company a lot of money. If he had sent everything to Monaco, the company could have avoided significant costs in relation to import tariffs and a value added tax. Moreover, the cost of then sending the drugs out to a number of hospitals in France would have been almost the same as those costs would have been in shipping them from Paris.

Frank decided to pretend there had been a shipping error. He told the shipping agents that *they* had made a mistake, and that the drugs had been intended to go to Monaco. He also told them that there was a way round this mistake. If they amended the delivery order and replaced it with another sending the goods to Monaco, he would arrange to send them on from Paris. By this means, the various taxes would no longer have to be paid.

All went according to plan. The shipping company agreed to amend the delivery sheets, and Frank sent the boxes over to the sales office in Monaco. However, instead of containing the drugs, the boxes were full of old newspapers. The drugs that had been in the boxes remained in France, and were sent out from Paris to various hospitals and medical centres. To cover up his duplicity, Frank told the Monaco office that some boxes were coming, and they could be thrown away. The staff in Monaco were puzzled, but then Head Office often did strange things! However, when the boxes arrived one of the sales staff couldn't contain her curiosity. Heidi opened a carton, peeked into the box, and discovered what was inside. She told her boss; he made some calls, and then he told her what had happened.

Heidi found herself in a dilemma. While she was happy that the new drugs were going to be available in France, she was very unhappy that lies had been told to get out of paying the appropriate taxes. She asked her boss what he was going to do. He was a little evasive, and merely said that he was not going to throw the boxes away, but would store them (she later found out he actually took them home!). She told him that she was going to do something, and he agreed that the situation needed to be addressed – but he made it clear that he was not going to be the one who did anything.

At the start, it all seemed so easy. She would get in touch with Frank's manager and tell him what had happened. Then she started to think. What would happen if she did talk to his manager? Would Frank lose his job? Would her boss get into trouble because he had not said anything? Would this also get back to staff at the shipping company? Quite obviously, if she did say something it was going to cause trouble of some kind. Heidi was about to become a whistleblower. To add to her concerns, a friend told her that whistleblowers often suffer as a result of their honesty: they usually lose their jobs, and find it hard to be employed elsewhere.

Heidi's friend was partly right: many whistleblowers do find it hard to get another job. Some start a new career promoting ethics and responsibility - like Sherron Watkins, the whistleblower at Enron[4]. Some blow the whistle and incriminate themselves, as happened to Bradley Birkenfeld, who blew the whistle on UBS, but was prosecuted and spent nearly three years in jail for helping a client defraud the IRS. At least he received the benefit of the 2006 review of rewards for whistleblowing. In the US you can obtain a reward of 15-30% of the recoveries made by the IRS as a result of your actions: he received $104m just as his prison term was coming to an end[5].

Whistleblowing is tricky. At first glance, it seems that the whistleblower is simply going to tell the truth, which is surely the right thing to do. However, whistleblowing raises a number of issues, of which "telling the truth" is but one component. In most companies there is an ethic of "not telling on others", the very topic we mentioned at the beginning of this chapter when we mentioned that you learn you don't tell on your mates at school. It is a "right way to do things" that is deeply embedded in many work and social cultures. Whistleblowers find themselves shunned by their company because they did "tell on others", and broke an unwritten rule in the corporate culture. Such actions are seen as disloyal.

There was another element of corporate culture that Heidi realised was at stake, which is that you do not jump over your boss to talk about something that has happened. There is a hierarchy, and it is to be respected. Being loyal to the boss is another way in which we accept how we should behave, adapting to group norms even when such behaviour can lead to quite unacceptable outcomes. Indeed, when Heidi went back to talk to him about it further, he commented, "Perhaps this is something that we should leave alone. Poking our noses into other peoples' business can lead to a lot of trouble". While he was troubled about what had happened, he could see some of the possible consequences that were playing on Heidi's mind, and he was suggesting they should not be the ones to initiate events.

On the other side, Heidi was also concerned that she (as well as her boss) was already being drawn into the events that had taken place. By not saying anything, they were sitting on some important information, and her boss was holding some critical evidence: they were in a position to do something. In fact, it was worse than that. If he was not going to address the issue, and she also failed to say something, then they had become accessories to an illegal activity that had taken place. Heidi couldn't help feel that if she did not act quickly, the situation would simply get more complicated, and it would be impossible to stop things unfolding in a possibly catastrophic fashion.

Heidi decided to seek some "off the record" legal advice. She quickly learnt that this was a very serious situation. The legal counsel asked her to tell him what had actually happened – it was clearly not a hypothetical situation. He suggested that action should be taken now, before the situation became out of control. The company could be sued. Rather than reassured, Heidi felt even worse: now people were going to suffer – Frank, who had engineered this piece of trickery, and quite possibly Heidi and her boss as well. Frank probably had a family, and might have been the sole breadwinner. In today's world, he might find it hard to get another job. He might end up in court. The shipping company itself might be involved in some kind of action.

Is it possible to do the right thing? Is it possible for Heidi to do the right thing? You could say that once Frank had decided to act – by doing the wrong thing – he created a situation where it was difficult to do the right thing. Heidi *can* do something now, but to do it now has many consequences beyond just aborting an illegal action. Telling the truth cannot prevent what has happened but only lead to some kind of remedial action. However, whatever is done next will lead to other consequences, not all of which will necessarily improve what had happened.

Surely it is quite simple: tell the truth, and be done with it. Is telling the truth the right thing? We are back where we started. Sometimes, we tell a white lie in order to do what we see as the "right" thing. In Heidi's situation, the same problem arises: it is not just a matter of telling the truth (important though that may be), but it is also a question of doing the right thing. In many organisations, doing the right thing has more to do with respecting the "chain of command", not telling on others, and reducing costs, rather than with just being truthful. Organisations aren't democracies. If we started to tell the truth, for example telling people what we really thought about them, then today's office politics would seem like that proverbial vicar's tea party compared to the maelstrom all that "truth" would create.

Of course, the real question to be addressed is "what is the *right* thing?" Somehow the right thing seems to involve more than truthfulness: it has to do with being fair, and showing respect. Frank was not being fair, and was not showing respect, but events have run away from Frank and his actions. Now Heidi is in a tangled web of competing principles of fairness, truthfulness, illegal behaviour and respect for others. To add to her difficulties, by seeking some hypothetical advice she has drawn someone else into the situation, whose very training requires action on the basis of what is legal, regardless of the consequences. The legal counsel had no doubt about what was right.

Heidi did tell someone, a director of the company with whom she had had contact in the past. She was hoping to keep the issue internal to the company so that it could be resolved, rather than becoming a true whistleblower and going public. The director thanked her. She was not told what had happened as a result of her actions, but soon after she was invited to take up a more senior position in the company, in Italy. Was that a bribe – to thank her for saying something, and paying her to say nothing more? Or was it recognition of her value to the company? Now what should she do? Turn down the offer? Tell someone else? I am sure you can imagine that she wished she had never heard of Frank, never seen the boxes of old newspapers, and knew nothing about what had happened. Ignorance is bliss – but she is no longer ignorant.

Later on Heidi did find out a little more about what had transpired. Others made sure that the situation was not resolved as she had hoped, but rather that it disappeared, at least for a while, quietly covered over. Frank was cautioned, but didn't lose his job. The company did avoid some tax. The new drugs were available to French hospitals. Heidi decided to look for another place to work, and eventually left to work in another business. However, the real story is not our interest here. Rather, it is the way Heidi's story illuminates the challenges of doing the right thing.

Perhaps it is a bit difficult to start with talking about doing the right thing. We can begin by asking: "What is the right *way* to do something?" One answer to this question comes from looking at what philosophers have said. A particularly interesting perspective comes from Immanuel Kant, who proposed that there was a form of behaviour based on following a fundamental principle, a principle that he described as a "categorical imperative"[6]. This is something that must be done, whatever the circumstances. In his mind, telling the truth was a categorical imperative. You must tell the truth, because that is a critical ethical consideration. Not to tell the truth is to lie. To lie is ethically wrong.

The Kantian approach is an interesting one. It is comfortable – to some extent – from the viewpoint of the person telling the truth. He or she can feel morally good for doing what was right. It is unfortunate if others suffer because you tell the truth, but at least you did the right thing, because you tackled the situation in the right way. Sadly, most of us are not so morally pure and absolute in our actions, and we cannot help but think about the consequences of what we might do. Always telling the truth, whatever the circumstances and consequences, is my first example of an elephant on roller skates, something that we might accept without further thought, ignoring contexts and possible outcomes. I am sure Julian Assange must have given a great deal of thought recently about his claims that his role was to publish the truth, given the consequences that have resulted from the disclosures on Wikileaks. Having acquired the information he did, was he obliged to publish everything? Would he have been lying if he did not publish it?

The need to put limits on always telling the truth is a common theme. It is usually explored by considering a story that highlights the importance of consequences. Your son has been involved in some kind of malpractice at work, and comes round to seek your assistance. There is a knock at the door, and you open the door to see a policeman. He explains that he is looking for your son "Is he here?" Your reply is "No". You are lying, just a little white lie, because you and your son need some time to work out how to deal with the situation. It may well be that you decide the best thing to do is for him to go to the police and explain what he has done. Maybe you will decide to speak to a lawyer to get some advice. However, right now you are lying because you want some time to think this whole situation through.

It seems reasonable enough: it was just a 'white lie'. Kant would disagree, and say you should have told the truth and that lying was wrong. Of course, we can brush that aside by pointing out that this is a familiar problem with philosophers: they live in a world of ideas, and you live in the real world. We could have made the situation more dramatic, to force the point: the usual version is that we are living at the time of the German Occupation of France, and you are harbouring some Jewish people. The Gestapo comes to the door. "Are there any Jews here?" "No!" That lie is a lot more fateful. If they come in and find them, or find out later that you were lying, you will be executed, and so will the Jews you have been protecting. What would *you* do in such circumstances: tell the truth whatever the cost? It is an impossible question. You would have to have been there to really know what you would have done. However, using drama to illustrate the issues at stake can sometimes lead us to miss a crucial point. A lie is a lie, whether or not the consequences are life or death, or merely embarrassment.

However, while there might be a right way to do things, so let us, for the moment, accept that it is to tell the truth, well that only works well when the situation is relatively simple. By the time Heidi was in a position to tell the truth, the situation was already very messy.

We often refer to tangled situations of that kind as wicked problems. A wicked problem is different from a simple one (a tame problem) in a number of respects. First, a wicked problem is complex, and it is actually best seen as a whole set of intertwined problems. Second, it does not have a stopping point, there isn't a simple solution that will resolve the problem, but, rather, anything you do to address the problem may manage or fix one element, but will have consequences for other parts of the problem. Wicked problems do not have solutions, they simply have better and worse alternative actions. Dealing with climate change is an example of dealing with a wicked problem. There is no simple solution to climate change, there is just a range of actions that may alleviate some of the issues that sit inside this complex problem, but any action you take will have consequences. The challenge is to pick the ones that are least bad, and that appear likely to do some good.

This helps us understand Heidi's situation. She may feel she cannot find the right thing to do, but she can identify some courses of action that are better, and some that are worse. As she saw the situation, just telling the truth about what had happened (and being willing to tell the truth publicly) would not be a particularly good approach. A lot of people including herself, as well as her company, might suffer. As we know, she chose to let someone senior in the company know about what had happened, and let him deal with the situation.

Perhaps we can see some other approaches that would have been equally effective (if not wholly truthful), and might have less serious consequences than just telling the truth. One might be to let the French government know there has been a shipping error. That would be hard to explain. Goods that were intended for France had been sent to Monaco. They were now being sent to the correct destination, and as a result there was some tax due. Even thought such a story sounds unreasonably complicated, the chances are the French Government would be happy to get some additional tax revenue, and would see no reason to investigate further. Of course, Frank would have to do this, which would mean he was telling another lie, but at least one that ameliorated the situation. Would that be a white lie?

Most of the time, real situations today are wicked, not tame. They demand that we do the "right" thing by weighing up alternatives and their likely consequences, and then taking the 'best' approach (the most positive, the one with the least downside), and hope that there are no unpleasant unanticipated consequences that appear after the event. Most of the time, such situations are considerably more complex than the issue that Heidi was facing. In practice, when we are thinking about how to do the right thing, there is no right thing to do, just a judgment to be made about what is likely to work best.

We all understand this approach when we apply it to areas other than business. Consider the case of bringing up children. There are many occasions when it is far from clear what is the best thing to do – when you catch your teenage son using drugs, for example. You don't want to push your child into becoming a secret drug user. You do want him to stop. You don't want him to form covert alliances. You do want him to mix with "the right crowd". You don't want him to be found out at school, and suffer the indignity of punishment, or even expulsion. As is the case with so many of the challenges of bringing up children, when something goes wrong, you wish it hadn't gone wrong. But it has, and you have to try and find the best way to deal with the issue. In this situation, as in so many we face, the question is no longer, "Can I do the right thing?" but, "What is the best approach I can adopt to address the issue now, and to ensure I minimise further problems down the track?"

Are there some other approaches that philosophers have developed to which we might turn in dealing with complex problems? Kant is clearly at one extreme, demanding that we tell the truth at all times. The utilitarians, who developed their ideas when writing in the 18th Century, had a rather different approach. They suggested that the best course of action was the one that maximised the benefit (the happiness) for the greatest number of people, and caused harm to the smallest number. This suggests a measure that can be used to assess alternative actions in wicked problems. Weigh up the costs and benefits of each alternative, and proceed with the one that has most on the benefit side[7].

The utilitarian approach is very practical. It does not rely on some kind of fundamental moral principle; it just rests on the very pragmatic consideration – how much harm, how much benefit. Just as in the case of Kant's categorical imperative, however, what seems simple is not as easy as it appears at first glance. How do you assess harm? We will have a lot more to say about that in a later chapter. For now, imagine how Heidi might apply this principle. She would quickly run up against a very tricky issue, which is that we never know the consequences of an action: we can guess what might happen, but the future is both unknowable and unpredictable.

She thinks about Frank, and the harm that this is going to cause to him and his family if 'the truth' gets out. However, it may be the case that Frank was following a system that had been used several times before in the shipping department, condoned by his manager. Perhaps Frank was working in a psychologically toxic atmosphere, and this would give him the chance to get out, and tell the world about how his company operated: he would be the whistleblower. Perhaps Frank believed that the concept of "moral hazard" applied to his situation. He was able to take a risk because he would not be liable for any costs that might be incurred if things went wrong. The idea of moral hazard might have led him to believe that the company would pay if the consequences of his actions came to light. Moral hazard is often cited as the reason banks were willing to sell risky securitized mortgages which are seen as one of the factors that caused the Global Financial Crisis in 2008: they were happy to take on the mortgages, because they knew, once sold, they would not have to bear the costs if the borrowers were unable to meet their obligations.

The utilitarian balance is simple in concept, but the balancing of costs against benefits requires us to look at both what *is* going to happen and what *might* happen, and the latter is something we cannot know. Like rigid moral precepts, utilitarianism works best in uncomplicated situations. To put that rather differently, both rigid moral precepts and utilitarianism are examples of elephants on roller skates. If we simply follow these ideas without careful thinking, we may lead do things that, with thought, we would have avoided. We may find ourselves on the edge of a steep slope, with an elephant trying to pull us down!

Can we do the right thing? I have found it useful to consider the approach of 'practical reasoning', a field that was revitalised in the 20th century by Stephen Toulmin and others. It had been a very important area of analysis by theologians some centuries before, but had fallen into disrepute as a form of 'academic disputation'. Albert Jonsen and Stephen Toulmin argued that certainty is an infrequent characteristic of reasoning (it only applies in such areas as symbolic logic and mathematics). He suggested that most reasoning is contextual, or practical, as it has to take account of the nature of the problem and the circumstances that surround it[8].

This is an approach that would be familiar to students of jurisprudence. In legal reasoning, the task is to assess the application of laws (some of which may be contradictory or overlapping with others) in the context of the specific events to which the law is to be applied. In law, this leads to precedent; decisions that help us consider a situation in a way that is based on the logic that "in these circumstances, it would be reasonable to apply the law in this way". Precedents themselves are always open to re-examination, and situations are never exactly the same. Thus practical reasoning, like legal reasoning, always demands that we look carefully at both the theory and the realities of application, thinking through what makes best sense at the time. The analogy with legal reasoning is a topic that we will return to later.

This, surely, is what we might expect Heidi to do, to rationally analyse the best way to proceed, and it was that kind of analysis that led her to choose to tell a director about what had happened. You can't be dragged by an ideological elephant into believing it is just a matter of "always tell the truth, regardless of consequences". As human beings, in order to do the right thing we need to combine reason with pragmatics, logic with an appreciation of the complexity of situations, and think through the best thing to do, at the time, and in the circumstances. We can do the right thing, but to do so requires thought and reflection, not an "off the cuff" reaction.

There is, I would like to suggest, one more issue sitting inside this question of what we should do. Throughout our exploration of Heidi's dilemma, we have touched on morals, but not really confronted the issue of what is the moral thing to do. Kant has a pure, and for that reason almost impossible, moral view; Heidi recognised a duty of care for others in trying to think through the right actions to take. In the next chapter we will take the issue of being 'moral' a bit further.

3. What do we mean by moral?

Recently a friend of mine asked "How can you be moral, and be a Republican?" He is a very thoughtful and well-read person, and yet he said it with such vehemence that I realised that it was clearly a comment based on deep feelings. As a result that phrase has lingered in my mind for weeks, making me question what is meant by such an easily used term as 'moral'. While I want to explore my friend's question, I should forewarn you that I intend to ask the opposite question at the end of this chapter: "How can you be moral, and be a Democrat?"

If morals are the principles we use to determine what is right and what is wrong, today we seem to accept that morals are a matter of individual choice, and comfortably adopt that relativistic frame of mind by saying, "Oh well, that's their choice". However, there are occasions when differences in the moral codes we observe can be very important: ask a Christian in Egypt, a Shi-ite in Iraq, or, for that matter, a Roman Catholic in Northern Ireland. Of course, my friend was not talking about religious differences, but rather the differences between Democrat and Republican views of the world in the USA, a somewhat less challenging divide to encompass than the sectarian differences that have torn societies apart. However, politics can still be very divisive, and at the heart of his comment was a deeply felt view about the basis of morality, and that is something that is critical to how we live our lives.

Both my friend and I are making one important assumption, of course, which is that politics is not just about power and control, it is also about acting morally, and that there should be a relationship between the moral code of individuals and the moral code that underpins a political philosophy. Neither he nor I believe that politics is just an instrumental activity, but we both know that many would not share that view.

What is this strange thing called a moral code? As a working definition it can be described as a set of principles or rules to which people adhere, principles that shape the way we interact with other individuals. As a result, those interactions collectively lead to the creation of a moral (or a good or decent) society. Of course, there are some people who we describe as 'immoral', and we call them that because they don't adhere to set principles or rules to live by that we consider appropriate: following their principles in dealing with other people does not create a good or decent society. If we talk in this way, then we are certainly not relativists. We are making it quite clear there are right ways to live (assessed by such terms as good and decent), and wrong ways. As Socrates might have said, a moral code defines, for us, the way we ought to live. Moreover, we usually prefer to live with others who share the same moral code as our own, at least in broad terms.

How do we find this mysterious thing called a moral code? Some people find it easy to identify their moral code, as they adopt it from the religious affiliation they hold. In many societies, there are groups that follow different moral codes because they justify them on different religious grounds (Protestants versus Roman Catholics in many western societies). Despite these differences, in practice we often find that we are able to tolerate another person's moral code even though it has a basis different from our own. This is because we can see that we share a number of fundamental principles, even if we disagree on some of the details: for example, Catholics talk about "transubstantiation" and Lutherans "consubstantiation". This is not to ignore the power these apparently small differences can have, as countless religious wars have demonstrated.

If moral codes for many people derive from their religious beliefs, then within a country with a diversity of religions this raises the question as to whether there has to be a moral code that applies to all the citizens of that country, irrespective of personal religious beliefs, or it there is scope to allow difference and dissent?[9] This is an important issue in a country like the United Sates of America, where there the Constitution provides for a rigorous separation between church and state (I am not claiming that this is always followed in practice, of course, as current debates about prayers before meetings of School Boards and others make clear). An example of the consequences of that Constitutional separation between church and state makes this clear.

Religions differ on their view of what constitutes marriage. In the west, most religions define marriage in terms of heterosexual monogamy, one man and one woman. In the Middle East, some Islamic countries allow polygamy; one man may have more than one wife. Clearly then, given that the US has citizens whose religious preferences include Islam as well as various forms of Christianity, then the only way to keep religion out of marriage is to decide that it is a state matter, a legally recognized union, not a religious one. However, if marriage is a legal issue, then this raises an interesting challenge – why should a legally recognised union have to be based on the practices of some religions and not others? Surely, a legal union can be between a man and a woman, a man and a man, a woman and a woman, or, for that matter, a woman and two men. In a multi-religious nation where state and religion are kept separate, "marriage" should be a legal matter and nothing more – recognising a union, and identifying what that union means in terms of such matters as property rights, responsibilities for children, etc. That doesn't preclude having a religious service as well, but the actual union is a matter of law, nothing more[10]. I am sure I don't have to tell you that this is not the way most people see this issue in the US at present, although some changes are starting to take place!

Of course, moral codes do not have to be based on religious principles. Some find the basis for their moral code grounded in a different kind of philosophy, for example there is one approach called 'humanitarian'. This is a moral code that is based on what makes us human, and what we should respect in other humans. Others look to the principles set out in some key document: the American Constitution; the accumulated precedents developed through the application of common law; the International Declaration of Human Rights; these and other sources are used to justify the principles that underpin our notions of equity or fairness. Yet others establish their moral code from a very simple but basic precept, "do unto others as you would have them do unto you" (although I still prefer Confucius' view of this: his version was "do not do to others what you would not have them do to you": in many respects the negative is far more powerful!).

If moral codes are principles or rules to live by to create a decent or a good society, then this suggests two further topics to explore. First, how is it that we can live alongside other people who have a different moral code? Earlier I suggested this may be because we recognise there are some underlying moral principles that appear to be fairly similar across different codes. Is this because there are some features of morality that are more universal, or deeper, if you prefer? Certainly, if we look at the underlying moral principles of a number of religions and others groups in society, we do see many issues that keep reappearing: respect for the lives of others; liberty; fairness or justice in how people are treated. However, science fiction writers enjoy presenting us with imagined worlds with moral codes that seem very different from our own. As I type these words, I am starting to wonder how often we slide over words like just, moral or fair without carefully analysing what they may mean to different people.

Let me use as an example the concept of the "sanctity of life", a way that some people describe the view that any good moral code should respect the lives of others. If the right to life is shared among many religions, the term "sanctity of life" turns out to be a loaded phrase. It is code for a set of beliefs about when life begins, and who has the right to determine whether or not a fetus can be aborted. This is a contentious issue. If people in the US are no longer killed for being Roman Catholics, some have certainly been killed for assisting in abortions. From the moment the Supreme Court determined that it is a woman's right to decide whether or not she should have an abortion (at least up until the point that the fetus could survive outside the womb), there has been a steady process of restricting and narrowing that right.

This may seem to be an argument about facts. When does life begin? Is a fetus a sentient human being? At the same time it is also a moral argument and a practical one: who has the right to make such decisions, and on what basis? Those who are arguing for a change in this regard put forward an interesting argument: the belief that life begins at conception is behind the suggestion that the Supreme Court should overturn that Roe v. Wade decision, and that this was a decision that should have been "left to the people" rather than having it placed it in the hands of unelected judges. "Left to the people" can only mean, of course, leaving it to governments at the Federal or State level to determine their own abortion laws (we do seem to accept that we need governments - the alternative would be mob rule!). Better here to step away from allowing this to be a matter for the Supreme Court, whose task it is to be interpreting the Constitution, and move this back to elected assemblies. In fact, we can see that while the Supreme Court did made a clear decision, many States have been whittling away at Roe v. Wade, constraining and limiting practice. However, while this has been the practice, the reason we have a Supreme Court is to ensure that matters are not determined solely by votes and legislative assemblies. For this reason, we allow the Supreme Court to check and even to overturn legislation that does not meet some fundamental (moral and Constitutional) principles.

This example leads us to a second topic: is a moral code a static thing, or does it evolve and change over time? Certainly this has led to many schisms in the world of religions: the issue of change pits the orthodox, the fundamentalist (those who see that everything must be understood as it was first written down), against those who are reformists (willing to reinterpret what was said against the changing nature of the world in which we live). The battle between traditionalists and reformists (of whatever kind, religious or not) is constantly fought over matters of interpretation. There are many interesting examples, but one example, an issue that still causes a great deal of concern and political maneuvering, involves the second amendment to the US constitution which states: *"A well regulated militia, being necessary to the security of a free state, the right of the people to keep and bear arms, shall not be infringed."*

What does this amendment mean? The US Supreme Court, which is constantly asked to examine the meaning of the Constitution and its amendments, recently stated that the Second Amendment protects the individual's "right to keep and bear arms." This interpretation is seen as supporting the right of all law-abiding Americans to exercise the right to own firearms and to use them for such activities as hunting, recreational shooting, self-defense, and the protection of family and property. Is that what the Amendment says? The Supreme Court says, "Yes".

Some people would argue that such an interpretation can only be justified if you remove the first 13 words – "A well regulated militia, being necessary to the security of a free state": if the security of the state is now maintained by a paid militia (the armed forces, and all those other agencies like the CIA, FBI, etc.), then there is no longer a need – or a necessary right – for people to be able to keep and carry firearms. This has returned on to the political agenda in recent years as massacres (especially the one at Sandy Hook Elementary School in 2012), raise the question as to whether the freedom to have any kind of firearm is really appropriate.

The gun lobby, the NRA and other advocates of the freedom to carry firearms, resort to the Second Amendment to justify their views. They do so on the basis that this right is enshrined in the Constitution. Ironically enough, if you were a fundamentalist, someone who reads the *whole* text and defends it as it is written, wouldn't you be on the side of restricting the use of arms? However, interpretation is always open to alternatives and argumentation. One of the challenges the Supreme Court faces is as to whether its role is to apply the rights set out in the Constitution as they are written, or also to interpret them in the context of US society today. Reflecting on the two issues of the right to life and the right to carry firearms, it seems we support the Supreme Court when we like what it says about the application of the Constitution, but disavow its right to interpret when we don't like the outcome!

It is not just a matter of fundamentalism, of course. On top of questions of interpretation (what do these words mean?), moral codes can rest on principles that are themselves contradictory or overlapping. As many Christians know, The Bible contains such statements as "thou shalt not kill" and "an eye for an eye, a tooth for a tooth". So we pick and choose, emphasising the one over the other as we see fit. You are not to kill another person, except in such cases as accidental death or justifiable homicide. However, killing other people is acceptable in war isn't it? Well, it is acceptable to kill those opposing soldiers, but not civilians, except that today we accept 'collateral damage' (which sounds so much better than "civilians killed in military action"). If you are the President of the United States you may choose to kill people who are potential threats to our society, not people with whom we are at war, and you may choose to do so knowing that there will be extensive 'collateral damage'. President Obama has made it clear that he recognises the importance of the debate over the use of drones and missiles, and the debate about the limits to the use of drones continues; but so does the use of drones to kill people with whom we are not at war.

On the other hand, while we accept killing as a necessary part of war, many societies no longer support capital punishment in relation to criminal offences such as murder, except that more than a few still do so. This is even the case in some of the States in the US. Despite the fact that there is no evidence to suggest that capital punishment for murder is a particularly effective deterrent, many State legislatures still believe it is the case. One part of that might be because of the lingering view that punishment should be of a kind that fits the crime (the Christian Old Testament principle mentioned earlier: "lex talionis, or an eye for an eye").

For some advocates of capital punishment this is not an issue about the principle of the right to life, but a matter of utilitarianism, doing what is best for the majority even if it is harmful for a minority. Almost inevitably, the topic of capital punishment, and punishment by incarceration, raises the topic of liberty, one that sits firmly in the wording of the First Amendment to the US Constitution. That is a wonderfully complicated area in terms of interpreting our moral code – so much so that it is reserved for the next chapter. It deserves a discussion all by itself!

The Supreme Court decision about the Second Amendment raises yet another issue, which is the misrepresentation that can occur through omission. In the previous chapter we referred to "white lies", untruths told for "good reasons". These are quite different from deliberately misleading through failing to provide all the necessary information that will make a truthful disclosure. This is a technique practiced by politicians of all persuasions. Paul Ryan gave a wonderful example of this at the Republican Presidential Convention in 2012, when he accused President Obama of failing to act on the recommendations of the National Commission on Fiscal Responsibility and Reform (Bowles Simpson, as it is known). He neglected to point out that he was among those who voted against the Commissions recommendations being put forward to Congress, effectively derailing the reform process. Not surprisingly, he also failed to mention that President Obama had taken up many of the ideas in other proposals and actions. Selectively telling the truth may not be lying, but is it moral? If you think Paul Ryan's actions were not moral, what do you think about the Supreme Court's decision on the right to bear arms? This *is* a complex area!

Discussion of the complicated nature of moral codes allows us to sweep away one view, which is that we can talk about a moral code as if it were a paradigm: as some say when discussing what they see as the breakdown of moral codes, "the paradigm is broken". We have to thank a philosopher of science, Thomas Kuhn, for getting this word into our lexicon. He defined a scientific paradigm as: "universally recognized scientific achievements that, for a time, provide model problems and solutions for a community of researchers", i.e.,

- *what* is to be observed and scrutinised
- the kind of *questions* that are supposed to be asked and probed for answers in relation to this subject
- *how* these questions are to be structured
- *how* the results of scientific investigations should be interpreted

Two paradigms cannot be reconciled with each other because they cannot be subjected to the same common standard of comparison: they are incommensurate. However, moral codes are not like paradigms. They may suggest how we should look at the world, but they are full of inconsistencies and contradictions, and one moral code can sit quite happily alongside another: there is no paradigm to be broken.

So, with all that initial bit of ground clearing, let me return to my friend's comment: 'How can you be moral, and be a Republican?' What did he mean by that? Perhaps it might help if we sketch out the key elements of a Republican view of the world. Here is a quote from

Mitt Romney's website when he was seeking to become President in 2012:

> *"Mitt Romney believes in America. He believes that liberty, opportunity, and free enterprise have led to prosperity and strength before and will do so again. America, however, must take decisive action to roll back the misguided policies of the last three years, empower our citizens, and restore the foundations of our nation's strength."*

> *"He favors a set of economic policies that will enable every American to get ahead through education, hard work, and a willingness to take risks. Accordingly, he opposes higher taxes that discourage investment and kill jobs. He believes that the tax code needs to be simpler, flatter and fairer. As President, he would work hard to make America once again a country where everyone who takes initiative can flourish."[11]*

This quote is very illuminating as it contains two very important points. First, it makes a clear claim about a decent society: it should be a place where *anyone* (my rewording) who gets on and takes the initiative can (not "will") flourish. It is a world where you are rewarded for your efforts and capabilities. That is an underlying moral value we will examine in a moment. At the same time, it is making another point – that the current system is broken, and that there is a need to restore America to the way it was: a clear comment on what is seen as years of increasing government intervention and control over peoples' lives. Restoring the traditional approach will reduce the cost of government – which it is argued is becoming too large a burden to bear, and we will have a sustainable country again (and, by the way, you will have more money in your pocket, as taxes go down, thereby offering an approach that appeals to our natural stinginess).

This, essentially, may be called a 'libertarian' view of the world. I should add that, in today's complicated world, there are now many versions of libertarian: for the sake of simplicity I am referring to that core version of libertarian that seeks to maximize individual choice and reduce the role of government.

Perhaps we should begin with the issue of the morality of a society in which people are rewarded according to their efforts. Surely this is the basis of the market economy, which has delivered so much. If one works hard, he or she will be rewarded in the marketplace. If he or she is lazy, fewer rewards will be provided. Fair enough? What could possibly be wrong with the idea that we get what we deserve, and what we deserve is determined by the effort we put into what we do. Not only does that seem fair, but it is also a huge incentive to those who start off with little in life: work hard, and you can become rich, as many others have done before. You, too, can be a Rockefeller, a Carnegie or a Ford, or for that matter seek to emulate those fictional heroes created by Ayn Rand, and become a John Galt, or a Howard Roark: this is "The American Dream".

Is that how the market works? In the marketplace, you will be able to sell what you have (your labour, your goods, your services) at a price that others are willing to pay. Just so, said Milton Friedman, the economist who has been credited with playing a key role in the development of the political acceptance of the market economy approach in the 1970's. But he did add a rather important rider: Friedman's view of the market was that it was the best system, provided exchanges were made on the basis that the parties negotiating in the market place were doing so voluntarily, equally, and both were fully informed.

Is that your experience of the marketplace? If we look at someone at trying to obtain a job, he or she may be highly skilled, having trained for several years, and then gained great experience in the workplace, but, if the economy or structural reform has created change, those skills may not be in demand. He or she may not get a job at all, or receive a much lower salary than expected. He or she may be new to the marketplace; employers will probably pass him over in preference for those with a track record of experience. In other words, one may lack the attributes of the privileged and find the door to opportunity closed to you. F. Scott Fitzgerald illustrated all that so evocatively in *The Great Gatsby*[12]. Seeking employment is not just a process that highlights inequalities. On top of all the challenges that derive from training, capabilities and experience, people often do not enter the marketplace voluntarily – they are there because they really need a job.

It seems odd that we even use the word 'the market' to describe the extraordinarily complex system that exists in a country to deal with the buying and selling of goods and services, for labour and for support. There were markets, physical marketplaces, long ago, and there are still some today, and these "real markets" are something we will talk about in Chapter 8: for now, we will focus on the system called "the free market".

Perhaps we could begin by looking at how we buy goods or services in the marketplace. When we ask questions about something we wish to buy, we have to know what to ask. If we don't explore some issues that may be very important – through ignorance – then it is our bad luck if the product does not perform as we expected. The seller is not going to tell us everything, and is least likely to tell you about the limits of what is on offer. Most of the time in the marketplace, we are far from fully informed, and quite often we are misinformed. The buyer of sub-prime mortgages had little idea of what was sitting inside that parcel of debts.

The free and open market is a perfect mechanism for allocating resources – in theory. In reality, there are few such mechanisms. Most transactions are involuntary, unequal and characterized by imperfect or skewed information. That means that, leaving on one side the dreams of economists, most markets are far from wholly efficient. However, we are looking at the market for another reason – that it allows each person to achieve on the basis of his or her effort. Accepting that markets are often imperfect, is that not a better approach than having the government decreeing what you can make, what you should buy? What are the values of the marketplace? Surely - at the very least - markets are blind to moral issues?

Perhaps markets are far from being morally blind. Perhaps they have at their core that very simple 'moral' basis we summarised earlier – you get what you deserve. Hard work and initiative are rewarded. Indolence and passivity are not. There is biblical justification for this – just remember the story of the master and the servants to whom he gave a number of talents (money, not skills). The servant who was rewarded was the one who used his talents to make even more money. The servant who acted conservatively as a trustee for the money he was given was cast out. It seems my friend's comments about the impossibility of being moral if one is a Republican may not be correct.

Let us now go on to the second part of the Romney promise. If one accepts that there has been a trend by government to intervene in more and more areas of our lives, then one can understand the other component of the Republican critique. We need to roll back the reach of government. If we do this, then we really can reward people for what they do: let them make the choice for themselves as to the extent to which they want to work hard and be rewarded for their efforts. This, too, is a moral issue. It is restoring the right of the individual to make choices, not have the government make them for you (except in the case of abortion, of course). This is the libertarian agenda, that each person has the right to liberty, the freedom to choose what he or she does. A person who shares the Romney promise would regard this as highly moral.

So, why is my friend so vehement that this is not a moral course? Does he reject freedom of choice, liberty? Perhaps he has read the same text that the Republicans have – John Stuart Mill writing *On Liberty*:

> " the sole end for which mankind are warranted, individually or collectively, in interfering with the liberty of action of any of their number is self-protection. That the only purpose for which power can be rightfully exercised over any member of a civilized community, against his will, is to prevent harm to others. His own good, either physical or moral, is not a sufficient warrant. He cannot rightfully be compelled to do or forbear because it will be better for him to do so, because it will make him happier, because, in the opinions of others, to do so would be wise or even right. These are good reasons for remonstrating with him, or reasoning with him, or persuading him, or entreating him, but not for compelling him or visiting him with any evil in case he do otherwise. To justify that, the conduct from which it is desired to deter him must be calculated to produce evil to someone else. The only part of the conduct of anyone for which he is amenable to society is that which concerns others. In the part which merely concerns himself, his independence is,

of right, absolute. Over himself, over his own body and mind, the individual is sovereign."[13]

The topic of liberty will be explored much further in the next chapter, but sufficient for here is to note that this is a strong call to leave people alone – except where they might harm others. Of course, the devil is in the detail, and we have to wonder what 'harm to others' might entail: that was a question that came up when we were looking at Heidi's dilemma. However, it does make it very clear that Mill sees the issue of harm to oneself as a personal matter – and certainly not something on which the government should act and seek to constrain behavior. Today's Republicans are simply reinforcing this approach.

Perhaps my friend was thinking of another principle, that of equality. He might have been thinking that it is a key feature of society that we should seek to minimise disadvantage and ensure equality of opportunity. This raises the important question as to what is 'fair', and this is another topic we will explore in a later chapter. Perhaps a good way to make sure things are 'fair' would be to take them out of the market to ensure everyone is treated the same, and even to introduce positive measures to enhance equality of opportunity. This is the justification of equal opportunity laws. It is a very different moral code from that of the libertarians as I have described them so far. If the view that I have ascribed to the Republicans is one of 'reward for effort, and liberty of choice', then this view wishes to reduce inequality, encourage caring for others and maximise opportunity for all.

Are Republicans immoral? I don't think so, and in that sense, I think my friend is wrong. One can be moral, and be a Republican. However, in placing all the emphasis on the individual and his or her participation in an open market world, they have arrived at a blinkered morality. Belief in the power and effectiveness of the market is not an "elephant in the room". In fact it is talked about all the time. However, it has become more than just a desirable approach, it has become an ideology, a view that the market is the only way to provide resources, products and services. As it is an ideology, it is most certainly an elephant on roller skates. Once belief in the value and power of the market moves on to becoming an ideology, it soon runs away from you. It leads us to believe in a world in which everything has a price, there is a market for everything. There is only one unfortunate consequence and this is that those who are disadvantaged are going to be run over by an elephant on roller skates!

There is a long history of critics pointing out that markets should have their limits, and that that there has to be a moral dimension to how we live. In recent years, one of the most articulate has been Michael Sandel, who observed that, "some of the good things in life are degraded if turned into commodities. So to decide where the market belongs, and where it should be kept at a distance, we have to decide how to value the goods in question—health, education, family life, nature, art, civic duties, and so on. These are moral and political questions, not merely economic ones. To resolve them, we have to debate, case by case, the moral meaning of these goods, and the proper way of valuing them."[14] Similarly, Jeffrey Sachs has argued recently that, "the market by itself is not equipped to achieve the triple bottom line of efficiency, fairness and sustainability"[15]

Michael Sandel's concerns about the limits to markets have led him to observe that in recent times a whole number of things that used to be "out" of the market are now "in". He suggests that the use of "markets to allocate health, education, public safety, national security, criminal justice, environmental protection, recreation, procreation, and other social goods were for the most part unheard-of 30 years ago. Today, we take them largely for granted." He suggests that we should think about two things when we look at the pervasive ideology of the market – inequality and corruption.

Consistent with his view that a fair society would seek to reduce inequality, Sandel is concerned that the market based approach will increase it. People are not equal, not just in determination to work hard, but in terms of their capabilities. The market rewards those whose capabilities are in demand, and ignores those whose capabilities are not. The market rewards those who use their capabilities effectively, and it leaves those with limited capabilities on the curbside. As has been observed many times, "the strong do what they will, and the weak do what they must" (that particular formulation comes from Thucydides writing 2,500 years ago!).

The damage done to society by corruption is even more telling. Sandel is not just talking about corruption in the form of bribes and deals. That kind of corruption thrives in marketplaces, even if it is something that has to be conducted under cover. Despite laws and regulations, there is every reason to believe that the more the market is the sole driver of society the more corrupt practices will prevail. The only change in recent years is that the forms of corruption are more subtle and therefore all the more insidious.

However, Sandel is more concerned about another form of corruption. This is what we might call moral corruption, a process by which we assess every thing only in terms of its tradable dollar worth, and in so doing ignore its intrinsic worth, assessed by other measures of value. We used to believe that children should not be bought and sold in the marketplace, but now we accept surrogacy and other measures to "buy" a baby. We don't allow people to sell their right to vote, not yet, anyway, but we certainly allow people's votes to be "bought". The market corrupts the value of things by giving everything a dollar value. In that sense, we could argue that the market is amoral, rather than immoral.

When we enter the world of moral issues, then it is values that are at stake, and values are not, in themselves, objects with a price attached to them. One cannot put a price on social well-being, aesthetic appreciation, or happiness. Clearly, the logic runs, if everything is put into the market, then values other than monetary ones are completely ignored. Since this seems self-evident, why then do so many people believe so fervently that the free market is the panacea for all our ills? Well, perhaps not all our ills. It turns out that even the most fervent advocates of the free market agree that there are some things that should be kept out of the market: these range from government measures to ensure that the market operates effectively, through to the defence of the nation, the right to vote and the education of the young. Perhaps a better question to ask is, "how do we determine which are the 'good' things that should be kept out of the market?" Sandel has argued that we need debate over these issues, rather than having that slippery slope leading to more and more to be falling down the slope to be priced in the free market.

One way to explore these questions may be to consider a couple of specific examples: the first is about physical things (in this case body parts); and the other is about capabilities (in this case learning). Both of these examples came up in an interview with Michael Sandel,[16] and they provoked some interesting questions and comments.

The first example concerns kidney transplants. In such operations, there are many charges and these include a fee to the doctor carrying out the transplant operation. However, if a live person has agreed to provide a kidney for the operation, should he or she not also be paid? As an advocate for limiting the scope of markets and the importance of moral considerations, Sandel's view was donors should not be paid, that we should be concerned about coercion and the erosion of values, the commoditisation of everything.

First, there is the matter of coercion: how can we be sure that the person selling an organ is not being forced into this action? If organs have a price, then those who are poor, needing money, and with limited alternatives to increase their resources will feel compelled to enter the body parts market, even though they might prefer not to do so. Surely it would be much better to donate a kidney, as this is a morally good action, rather than sell a kidney and thereby reduce our gift to a commercial transaction?

Richard Titmuss explored this issue some forty years ago in looking at blood donation.[17] He compared blood donation in the UK and USA: at that time donation was free in the UK, whereas blood donors (blood sellers?) were paid in the USA. He argued that donating blood in the UK was a form of the 'gift relationship', where the act of giving established a bond of reciprocity between the donor and society. Most of the time, when we give a gift to another person, there is an immediate sense of reciprocity established between the donor and the receiver, establishing a sense of obligation on the receiver's part to return the gift in some way[18]. However, to donate blood is an impersonal activity, possibly one undertaken out of a sense of social obligation. To donate blood is not to seek something in return, other than a sense of giving back to the community, and perhaps helping to create an environment in which a donor can expect to receive donated blood should the need arise. It is an altruistic act, but one that places the donor in a network of altruistic relationships.

Titmuss also argued that people would be more willing to donate blood than to sell it, that selling would act as a disincentive. Indeed, he suggested that not only fewer people would provide blood, if payment was involved, but also they would be more likely to lie about any illnesses they had experienced, illnesses that could have contaminated the blood they wished to sell.

Titmuss's book started an extensive academic debate about the roles of altruism, the market, and reciprocity. Critics made two key observations. Among these, Kenneth Arrow pointed out there is no evidence that payment reduces the propensity to donate blood, and quite a lot of evidence to suggest it is a real incentive.[19] Secondly, there is evidence that paid blood donation tends to shift the groups from which donation is more likely - towards those who are poorer, and for whom the income is more important. It is still not clear if they are any more likely to seek to mislead a blood bank about any risks their blood might carry - especially since we now have very sophisticated testing procedures. Today, selling blood appears to be an acceptable activity.

Beyond the need for blood, compared to forty years ago there is now a considerably more complex market in human products: a striking example can be found in relation to markets for human ova and sperm. Both of these can be bought, and people shopping for either ova or sperm can stipulate requirements in terms of the donors' physical attributes, intelligence, personality and so on. The price that is paid is a function of these attributes, and in this increasingly sophisticated market many who sell are neither poor nor desperate. It would be very hard to argue that many participants in this market are being coerced.

Indeed, in relation to our bodies, the issues about coercion prove to be very complex. To take a different example, I need to have money to live in contemporary society. As an able bodied person, I choose to sell my services to a company: they buy my physical and mental capabilities, and determine what they will pay. They require my performance over specified periods of time, and they even require that I remain on their premises during the period of my contract with them. I am being assessed in economic terms, and, according to how well I perform I can keep my job, or even be paid more to do new tasks or undertake new responsibilities. I accept that is the way the market works, and do not consider it immoral. Unfair? Well I probably believe I should be paid more, or given more privileges, or holidays, but not immoral.

I can sell my services, the use of my body, and some of my body parts (at least ova or sperm) and I accept that the market prices these according to the attributes that these might have. So, why not a kidney? When I think of what limits there might be on what I can do, I keep going back to Mill's statement that liberty means that, "Over himself, over his own body and mind, the individual is sovereign"[20]. Am I being coerced to work? Probably, at least in the sense that left to my own devices I might prefer to just laze around. However, the issue here is not that I am being coerced by someone making me do something, so much as the fact that I live in a society where one needs money to live, and in order to get money, legally, I will need to sell my labour, my ideas, and, yes, even parts of my body. We are all coerced in that sense, and I have no idea why I should consider the coercion that I feel is any better or worse than that which another feels: more to the point, I am unable to say that any particular level of coercion is unacceptable as compared to another.

Is there some point at which coercion is unacceptable, one that is a stopping point to prevent things going down that slippery slope? Or have we already allowed a dangerous precedent, and now we are to stop things continuing? If the latter, where was the point when the precedent was created. When we allowed people to sell sperm? Or blood? Or labour? If we were to focus on the views advocated by Republicans like Romney, you are rewarded for what you do and the choices you make: in those terms choosing to sell your body or body parts is entirely your business.

This leads to the second issue I noted above, which was about values, and the risk of commoditisation: things in the market are assessed only in monetary terms, and all other values are left out of the equation. This, too, is a tricky area. The usual objection made here is prostitution. Unfortunately, discussions about selling one's body for sex tend to conflate two quite different points. In the situation where a prostitute is forced to sell his or her services because he or she is, in effect, a slave to another person (a pimp), we would agree that this is wrong: as a form of slavery it is morally wrong, and it is illegal. However, to choose to sell one's body for money as a matter of free choice is a different matter. Once again, the market prices participation against criteria of attractiveness and risk (such issues as beauty, and the use of condoms). As a free agent, you can choose to accept the price and conditions or not. If I can sell my body, my skills and my knowledge to a company, why can I not sell the same to an individual?

There is evidence to suggest that "body commodification" is becoming more prevalent among university students, who can earn money by exotic dancing or performing erotic acts on web camera. Is this moral? Well, one observer noted, "transaction that many would see as corrupting might be viewed less judgmentally if it creates the potential for a positive result". Ms. Zelizer, author of *The Purchase of Intimacy,* commented that if a student exchanges sex for cash to cover her college expenses, she will regard that decision differently. "By saying, 'I'm doing it for tuition,' it kind of cleanses the money."[21]

Just to add to the complications in this, there is a converse problem. Many people do a great deal of work for which they are not paid, and, as a result, not given the recognition that they are due. This is the argument to put housework into the marketplace, so that unpaid people working on home duties are rewarded as much as their partners whose jobs take them outside the home. How could there possibly be a problem for charging when you use your body for work?

I used to chair the Human Research Ethics Committee of a major cancer hospital in Australia, which had some 750 researchers carrying out everything from desktop research to 'translational' research. Our concerns were largely about the extent to which patients could give informed consent to participate in a project (can you imagine the paradox of trying to make sure everything was crystal clear, while knowing how enthusiastic most patients were to carry out trials of a new drug, combination of drugs, or some other procedure, whatever it might entail). We also questioned the appropriateness of elements of a research project. However, a particularly vexing area dealt with using biopsy samples for further research. Would we be able to ensure that such samples could always remain de-identified? If one sample led to some kind of medical breakthrough, or even advance, should the patient receive some part of the reward? People were donating their genetic material for free, and I often wondered if they really understood what they were doing. At least the kidney donor is clear about what is happening, and the value of what is being 'given'.

This is a good point at which to introduce the second example that came up in that radio program. A listener asked, "why is it wrong to pay children to read?" After all, if this gets a child to start reading books, and if they find the experience enjoyable, they will continue to read books. If they do not find reading intrinsically enjoyable but like the reward, they will continue to read - and, without necessarily recognising it, continue to learn.

There is the key word: 'intrinsically'. What does it mean to say that we should read because it is intrinsically a good thing? Should we learn, develop our minds, because to do so is a good thing? It certainly is not the way the system works. Students study because they want rewards - rewards in the marketplace. They want to get scholarships to reduce the burden of study. They want to get good jobs. They may find the process of learning enjoyable in its own right, but the incentives are clearly important. Just as Kenneth Arrow pointed out in critiquing Titmuss's work, incentives are scarcely likely to lessen our propensity to do things, and they may well enhance them.

Fundamentally, the criticism of the market is that paying for something degrades it. However, we constantly seek to be reassured of the value of what we are doing, and market value may be one-dimensional, but it is pervasive. We may not like that everything has a price, but we lack any other all-embracing measure (or set of measures).

There is another issue to consider here. While the free market - ideally - ensures that economic transactions are made in the most efficient manner possible, we do accept some areas of inefficiency.

For example, the electoral process is costly and far from efficient, but the right to vote is too important to be thrown open to some kind of market mechanism. Most people seem to agree that it is important to have some mechanisms to ensure that disadvantage is minimised, through government schemes based on income redistribution, welfare support and so on - even if we continue to debate the size and scope of such schemes. Why do many people who are at the lower end of the income scale, who often rely on government services of one kind or another, still turn out in large numbers to support members of the Tea Party and other extreme advocates of 'minimalist government'?

That libertarian elephant is running away from us rather quickly right now, and it is hard to see how it is going to be reined back in. Republicans are not necessarily immoral, but they are accepting an ideology – a blinkered morality – that will slowly drain society of the very things that morality is meant to cherish. If the only measure of things is monetary value, then morality has no place left – other than to insist on the enforceability of contracts and the operations of the marketplace itself.

Is there more to be said? I think so, because Sandel's use of the word 'corruption' can be extended not just to talk about moral corruption, but also about the threat the market poses to how we see ourselves as human beings. This is not just to assert we are not tradable objects, but as human beings we have some unique claims – for ourselves and for all other human beings – that that must be kept out of the marketplace.

So now we return to the question as to what are the criteria that tell us those 'good things' that we should keep out of the market. This is the critical point that might help us avoid those slippery slopes, wedges and dangerous precedents we fear.

One answer is that we should keep out of the market those things that are our fundamental rights as human being - the right to life, liberty, to vote, to be protected from coercion by others, to be defended against invasion. These are the human rights to which we all lay claim, rights that have been fought for over hundreds of years. While rights are not cast in stone, many have proved durable: they should continue to be scrutinized and debated, but those that we accept should always be protected. One way to stop the encroachment of the market system is to build a secure steel wall around our rights, a wall that will stop any elephant on roller skates, however fast it is travelling.   These human rights are those that sit inside the International Declaration of Human Rights, (although we might note, in passing, that many are now arguing that one of the criticisms of these rights is that they are not accompanied by an associated set of responsibilities). Rights should not be traded, but at the same time those things that sit outside the box of 'human rights' should be open to discussion and constantly be re-examined, for fear we have allowed something fundamental to slip into the market.

What are these human rights? Here is my list, which you might want to consider. They are important, because their being kept quite separate from tradeable goods is one of the ways in which we might be able to prevent the free market from trampling all over us.

The first right is the right to life. I accept that people may willingly set aside that right if they believe their country is under threat, and they choose to serve in the military, to protect the rights of others. I do not accept the use of capital punishment – I do not think anyone has the right to deprive someone else of his or her right to life. As for the vexed issues of contraception and abortion, I believe that women should have the same right as men to choose not to create a new life, and I also believe that life exists when a fetus reaches the point that it can survive outside of the womb: prior to that point, the fetus is just a potential person, as is an ovum or a sperm.

The second is the right to liberty, and here I go a long way with Mill. We should have liberty in relation to our thoughts, our ideas, our ability to say what we want to say, and over our bodies: *"Over himself, over his own body and mind, the individual is sovereign."* Are there limits on this right? Yes, if someone breaks the laws of the land, knowingly and deliberately, then it may be that he or she should be deprived of his or her liberty for a period of time. However, I think we should be able to see, today, that depriving people of their liberty is done in order to help them learn to accept the rules of society in the future. Most incarceration today is a demeaning experience, and makes the lawbreaker more like to return to crime than to avoid it in the future.

We can make the experience of prison more focussed on re-education than on merely punishment: not to do so is to diminish those who break the law, to treat them as less human than the rest of us.

Mill also included the right to travel and the right to associate with others as part of the right to liberty. As with other rights, the only limits on these rights might be where there are laws, reasonably introduced, which seek to limit travel or associations because of the threat that they pose to others. As we have already noted, determining what is harmful to others is not easily resolved, and always open to further debate. The key issues here are fairness (and particularly that such laws apply to everyone, equally) and reasonability (that they can be shown to address a concern, or an issue of harm or potential harm to others in a manner that is demonstrably just and does no more than is absolutely necessary).

The third right is the right to citizenship, to be a full member of the country in which you are born, or to become the member of a country where you choose to move, or from which your parents came. I have no problem with setting some requirements to obtain citizenship outside a person's country of birth, as long as those requirements are concerned with ensuring the commitment and participation of the person in the new society in which they seek membership. At the same time, I would add that there should be political equality, so that everyone has the same opportunity to participate in the political systems of the country - including standing for office - and to vote.

Beyond these rights, there are others that require much more analysis than this chapter can embrace. There are rights to education (and in particular that everyone has equality of access to sufficient education that enables him or her to be a fully functioning and contributing members of society), to trial by jury of one's peers, to safety and protection (through defence, police and fire services), to social security (in the sense of such things as support for the disabled, an adequate form of retirement support, and also bridging support for low income earners of working age who lose their jobs through no fault of their own) and to health (and in particular that everyone has equal access to sufficient basic medical care to ensure they can live and participate in society without being held back by illnesses and injuries that can be readily and effectively treated).

Many of these rights are currently under debate. Indeed, the right to health deserves another book on its own, and many have written on this topic. Perhaps one of our greatest concerns today is that medical services are often directed towards illnesses and treatments that are determined by the size and operation of markets, and not by their impact on overall well-being: it is bizarre that erectile dysfunction should receive more attention than preventative medicine, and equally bizarre that expensive medical interventions are given to affluent people to prolong the last few months of their lives, when chronic and crippling conditions are poorly addressed. If you want to understand how the market distorts health care, just spend a couple of days talking to doctors and nurses working in the emergency department of a major city hospital in the US.

However, some would add that another thing that should be kept out of the market is our right to choose: this actually touches on the question posed earlier, where we asked why people on welfare still want the smallest role for government. Perhaps this is an indication that they appear to be saying one thing that is of great importance to them: each person should be allowed to make his or her own choices about what to do; and that choices should not be made on each person's behalf by anyone else, especially not the government. Is this a moral value? Perhaps it is. It is clearly a statement saying that what is good for me is something I should be allowed to determine. It is a view that Mill supported, but he added the rider that "the only purpose for which power can be rightfully exercised over any member of a civilized community, against his will, is to prevent harm to others".[22]

Like many people, I support Sandel's concern that we need to limit the extent of markets, and that there are some things that should not be 'for sale'. Sandel suggests that we may also want to keep out of the market things that will lead to coercion, or things that should not be valued in economic terms. The argument that this includes keeping our human rights out of the market seems accepted by even the most enthusiastic supporters of the free market. However, are there more things than these? Perhaps I am still left with a question - for things other than our human rights, what are the measures that we can use to determine what stays out and what goes in? To say that we may value some things in other than monetary terms, to say that there is a moral dimension to our lives, these statements seem immediately acceptable. Deciding when values and morality require they be exempted from the market processes cannot just be left to emotion and ideology: we need some criteria we can apply.

The capitalist market system has achieved extraordinary results. In at least this respect, Engels and Marx had it right, when in *The Communist Manifesto* they observed:

> *"The bourgeoisie, during its rule of scarce one hundred years, has created more massive and more colossal productive forces than have all preceding generations together. Subjection of Nature's forces to man, machinery, application of chemistry to industry and agriculture, steam-navigation, railways, electric telegraphs, clearing of whole continents for cultivation, canalisation of rivers, whole populations conjured out of the ground--what earlier century had even a presentiment that such productive forces slumbered in the lap of social labour?"[23]*

Indeed, the free and open market has proved to be the most efficient way of allocating resources that we have discovered. It can do this far more effectively than governments – provided efficiency is the objective. It can take monopolies and, through fair and open competition, change them into efficient and productive enterprises meeting needs in the most cost effective fashion. We have benefitted from the operations of the market, and will continue to do so.

Of course, that does not mean that the way the market operates in practice is ideal. The problem of "externalities' remains. Because we have allowed the operations of the market to assume some things are free (and this is especially important in relation to the air), and where government legislation has been inadequate to address the consequences, we have suffered. This is particularly clear today as we look at the environmental damage that has already taken place, and is likely to continue until better systems are put in place. Pollution has other consequences, too, and the consequences range from dust bowls treating soil as if it were an inexhaustible resource through to health problems caused by atmospheric particulates.

There are other issues. The idea that companies 'own' their staff, that the objective of business is to make a profit for return to its shareholders, that businesses operate outside of society rather than as part of it: all these ideas have rightly been criticised and far more appropriate models and approaches have been developed (especially through the writings of Charles Handy, and also through the work of the Centre for Tomorrow's Company). However, change is hard to bring about, and the vested interests (of capitalists – as Engels and Marx would remind us) that benefit from the current market model are proving very hard to address. Markets, in their proper place, and established on a reasonable basis, are great: markets that extend into areas that should be protected are not!

Engels and Marx were well aware of this, and while their prescription for revolutionary change was not followed, they certainly understood the corrosive effect of markets, and got that right:

> *"The bourgeoisie, wherever it has got the upper hand, has put an end to all feudal, patriarchal, idyllic relations. It has pitilessly torn asunder the motley feudal ties that bound man to his "natural superiors," and has left remaining no other nexus between man and man than naked self-interest, than callous "cash payment." It has drowned the most heavenly ecstasies of religious fervour, of chivalrous enthusiasm, of philistine sentimentalism, in the icy water of egotistical calculation. It has resolved personal worth into exchange value, and in place of the numberless and indefeasible chartered freedoms, has set up that single, unconscionable freedom--Free Trade. In one word, for exploitation, veiled by religious and political illusions, naked, shameless, direct, brutal exploitation. The bourgeoisie has stripped of its halo every occupation hitherto honoured and looked up to with reverent awe. It has converted the physician, the lawyer, the priest, the poet, the man of science, into its paid wage labourers. The bourgeoisie has torn away from the family its sentimental veil, and has reduced the family relation to a mere money relation."*[24]

I wonder if Republicans read *The Communist Manifesto*. What a foolish question! More to the point, I wonder if they realise that the libertarian agenda of the 21st Century, which they so enthusiastically prosecute, is no different from the economic development of the 19th Century that Engels and Marx so presciently observed – together with its consequences. I wonder if they realise that the (capitalist) free market they so enthusiastically support is encouraging exploitation and the reduction of everything to "a mere money relation". Perhaps they do, and consider that such outcomes are an inevitable result of "progress".

"How can you be moral, and be a Republican?" Have we progressed in our understanding of my friend's question? I think we have seen that there is at least one strand inside the Republican party that follows the traditional libertarian approach: roll back the role of government and maximize individual choice, using the marketplace as the mechanism to allocate resources and choose what you want. It is a moral position – about the centrality of individual choice – but it is a 'blinkered' morality, in the sense that it contains the seeds of its own unraveling. Taken to the extreme, it is an ideology, and an ideology that treats everything – and everyone – as determined by monetary value. My friend's concern is, of course, about that extremist position. I hope you would agree that reducing people to things, and their value determined by price, is not moral – it doesn't meet the criterion of "a set of principles or rules to which people adhere, which create a good or decent society". Well, perhaps that depends on how you define a good society: there may be many people who believe it is entirely moral to measure everything by the common yardstick of monetary value, and only some of us regard that as taking an approach to the extreme.

However, even if you share my views, we should be careful: not all Republicans are extremists. Extremism is always an easy target. Perhaps we should ask another question: How can you be moral, and be a Democrat?"

Perhaps you can already see that the same arguments can be used here as in the original question – just inverted by a mirror, as it were. The Democrat position, at the extreme, is one where the government could and should intervene in the affairs of the people in any way it sees fit in order to prevent harm or reduce its likelihood. It should ensure that the costs of important goods (like medical care and education) are the same for all. I will explore this topic in a later chapter, but for now let us imagine a situation where the government mandates wearing seat belts and helmets in your car, bright orange sweatshirts when walking along the pavement, and bulletproof vests at night! It should determine what foods we should eat, and how they can be cooked (all that regulation about the use of trans-fats). Sadly – for both my friend and me – it should remove all harmful and addictive substances from the marketplace, which will obviously go beyond cigarettes and recreational drugs (which we do not use!) to alcohol, and full fat milk (which we do!).

I could continue in this vein, and in so doing expose why people on the Republican side of politics are concerned about the extent to which government is already intervening in and limiting the liberties of the individual, and could do so even further in the future. They might argue that people should be free to wear seatbelts or not, or to choose what foods they wish to eat, as long as the costs of the consequences of their behaviour were entirely covered by themselves. Indeed, we are already seeing insurance companies introducing more and more complex policies with the effect of requiring people to pay higher rates for medical coverage if they decide they wish to continue to smoke, and car insurance companies increasing premiums for drivers they see as being "at risk".

The problem about being moral is that it is not a neat and tidy business. Being moral means confronting all sorts of inconsistencies and challenges, and accepting the broad ideologies of political parties (or companies, or churches for that matter) is a way of avoiding addressing moral issues, and letting them slip past unexamined. The very reason Heidi's story was so interesting in the previous chapter was because it did throw up the messy nature of moral codes and moral choices.

One key theme in much of this seems to be individual liberty, and I would like to explore this in the next chapter. Before doing so, I want to refer to something that I think is important, which is our willingness to confront and analyse moral conflicts. In looking at the challenges Heidi faced, I referred to practical reasoning. The antecedents of today's practical reasoning can be found in 'casuistry', a method followed by the Western churches in the past.

Casuistry was using debate to explore and resolve moral quandaries, especially those where competing principles meant there was no clear course of action. You will recall that Toulmin suggested casuistry can be compared to the practice of common law: in common law, the issue is to establish what is reasonable and fair to do in a situation where laws and circumstances are complex, and defy straightforward resolution. In the field of moral behaviour, casuistry addressed the issue of what is reasonable and fair to do in a situation where moral principles and circumstances are complex, and defy straightforward resolution. There is a fine body of precedent established in common law. It would be good to see the same body of precedents established in casuistry. So far, it has been left to academic theologians and philosophers to try and do this: their results often seem arcane and impracticable. Perhaps we need some 'common' casuistry.

4. Can we be free?

One of the truly explosive ideas that emerged in the 19th century was that of individual freedom. The idea of liberty had already taken hold – but that was largely freedom from oppression, freedom from kings and aristocracies, the freedom that was to animate the French Revolution. Over the years various writers had explored and developed the idea of freedom, some before and many after the French Revolution. One of the most important and confronting of these proved to be John Stuart Mill, when he wrote his essay 'On Liberty' (which we looked at briefly in the previous chapter)

Mill set out a manifesto for individualism in his essay, and established a basis for what we mean by liberty that has influenced political discourse ever since:

"This, then, is the appropriate region of human liberty. It comprises, first, the inward domain of consciousness, demanding liberty of conscience in the most comprehensive sense, liberty of thought and feeling, absolute freedom of opinion and sentiment on all subjects, practical or speculative, scientific, moral, or theological. The liberty of expressing and publishing opinions may seem to fall under a different principle, since it belongs to that part of the conduct of an individual which concerns other people, but, being almost of as much importance as the liberty of thought itself and resting in great part on the same reasons, is practically inseparable from it. Secondly, the principle requires liberty of tastes and pursuits, of framing the plan of our life to suit our own character, of doing as we like, subject to such consequences as may follow, without impediment from our fellow creatures, so long as what we do does not harm them, even though they should think our conduct foolish, perverse, or wrong. Thirdly, from this liberty of each individual follows the liberty, within the same limits, of combination among individuals; freedom to unite for any purpose not involving harm to others: the persons combining being supposed to be of full age and not forced or deceived.

No society in which these liberties are not, on the whole, respected is free, whatever may be its form of government; and none is completely free in which they do not exist absolute and unqualified. The only freedom which deserves the name is that of pursuing our own good in our own way, so long as we do not attempt to deprive others of theirs or impede their efforts to obtain it. Each is the proper guardian of his own health, whether bodily or mental and spiritual. Mankind are greater gainers by suffering each other to live as seems good to themselves than by compelling each to live as seems good to the rest."[25]

In setting out this definition of liberty, Mill left us with three major challenges to address. First, what do we mean by 'harm to others'? Second, what do we see as the responsibilities that society – and particularly government – has to the individual? Finally, third, what responsibility does the individual have to society? For such a forthright exponent of the importance of liberty, the challenges Mill gave us are complex and yet critical: they continue to haunt us today, and are likely to do so for a lot longer.

Mill states that the limitation on our freedom to do as we wish is that we must not cause harm to others. So, what do we mean by 'harm to others'? This was the issue that Heidi was grappling with in Chapter 1. The challenge Mill has set us is to determine *how* harm is to be identified – by whom, and against what criteria.

We can begin with a simple – and commonly used – example. Driving a car is an activity that can cause harm to others. In order to reduce the likelihood that any harm is caused, society has agreed (in most parts of the world) some fairly reasonable limitations. You cannot drive a car until you have passed some kind of test or certification to demonstrate that you can drive a car safely and understand the rules of the road. You cannot drive a car if you are under the influence of alcohol or drugs at a level that will impair your ability to drive safely. You cannot drive a car if the car itself is not in safe working order (usually assessed in terms of such things as working brakes, appropriate working lights and signals, and so on). Most people seem to think that rules of this kind are reasonable – we don't want to be killed by a dangerous driver, nor do we want someone to be driving an unsafe car. However, these are rules about *possible* harm to others – not about directly causing harm to others

There are some other rules that are a little more contentious. In some countries, you must not drive with more than one passenger until you have been driving safely (i.e. you have not been found to have been driving unsafely) for a minimum period of time (usually a couple of years). Again in many countries, another rule is that you must not drive a car without wearing a seat belt, or even without all people in the car wearing seat belts (or an appropriate safe baby capsule for someone under the age of 1-2 years). Can these rules be justified against Mills rule of 'harm to others'?

Let us begin with one of these examples, on limitations on passengers for 'probationary' drivers. Many people would say that this is a matter for a personal decision, not a blanket rule. As a passenger, I believe I should have the right to determine whether or not I get in a car with someone else as the driver, and that right is something I will exercise whether or not the driver concerned has been driving for six months or six years (or sixty years, for that matter). I am best placed to determine if there is a risk of harm to me, not have it determined by an arbitrary government law. If you think about it, this is merely an extension of the rules about being allowed to drive – this is another rule to deal with "possible harm to others". Surely possible harm to others is something that should be left to those same 'others' to assess and act on as they see fit.

There is a standard response to that argument, of course. The harm to others that unregulated driving can cause is not just a matter of someone being hurt in an accident. The costs of the medical care of people involved in traffic accidents can be very high, as well as the costs to the members of that person's family. There is both harm to society as a whole (higher costs of medical care) and an immediate harm both to the victim and the immediate family (not just in terms of medical costs, but the wider costs of potential loss of family income, psychological costs and so on).

It seems 'harm to others' can be defined as both specific – those directly impacted by someone's actions – and broad – the costs to society as a whole. The discussion over wearing seat belts in cars moves us much further into the territory of the broader definition of 'harm to others'. For the driver, being required to wear a seat belt is, first and foremost, a means to ensure that the driver does not cause harm to himself. That would seem to be something that Mill would argue is an issue we can bring to someone's attention, suggest to him, try and persuade him, but cannot require him to do. The only basis on which this might cause harm to others is to address a consequence beyond the individual, just as we discussed in the previous chapter – that there is a risk of both harm to society as a whole and immediate harm both to the driver and his or her immediate family.

The same argument presumably applies to other passengers and the requirement they wear seat belts. This is not a matter of their safety, which should be a matter for their own decision, but, again, the wider costs that would be entailed in the case of an accident. However, we are still talking about restrictions we are placing on the liberty of an individual because of potential harm to others, not because they are actually causing harm to others. I think it is likely that Mill would have argued that government should keep out of such matters as the number of passengers for provisional drivers, and the requirement to wear seat belts. Incidentally, he might also have been very interested in how these things were accomplished: people wear seat belts today because early on there were fines for not doing so. In other words, the approach used was not about harm to others (which was tried at an early stage), but simply about avoiding a costly fine!

The theme of 'harm to others' has been under debate from the moment Mill's essay was published. In the narrowest definition, Mill is read as saying the only form of harm to others to which we should pay attention is where what we do limits the ability of another to do what they would like to do. Under that definition, we would probably accept the rules about driving (certification, in full possession of faculties, and safe car) simply because without those rules, others would find it hard to be able to drive safely themselves. However, we would be unlikely to accept rules about seat belts and the number of passengers in the car (but we *might* be able to find an argument to justify both of these, if we really tried hard to do so: after all, we now have many years of statistics to show the consequences of the requirement to wear seat belts in terms of injuries, death, and the costs of medical care from motor car accidents).

With such a broad definition, almost any restriction on our liberties can be justified. There is always some cost to society, some disadvantage to a person's kin or friends that can be brought forward. These arguments on restricting our liberties are fought in the middle ground, comprising battles and skirmishes about the limits we will accept, whether we want to maximize our free choice, or we prefer to live in a 'nanny' state that accepts a duty of care towards its citizens.

This takes us to the second of the challenges that Mill's essay has left us, which is to determine the responsibility the state has to the individual. Do we expect that the state will police our liberties and make sure they are not being infringed? Or do we expect the state to actively seek out and define areas of actual – and possible – harm, and put in place appropriate limitations on our freedoms on that basis. In today's rather heated atmosphere, these matters are debated by contrasting the role of the state as an active instrument of protection and support, with that of the state as a place of last resort in areas where individual freedom is not enough.

Many factors can influence the ways in which a government acts. For example, the period after the Second World War saw a major expansion in the role of the state in many western countries. There were good reasons for that. Services had been damaged or attenuated by the war itself, and there were many more people who needed assistance (orphans, single parent families, injured and handicapped people, people with chronic conditions, potential home buyers in a situation of inadequate housing provision, and so on). However, from the 1980's onwards, many of those problems had been reduced, and demands for some services slowed or even reversed.

Today we would say governments have not proven particularly effective in actually delivering services – generally speaking the market proves to be far more efficient in the allocation and use of resources. Partly as a result of this (and partly for ideological reasons), more and more services have been privatized. This has led to a situation where many formerly free services are offered on a 'user pays' basis (the range goes from home based medical care through to university courses). Governments argue that as affluence has increased, so peoples' ability to pay for services has grown.

The consequences of privatisation have not been as positive as many had hoped. Today, there seems to be something of a split between those with higher incomes, who pay for many of the services that used to be free (and this group would like to be taxed less as a result), and those with lower incomes, who still rely on (increasingly restricted) government services, but who would like more money so that they could pay for more of what they want (and, as a result, would also like their taxes reduced). The last few years have seen the role of the state reduced, and the market playing a bigger role in everyday life.

While that has been the process in recent years, it begs the question – 'what should the state's responsibility be?' In the previous chapter, we saw how the ever increasing reach of markets both fosters inequality, and leads to a corruption of social values. Is that the inevitable price of individual freedom? Clearly almost everyone agrees that the state must have some responsibilities: as we explored in the previous chapter, Milton Friedman, one of the architects and advocates of the current model of the free market, argued that the state has some clear responsibilities. Not surprisingly, these were about ensuring the free market could operate effectively (and certainly not about providing education or health services). In his eyes, two things were essential. First, he argued that the state should ensure that conditions in the marketplace maximise the extent to which transactions can be carried out on a voluntary, equal and transparent basis. Second, there is also a responsibility to ensure there is an adequate legal framework to support the operations of the market. At a minimum this includes laws to require that contracts are binding, that there is a right to individual property (both physical and intellectual), and that there are adequate provisions for redress through the judicial system to deal with failures in carrying out the obligations of the marketplace.[26] In other words, the role of the state is to ensure that the market operates within an adequate system of rules and regulations.

While Friedman spent a lot of his time arguing about the things the state should not do (the list got very long), he did concede that there are some things that are not goods or services, and these are also the responsibility of the state: this included the defence of the realm, the legal system, and the democratic process to appoint governments. In other words, the role of the state – through government – is to protect the workings of the market, and to protect the state. Other than that, everything else should be provided in the most efficient manner possible – and that is through the open market[27].

If Friedman represents one extreme in looking at what the state should provide, so socialist countries show us what the other extreme might comprise. There the state takes on the role of providing many of the resources necessary to ensure that each person has equality of opportunity in participating in society and in developing their potential to contribute. This must include, at the very least, civic education, education more broadly up to a certain level, health services, welfare services, especially for those who are disadvantaged, accommodation services, especially for those who are poor, ill or handicapped, and various support services such as libraries, meeting places, parks, and facilities for entertainment. To do these things, the state must have adequate resources - which, almost always, means high levels of taxation.

Today we see battles across the US over whether government should continue to offer subsidized services, especially in relation to health care of social security. The challenge in these disputes is the extent to which freedom from government control will lead to the same services being offered cost effectively through the private sector: it is a battle over conflicting ideologies over how a good society should operate. On one side sit advocates of a "caring society', who believe that it is a responsibility of society, through government, to look after those who are disadvantaged or unable to meet the costs of meeting their basic needs for food, health or accommodation. On the other side sit proponents of individual responsibility, with the underlying assumption that society is a place where survival depends on effort, and those who do not work hard will receive less of the benefits, a form of social Darwinism.

While this is important to consider (and we have looked at some of this issue in the previous chapter on morals) perhaps another key question is not just what the state should provide, but *what freedom of choice* should be left to the individual. This, after all, is the very issue that the US Supreme Court was asked to consider in looking at the Obama Health Care proposals: can the Federal Government *require* that people take out medical insurance. As that judgement made clear, the Constitution (and hence the Supreme Court) cannot determine the morality or the appropriateness of legislation – that really is a matter for lawmakers. What the Supreme Court can do is see whether or not the Constitution permits particular kinds of law – in this case, as they saw it, a form of taxation. This decision made it quite clear that this is a very different requirement than that often called the 'broccoli' argument – that the state can make you do things because they are good for you, like eating broccoli! Yes, people can be taxed, and yes, if they fail to pay a tax, they can be fined. In that sense the 'individual mandate' is legal, it is within the actions permitted by the Constitution. This was a very interesting, and important, line of clarification, setting out what the state (the nation in this case) can do, and what freedom is left to the individual.[28]

In the previous chapter I argued that there were a number of rights that should not be in the market - because they are fundamental rights. Some are probably uncontroversial, at least in broad terms: the right to life, the right to liberty, and the right to citizenship. There were others that are certainly contested today: that everyone has equality of access to sufficient education that enables them to be fully functioning and contributing members of society, to social security (support for the disabled, retirement support, and bridging support for low income earners who lose their jobs) and to adequate health care.

Why are these contested? America has a long history of promoting liberty, and this has resulted in making many rights that are seen as fundamental and universal in other countries a matter of individual choice. The arguments that rage today are about where choice should be allowed, and where the provision of some kind of service is too important to be placed in the market: while this is often couched in terms of a debate about equality versus efficiency, it is also a debate about entitlement.

Clearly there is no easy rule that helps us draw the line on where the responsibility of the state ends, and that of the individual begins. This is – and should be – a matter of continuing debate. As we saw in the previous chapter, things start to go wrong when discussion ceases, and we simply accept an ideology without questioning its applicability. People should have an appropriate domain of free choice; the state should have some responsibilities. Claiming that the state knows best or that the free market is the best way to allocate resources are both simplistic ideologies that stop us thinking about where the right balance is to be found. They are elephants on roller skates.

So now we come to the third point that Mill's essay raises – what are the obligations of the individual to the state? Part of the answer to this has to be that the obligations of the individual have to be symmetrical to what the state provides to the individual. If the state ensures the proper operation of the market, then the individual must accept the validity of the rules that are set out, and should abide by them. Even the most ardent libertarian would consider that 'playing by the rules' is reasonable. If the state is going to undertake some other basic activities whose purpose it is to ensure the safety and reasonable operation of the state – previously we included such things as defence, the legal system, the democratic government system under this heading – then the individual must be willing to accept the rules that establish these activities.

For all these areas, (the operations of the market, defense and so on), the individual must also accept the responsibility to contribute to the costs of these operations: this is the basis of tax. To go beyond saying just 'tax' raises some quite different issues. Some would argue that tax has to be 'fair', and would argue that the best system so far devised is a progressive income tax. Others argue that the fairest system is that everyone pays some tax on the goods and services they consume – this will be fair, because it will mean each person is taxed according to his or her level of consumption. Finally, some argue that there should just be a 'flat' level of income tax, so that the incentive to earn more is not reduced by a progressively higher level of tax. Which of these alternatives we prefer, we have to concede at least one point, that our freedom is now limited in two ways: there are some activities that the state must undertake, and there are costs that must be met by some form of tax. These are two big constraints on Mill's freedom to do as we like.

There is another obligation on the individual that also bumps up against the agenda set out by Mill in exploring 'the appropriate region of human liberty', and this has to do with the vexed issue of freedom of expression, or as he described it "the liberty of expressing and publishing opinions". Interestingly, this freedom was not in the American Constitution, but was embedded in the First Amendment, which states: *"Congress shall make no law respecting an establishment of religion, or prohibiting the free exercise thereof; or abridging the freedom of speech, or of the press; or the right of the people peaceably to assemble, and to petition the Government for a redress of grievances,* (my emphasis). It turned out that the convention that met to draft a constitution did not think to include individual rights – much to subsequent general consternation – and the Constitution was only approved after the first ten amendments were added, (all of which came from the Declaration of Rights that George Mason had drafted for the State of Virginia).

This freedom – the freedom of speech – has been constrained from very early on, with laws against saying or publishing things that are regarded as treasonable, seditious, racially inflammatory, or using words that are considered pornographic or demeaning. Of course, there have been continuing battles over this. It is to the credit of the US that it has some of the most open provisions for free speech anywhere in the world. However, it has certainly been a liberty that has been reviewed and limited, if only to have some of those attempts to limit freedom of expression dismissed as the First Amendment has been challenged and interpreted in the face of new laws and appeals.

This is not just a matter of the law. To add to the complexities of this area, in the past twenty years the issue of 'political correctness' has added to the thicket of prohibitions and conventions about what can be said. A wonderful example of this came recently when Mitt Romney's media attack on Newt Gingrich in his home state of Georgia during the Republican presidential primaries was described as a 'Mittskrieg'. Jewish people in the US saw this as offensive as it reminded them of the 'Blitzkrieg', and a formal apology by David Axelrod had to be made.[29]

The issue of freedom of speech has also been turned the other way in debates about what can be taught in schools. Perhaps the most famous example of this comes in the field of science, where from time to time, schools and school districts express a desire to teach 'creationism' rather than 'evolution', or teach them side by side. This has raged ever since the Scopes Trial of 1925 first sought to address the prior prohibition on the teaching of evolution. The Scopes Trial did not succeed in overturning the Tennessee Butler Act, preventing the teaching of evolution in that State's schools. However, from that moment on the teaching of evolution became increasingly firmly established in schools' science classes.

Despite this, even today creationists keep trying to reinstate the creationist approach, based on biblical revelation, into science curricula; creationism has been successfully rejected as a 'scientific' theory, but many schools teach it as 'another approach'. If political correctness has narrowed our right to express our views, proponents of creationism are pushing in a different direction, arguing that other viewpoints should be taught to children irrespective of any factual basis for their justification.

While this is at the extreme, it does uncover a more fundamental issue about liberty of thought and liberty to express views: we know what we know because of what we have been taught. At a trivial level, we know about this when we spend time in countries whose language(s) are different from our own. Some words do not translate, which means either we cannot understand some things we are told, or, alternatively, we cannot explain some things to others. At a more basic level, it means that our freedom is limited by our language, and by the theories and accumulated knowledge of our society. We are 'free' inside a framework we cannot see, even if there are times when we realise there is something we are unable to apprehend.

The final element of Mill's approach that deserves comment is that we are free to follow our tastes, pursuits or plan of life without being prevented by others – however much they may try and show we are mistaken. That is an interesting freedom. Friends, relatives and conventions all conspire to limit our choices quite effectively. Some conventions rest on us lightly. It is a convention in Australia to walk on the left side of the footpath; in the US the convention is to walk on the right side. Today, however, in most cities where you walk, the convention only seems to get supported 60% of the time – at best! Perhaps that is indicative of the multi-cultural nature of most cities. I still like to wear a tweed jacket, something that is decidedly unfashionable. Despite occasional suggestions about my poor taste, most people just see it as a harmless aberration: perhaps they think that I am waiting for tweed jackets with leather elbows to come back into fashion!

Conventions are important. They enable us to live together within some comfortable ways of behaving. They also establish some important areas for contestability and rethinking. New generations tend to push against the conventions of those that precede them, in dress, in behaviour and values. That challenging is healthy - it is the very kind of thinking that ensures we don't allow the elephant of freedom to run away from us.

However, push a little harder, and you will find that some other 'freedoms' are subject to a lot of pressure: not just the resistance of conventions, but real challenge and determination. Tell your family that you have decided to sell your house (holding property is so 20th Century, you tell them), and instead you will live in a caravan in your brother's back yard. A lot of wise people will be able to explain that this is a foolish course of action. Tell your family you are going to give up your well paying job and become a writer (a field in which you have demonstrated absolutely no ability to date) and even the most supportive partner is likely to exert a lot of pressure. Start sending flowers to the nice young lady at the end of the street (young enough to be your grand-daughter) and you may find yourself at the wrong end of a restraining order.

We understand the conventions of living with other people, and yet we don't want to be too conventional. We are willing to follow a lot of generally agreed practices, but we like to push against some of them: however, we don't want to be seen as too unconventional. Where is the point of balance? Many people who see themselves as 'unconventional' often share a lot with others of the same persuasion - in dress, language and life style: they seem as conventional as the very people from whom they purport to differentiate themselves. Many people who appear quite conventional on the outside often turn out to be quite unconventional when we look more closely. It seems that superficial conventionality often allows real freedom to be practiced under cover.

Exercising our freedoms is integral to asserting our individuality. Some of this takes place in the public domain, presenting our unique selves to others (but, oddly enough, offering enough clues to allow us to be categorised and 'put in place'). Some of this is in the more private domain - in our interactions with close friends and family, at home - where we feel freer to expose the specifics of who we are and what we do. There may be a third area of freedom that is important in dealing with conventions, which is the way we think about ourselves 'in our heads'. That exploratory, imagined and sometimes fantastical self is only in our mind's eye, but it can push and pull the things we do in the physical world. Our imaginations can transcend conventions, even if such possibilities seldom make it into the physical world.

One of the foundations of libertarianism concerns choice, having the freedom to choose what you want, and that the best way to exercise these choices is to make them in the free and open market. Indeed, libertarians argue we should seek to maximise what is in the marketplace in order to ensure that we *are* allowed to choose what we want in almost every aspect of our lives, (as well as allowing the market to distribute resources in the most efficient way possible).

This is an approach that has some weighty antecedents. John Stuart Mill wrote on our right to liberty and to "framing the plan of our life to suit our own character, of doing as we like, subject to such consequences as may follow, without impediment from our fellow creatures, so long as what we do does not harm them, even though they should think our conduct foolish, perverse, or wrong"[30]. Many have written on the operations of the market, from Adam Smith on 'an invisible hand', (his way of describing the way in which businesspeople pursuing their self-interest nonetheless bring benefits to the wider society), right through to the Chicago school of economics in the 20th Century demonstrating the ways in which the market is, indeed, so efficient.

To make choices raises a number of issues, however. Many of these issues have to do with how we 'see' choices: on many occasions our choices are 'framed' and we are 'nudged' (to use the title of an excellent book on this topic by Thaler and Sunstein[31]) to choose one alternative over another. Marketing, product placement, associations, recommendations, these and many other factors influence our preferences. However, while such issues deserve attention, on this occasion I want to focus on the policy issues that arise when we examine the right to make choices.

There are many situations where we make choices just to suit our needs. Some years ago, I used to have some fun with my business school students on this issue, asking them a question: "what's the difference between Microsoft and the Australian Public Service?" It was one of those silly questions that you ask when you are looking for a very specific answer: in this case, the answer I was hoping to hear was, "Very little!" Each offers you a deal, and the only difference is in the details of the deal, and hence which of the two you prefer.

Microsoft appeals to the nerdy side of your character. "Would you like to work with other nerdy people on nerdy projects? Would you like to earn a lot of money? Well, join us, work hard - 24 hours a day, seven days a week, and make sure you eat, live and love within the company walls, and you will earn a lot. After a few years leave, and do whatever you would like, because you will be rich!" The Australian Public Service appeals to the security side of your character. "Would you like to have a job that is guaranteed for life? Well join us, work short hours, don't get paid a lot, but have income security and a good pension - and the only challenge you will face as you look out of the window every morning is how you are going to fill up your afternoon!"

The question *was* partly just fun, illustrating the differences between an entrepreneurial leading edge business and the bureaucracy of a government department. However, even in considering choices like these the way we approach our decisions is revealing. In many cases, we choose without giving much thought to the fact that our choice may be constrained by all sorts of rules and requirements. In the case of employment, that is obvious: there is a thicket of legislation affecting employment processes, work conditions and treatment of staff. Similarly, constraints often sit behind choices that seem, on the surface, just to be business transactions. Thinking of taking a river cruise on the Rhine? Well, that seems a good idea, with travel, food and drinks and excursions included. However, how many of us carefully read the fine print. Considering signing up a cable television offer you saw this week? Again, do we read all the terms of the agreement we are asked to sign? About to buy a ticket to fly to Washington? I wonder how many of us have taken the trouble to read through those minutely printed pages of conditions that are attached to the ticket.

That last example is quite revealing, because we certainly know about some of the terms and conditions - mainly those the government imposes on air travel. There are rules about what we can carry on to the plane, about congregating in the cabin and so on. We also assume there are a number of conditions that the airline has to follow to do with refueling, use of air traffic procedures, hours staff can be in the cockpit, etc. - again, these are rules set by various government agencies, on our behalf, that are intended to enhance the safety of air travel. Of course, Mill had allowed for the fact that we might be constrained in our choices if otherwise our actions can cause harm to others - and many of the rules about air travel are concerned with exactly this issue. However, in raising the issue of harm to others, Mill leaves some interesting questions on the table. Is it always clear that what we propose to do impacts others adversely? Who makes that decision? Are there any other limits on our right to make our own choices about how we live?

In relation to the question of 'harm to others', we seem to have ceded many areas of decision making to governments. This has created a highly contested area. Government legislation that is introduced to 'look after' the interests of citizens often becomes a touchstone for debate between libertarians and communitarians. The government introduces legislation requiring motorcycle or bicycle riders to wear a helmet. The libertarian objects: it is for me to decide if I am at risk in riding my bike, and to choose to wear a helmet or not. The communitarian argues that there is a cost to society caused by accidents - medical care, psychological damage to family members, and so on. Many of us are quite happy that determining whether an action causes harm to others is a contested area: we should constantly debate what is meant by harm to others, how this relates to specific situations, and the extent to which there should be rules introduced on this basis. Mill has set a measure - harm to others - but it will always be contextual, dynamic, and important to review.

However, on the third of the questions his examination of liberty raises, which was whether there are any other limits on our right to make choices about how we live, there is more to be said.

In the example of air travel, the small print we often fail to read can become important if something goes wrong. We feel aggrieved when the experience is not quite what we expected: the airline cancels a flight, and we have to wait a day to get another - at our expense! We complain, and then we are told that we should have read that 'fine print': a suggestion that often increases rather than diminishes our annoyance!! It would seem that some of these constraints on our choices are not because of 'harm to others': rather, they are protections - in this case for the business, protecting it from financial 'harm', rather than protecting us. We entered into a contract, but we because we didn't give the arrangement the close attention it required, we failed to understand what that contract specified.

The advocate of the free market would say *caveat emptor*, let the buyer beware: it was all spelt out, but you were too lazy to take the trouble to understand the nature of the deal! Milton Friedman has been one of the leading voices in explaining the virtues of the market, and he explained that transactions should be transparent - all the information should be available to both parties. He also made a very interesting comparison between government and the marketplace:

> *"The characteristic feature of action through political channels is that it tends to require or enforce substantial conformity. The great advantage of the market, on the other hand, is that it permits wide diversity. It is, in political terms, a system of proportional representation. Each man can vote, as it were, for the colour of tie he wants and get it; he does not have to see what colour the majority want and then, if he is in the minority, submit."[32]*

In other words, accept the contract when you are making a choice, and reflect on the fact that you could choose what you wanted.

Friedman is skating over a couple of issues here. First, in arguing that government requires (or enforces) 'substantial conformity', he is also implying there is something better about a system of proportional representation. Well, it may be good that minority voices get heard in the legislature, but it is still the case that the majority (whoever actually forms 'the government') will still do what it wants and the minorities will have to submit! Voting for a minority party only gets you their representation, but it certainly does not mean you will also get the benefits of their proposed policies (and yes, a minority party may be in a coalition in order to form a government, but there will still be some other parties outside the coalition)

Rather more important in his praise of the benefits of the market is the implication that anyone can buy a tie of the colour he wants, (or a scarf of a colour she wants, for that matter). In the world of goods and services, infinite choice does not exist. What is offered in the market - to a significant extent - reflects the preferences of the majority. Of course, if you are wealthy you can commission someone to make the tie or scarf you want: for the less wealthy, you have to choose among what is being offered, and if your preferences are not in the mainstream, bad luck. Choices are far from free, but constrained by what is on offer at a price you can afford, and the contractual conditions surrounding your purchase.

So far we have focussed on business transactions. However, we also make choices about those with whom we associate, and how we spend our time with other people. Suppose we decide we would like to become a member of a tennis club. As with business transactions, we may not read the rules very carefully. However, we are probably quite sensitive to the conventions and standards of behaviour that characterise this club. How do people dress - on and off the courts? Are mobile telephones banned in some areas? Is conversation in the clubhouse maintained below a certain level? And so it goes on. In fact, these issues about culture and norms can turn out to be very important: they may constrain the desirability of what is on offer, and they may constrain our subsequent participation.

Of course, conventions are important in business transactions, too, and they may or may not be covered in the rules. We want to travel somewhere, and decide to use an interstate bus line. There they are again, a whole lot of rules and conditions in small type on the pages after the ticket. Do we read those? Often not, but we do have some general ideas about what might be part of the important standards of behaviour those rules could cover: no smoking on the bus; no consumption of food or drink; no loud talking; no parties!!

So far we have been considering situations where we are able to make a choice. Some choices are made for us, of course. Some are determined at birth. Most of us grow up to find we are part of a family, with all that this entails. However, we later learn that what constitutes a family can be very different from one person to another, and the rules and requirements of our situation may be very different from those faced by another person in his or her family!

Simply by being born we find we are citizens of a specific nation. As a result, we have to accept the authority of the government of our country to legislate about things we may not do (while we are able to vote for leaders, this does not mean we can vote to have none!). However, unlike the case of being born into a particular family, as we grow older, we may make a conscious choice to leave one country and seek to become a citizen of another.

The issue of living in a country and having to accept its government is a particularly interesting one. This is well illustrated by the case of Hutt River Province in Australia. Resorting to Wikipedia we discover:

> "The **Principality of Hutt River**, previously known as the **Hutt River Province**, is the oldest micronation in Australia. The principality claims to be an independent sovereign state having achieved legal status on 21 April 1972, although it remains unrecognised except by other micronations. If considered independent, it is an enclave of Australia. The principality was founded on 21 April 1970 by Leonard George Casley when he and his associates proclaimed their secession from the state of Western Australia, in response to a dispute with the government of Western Australia over what the Casley family considered draconian wheat production quotas. Casley and his associates resorted to International Law, which they felt allowed them to secede. The government of Western Australia determined it could do

nothing without the intervention of the Commonwealth. The Governor General of Australia stated that it was unconstitutional for the Commonwealth to intervene in the secession. In correspondence with the governor-general's office, Casley was inadvertently addressed as the "Administrator of the Hutt River Province" which was claimed to be a legally binding recognition. Casley styled himself His Majesty Prince Leonard I of Hutt to take advantage of the British Treason Act of 1495 which allowed that a self proclaimed monarch could not only not be guilty of any offence against the rightful ruler, but that anyone who interfered with his duties could be charged with treason. Although the law in this matter has since changed, the Australian Constitution prevented its retrospectivity and the Australian government has not taken any action against Hutt River since the declaration. ....

In 1976, Australia Post refused to handle Hutt River mail, and following repeated demands by the Australian Taxation Office (ATO) for the payment of taxes, on 2 December 1977 the province officially declared war on Australia. Prince Leonard notified authorities of the cessation of hostilities several days later. The mail service was restored after a court case deemed that Hutt River stamps and coins were legal within the Principality and the tax requests also ceased. Hutt River residents are still required to lodge income tax forms but are classed by the ATO as non-residents of Australia for income tax purposes; thus income earned within the province is exempt from Australian taxation. The province displays documents supporting that no tax is paid but the ATO cannot verify the provinces tax status, as they can't by law comment on the affairs of individuals. The province levies its own income tax of 0.5% on financial transactions by foreign companies registered in the province and personal accounts. While the principality does not pay taxes, the Australian government's current official position is that it is nothing more than a private enterprise operating under a business name. "[33]

While this story might seem more than faintly bizarre, Leonard Casley seems to have successfully seceded from of Australia, and Hutt River Province is now a significant tourist destination in Western Australia. There are many other such micronations: 59 are listed in Wikipedia, varying from the absurd (like Hay-on-Wye which was declared a separate kingdom as a publicity stunt), through to more serious endeavours (like Hutt River Province). However, their existence is always challenged, and, more to the point, (and somewhat paradoxically), those who secede seem to replace the rules of the nation they left with similar rules of another. I wonder what Thomas Hobbes would think? In *The Leviathan*, he argued that we created government to help us drag ourselves above a life that was otherwise "solitary, poor, nasty, brutish and short"[34]. Now we secede from being governed to enjoy a better life - by being governed by someone else!

As we examine making choices to do something, it becomes clear that the act of exercising choice means that we are entering into a contract - formal or informal. Unless we take the effort to be fully informed, that choice may well involve accepting a whole lot of conditions that are not to our benefit. When we make a choice, we give up a bit of our freedom, and sometimes that cost can be quite high.

A rather different perspective on the right to make choices comes if we move from looking at choices to do something, to making choices not to do something - 'opting out' as it were. At first glance, it would seem that opting should be easy. Let us suppose I was a member of my high school alumni. One day I discover that the alumni body has decided that its principal role should be to raise funds for my old school, to cover the costs of equipment which the government is no longer willing to meet. I do not want to start paying money for these purposes, as I believe we should be pressuring the government to meet its obligations, not meekly accepting them. In this case I can choose to opt out, and I resign from the alumni association. It appears simple.

Perhaps a better example is that I like to drive. However, the government in my state has introduced a set of new rules about requirements for driving (they have determined that it is illegal to drive using a hands-free telephone or listening to the car radio). I have decided I will no longer drive. I am choosing to escape a whole set of regulations and requirements that infringe my liberty in ways that I am unwilling to accept. Sadly, I am also depriving myself of the convenience and pleasure of being able to drive, and so in opting out I am also losing out!

Rather than considering hypothetical choices to opt out, we can look at some real examples. For example, Jehovah's Witnesses have opted out of using blood transfusions, and they "request non-blood alternatives, which are widely used and accepted by the medical community. We do this because of the Bible's command to "keep abstaining from . . . blood.""" They go on to argue: "While we refuse blood for religious rather than medical reasons, many have acknowledged that this refusal has helped the Witnesses to avoid contracting many costly and fatal diseases such as AIDS and hepatitis."

This decision has led to many conflicts between doctors and members of the Jehovah's Witnesses, especially over the medical care of children. This is a very specific matter on which a group has chosen to step away from a common practice in the rest of the community. More extreme is the case of the Amish, another group that has chosen to opt out, who have rejected participation in many facets of contemporary American life. Resorting to Wikipedia, we see:

> *There are a number of distinctive practices shared by most of the Old Order Amish, the largest Amish group, (while some other smaller Amish groups have adopted practices which are either more progressive or more restrictive). Members usually speak a German dialect called Pennsylvania Dutch (Deutsch). High German is used during worship. They learn English at school. Formal education beyond Grade 8 is discouraged, although many youth are given further instruction in their homes after graduation. With very few exceptions, Old Order Amish congregations do not allow the owning or use of automobiles or farm tractors. However, they will ride in cars when needed. They do not use electricity, or have radios, TV sets, personal computers, computer games, etc. In-home telephones are not normally allowed. Some families have a phone remote from the house. Most Amish groups do not collect Social Security/Canada Pension Plan benefits, unemployment insurance or welfare. They maintain mutual aid funds for members who need help with medical costs, dental bills, etc. They do not take photographs or allow themselves to be photographed. To do so would be evidence of vanity and pride.[35]*

Generally speaking, these practices of the Amish are regarded as 'quaint' and a tourist attraction. Their criteria for opting out seem to raise less problems for most other people when compared to the

Jehovah's Witnesses attitude to blood transfusions, (although the prohibition of photography does cause a great deal of consternation at times).

How does all this affect me? Is there a limit on the things that I can choose not to do? Can I opt out of contributing to the government's medical care system? Given the judgement of Supreme Court discussed above, as a tax it is something I have to accept. It seems I can't opt out of taxes - even if I might think them immoral! Would Mill have accepted the right of the government to tax individuals?

Finally, I have to ask if opting out is doing something that is rather more serious than has so far been identified - by opting out, is this a way of ignoring my responsibility to others. Can I opt out of caring for others?

Peter Singer has been a forthright advocate of the view that we should recognise we have a responsibility to everyone else. He begins this extract from his book '*How are we to live?*' by quoting one of the women interviewed by Carol Gilligan in her book '*In a Different Voice*':

> ""*I have a very strong sense of being responsible to the world, that I can't just live for my enjoyment, but just the fact of being in the world gives me an obligation to do what I can to make the world a better place to live in, no matter how small a scale that may be on.*"
>
> *This could have been said by many people I have known, people working for greater overseas aid to poor nations, to allow farm animals the elementary freedom of being able to turn around and stretch their limbs, to free prisoners of conscience, or to bring about the abolition of nuclear weapons. ....*
>
> *These people take the broader perspective that is characteristic of an ethical life. They adopt - to use Henry Sidgwick's memorable phrase - 'the point of view of the universe'. This is not a phrase to be taken literally, for unless we are pantheists, the universe itself cannot have a point of view at all. ....*
> *People who take on the point of view of the universe may be daunted by the immensity of the task that faces them; but they are not bored,*

and do not need psychotherapy to make their lives meaningful. There is a tragic irony in the fact that we can find our own fulfillment precisely because there is so much avoidable pain and suffering in the universe, but that is the way the world is. The task will not be completed until we can no longer find children stunted from malnutrition or dying from easily treatable infections; homeless people trying to keep warm with pieces of cardboard; political prisoners held without trial; nuclear weapons poised to destroy entire cities; refugees living for years in squalid camps; farm animals so closely confined that they cannot move around or stretch their limbs; fur-bearing animals held by a leg in a steel-jawed trap; people being killed, beaten or discriminated against because of their race, sex, religion, sexual preference or some irrelevant disability; rivers poisoned by pollution; ancient forests being cut to serve the trivial wants of the affluent; women forced to put up with domestic violence because there is nowhere else for them to go; and so on and on. How we would find meaning in our lives if all avoidable pain and suffering had been eliminated is an interesting topic for philosophical discussion, but the question is, sadly, unlikely to have any practical significance for the foreseeable future."[36]

Singer's comments are almost overwhelming, as he is arguing that my freedom to do as I choose should be limited by the fact that I have obligations to everyone - to our common humanity. If there are people who are suffering harm, then I have an obligation to try to help them, even though that harm is not a result of my actions. This resonates with the Christian view that the first responsibility we have is not to ourselves, but to others, and that to serve others is the first step towards salvation. Rather than Mill's limitation on our freedom being the harm we cause to others, Singer is saying our liberty only exists insofar as we recognise our obligations to others first.

A libertarian would say that we can choose to help others, but that choice is ours to make: it is not a choice that can be made for us - by the government in particular. Singer is arguing that we have no choice in this, that we have an ethical obligation to try to reduce pain, suffering and all the other afflictions that face our fellow human beings. It is a communitarian ethic, expressing a sentiment that has been repeated by thinkers time and time again, in stark contrast to the selfishness of the libertarian ethic. It is taking Mill to task, and saying our liberty will always be constrained as long as there is a world in which the same liberty is not available to everyone.

Is our common humanity important, and should it be a constraint on our freedom of choice? Perhaps we should finish our discussion of this part of this topic with John Donne. In a Meditation written in 1642, he expressed a 'communitarian' perspective both elegantly and succinctly:

> No man is an island,
> Entire of itself.
> Each is a piece of the continent,
> A part of the main.
> If a clod be washed away by the sea,
> Europe is the less.
> As well as if a promontory were.
> As well as if a manor of thine own
> Or of thine friend's were.
> Each man's death diminishes me,
> For I am involved in mankind.
> Therefore, send not to know
> For whom the bell tolls,
> It tolls for thee.

Does being a libertarian mean you choose to no longer be involved in mankind? Can you make that choice without denying your membership of the human race?

The idea of liberty is tantalizing, a vision of what we might be able to achieve. At the same time, it is a siren song, pulling us away from our friends and colleagues and the broader community around us. Liberty gives us the opportunity to realise our unique capabilities and preferences, but it runs the risk of allowing us to ignore the rules and conventions that make society work. In practice, we have to trade in some of our liberty to be part of society: not just in ceding power and control over aspects of our lives to governments, but in accepting the constrictions of the culture and rules that characterise our social lives.

In his essay on liberty, Mill is describing an ideology, a view of the way the world might be. As we have already seen, an ideology is often an elephant in disguise. What is more, freedom, liberty to do as you please, is a strange elephant. It pulls us along, giving us the comforting sense that we are doing as we please, although we are solidly embedded in a network of habits, customs and rules that constrain our liberties, and we scarcely even notice them.

Do Mill's ideas still make sense in the 21st Century? In many ways this has been described as the time of individualism, so surely we are more likely to be pursuing liberty now than before. Indeed, there has been a lot of debate in recent years about what is meant by freedom, or to be more specific 'free will'. Some of the theories that have been put forward are clearly a little crazy – at least at the level that I can understand them.

One is that of 'determinism' – that if we could describe every molecule in the universe, its state, its location, etc., then we would be able to predict what was going to happen next, then next and so on. While that might make for some science fiction, it bears no relationship to the lived reality we experience. We know that powerful ideas can change the world – Mill was one such source of ideas that have had an enormous impact. We also know that the physical world, down at that molecular level, is rather indeterminate. We are not all part of a giant piece of clockwork.

Another idea is that of 'multiverses'. This is the idea that there are an infinite number of universes, and when a choice is made in 'this' universe, events in another universe go along a different path as if the alternative choice was taken. In this view of the world, there are lots of Peter Sheldrakes following different paths. It is a theory that reminds me of Ptolemy, and views of the place of the earth before Copernicus put things in the right place. In order to explain the movement of the planets in a universe where the earth was at the centre, end everything revolved around the earth in circles, Ptolemy had explain the motion of planets in terms of circles within circles within circles. Once we get into this kind of explanation – whether it be circles within circles or multiverses – we know that there is another, much simpler explanation waiting to be put forward.

Yet another that seems very popular at present is 'evolutionary psychology' - that what we do and the way we behave is a function of the biological process of survival of the fittest. While it may be possible to argue that language emerged as a result of evolution and the advantage that gave, it seems pretty silly to suggest that all that has happened in the past few hundred years is driven by the same process. As one commentator recently remarked, "it ain't necessarily so!" Biology has been important, but human culture is another level of development. Human culture both allows and promotes the concept of liberty in a way that bears no relationship to the drivers of evolution.

Since none of those ideas looks very promising, we might need to focus on some rather more prosaic questions that concern us today. The way in which individual choice is being realised in business is through the use of digital technologies – the individualised Google search, the individualized recommended book list on Amazon. Has technology enhanced our freedom of choice?

It might seem this is the case, as we are able to pursue our interests with greater ease than ever. The Internet is a cornucopia of information, knowledge, and entertainment, all there for the picking. In practice, we are being offered tailored products and services – and that means quite often that the market is working less than perfectly. We do not see the full range of choice; we just see the outcome that has been presented for our eyes alone.

Moreover, it turns out, as Sherry Turkle has told us, the digital technologies are actually making us less free in another sense: we are tethered by our iPhones and our computers, drawn into even tighter links with those around us – our boss, co-workers, families and friends[37] . It is a curious experience to sit on a train today, and watch the people around you. Most are focused on their smart phone, texting friends, twittering about their day, and reading the blogs, notes and comments of their circle. At home on Facebook, the freedom is even more constrained – there are posts to respond to, invitations to deal with, and the daily task of posting your contributions to the network. The technologies of the digital world promise so much, but, in the end, seem to reduce our freedoms even more than before. We are accessible at any time, on any day. Accessible also means answerable.

There is just one more twist in this, and that has to do with privacy. In Mill's day, a person could have a private life, out of the sight of others, free to pursue personal interests, hobbies, or activities. Today, privacy is rapidly disappearing, as businesses collect more and more information about our preferences, cookies alert computer systems to what we are doing, and smart programs record our every interest. If you are older, you probably fear losing your privacy; if you are young, well, it has never really existed for you. Mill's liberty presupposes a realm of privacy; without privacy, the scope of liberty shrinks even further.

The elephant of liberty must be smiling as we hang on to his tether, and all the while he keeps tricking us into believing we are free, whereas we are even more connected than before. There is an illusion of liberty. Shakespeare was a master of illusion, using illusion to mask reality, sometimes explicitly, as in the events in the forest in Twelfth Night, and sometimes implicitly, as Othello acts out his tragedy in a world of illusion. Is it always like this? Is there no real liberty, no real freedom?

While a debate about existentialism might be worth pursuing, my intentions are more modest. The concept of liberty is tangled up with many other issues. Two of these are the focus of the next chapter: fairness and entitlement.

5. Is that fair?

As a parent, or as a worker, how often do you hear the phrase "it's just not fair"? One child complains about another - something they were given, or permission to sleep over at a friend's house; one worker complains about another - a bonus paid, an opportunity to work in another division. To be treated fairly, to see justice being done, that is one of the enduring expectations we hold. Surely this is not an elephant on roller skates, but an issue we scrutinize continuously, checking our entitlements, looking to ensure equality in treatment and in opportunities?

In fact, we use the concept of 'fair' in two quite different ways. When we apply it to ourselves, we are thinking of our 'just deserts': I worked hard, and I am entitled to a bonus. I studied hard, and so it is only fair that I have a day off, and go into town with my friends. When we apply it to others, it becomes a matter of comparison - what is fair is what is equivalent. He worked less hard than I did, and therefore it would be unfair if he got the same bonus. I had to wait until I was sixteen before I could stay out until midnight, so it would be unfair if my younger sister were allowed to do this when she is only 15 years old. This is a critical division - it is the same as the difference between a Republican talking about creating a world in which initiative is rewarded (and laziness not), and a Democrat talking about a world in which everyone is entitled to same basic income, medical care or education. In a world of just deserts, you will get (only) what you deserve; in a world of comparative fairness, everyone should be treated in the same way.

One way to narrow our focus on what is at stake is to look at the issue of fairness as justice. This was a hot topic in the 1960's, as the civil rights movement was gaining momentum. One of the most memorable statements about what was fair, and what needed to be done to ensure justice, came from Martin Luther King. Speaking in Washington in August 1963, he said:

"In a sense we have come to our nation's capital to cash a check. When the architects of our republic wrote the magnificent words of the Constitution and the Declaration of Independence, they were signing a promissory note to which every American was to fall heir. This note was a promise that all men, yes, black men as well as white men, would be guaranteed the unalienable rights of life, liberty, and the pursuit of happiness.

It is obvious today that America has defaulted on this promissory note insofar as her citizens of color are concerned. Instead of honoring this sacred obligation, America has given the Negro people a bad check, a check which has come back marked "insufficient funds." But we refuse to believe that the bank of justice is bankrupt. We refuse to believe that there are insufficient funds in the great vaults of opportunity of this nation. So we have come to cash this check — a check that will give us upon demand the riches of freedom and the security of justice."[38]

While the call for freedom and justice was unequivocal, the nature of what he meant by justice was a little more complex. To be sure, justice was equated with fairness and equality. But King realised that there is something deeper here, and in his famous Letter from Birmingham City Jail, he analysed what made a law 'just'. Laws are prescriptions set out by a legislative assembly, and it is likely that - with the best will in the world - legislators will pass laws that are not just. This is how King examined this issue:

"One may well ask, "How can you advocate breaking some laws and obeying others?" The answer is found in the fact that there are two types of laws: there are just and there are unjust laws. I would agree with Saint Augustine that "An unjust law is no law at all."

Now what is the difference between the two? How does one determine when a law is just or unjust? A just law is a man-made code that squares with the moral law or the law of God. An unjust law is a code that is out of harmony with the moral law. To put it in the terms of Saint Thomas Aquinas, an unjust law is a human law that is not rooted in eternal and natural law. Any law that uplifts human personality is just. Any law that degrades human personality is unjust. All segregation statutes are unjust because segregation distorts the soul and damages the personality...........

Let us turn to a more concrete example of just and unjust laws. An unjust law is a code that a majority inflicts on a minority that is not binding on itself. This is difference made legal. On the other hand a just law is a code that a majority compels a minority to follow that it is willing to follow itself. This is sameness made legal.

Let me give another explanation. An unjust law is a code inflicted upon a minority which that minority had no part in enacting or creating because they did not have the unhampered right to vote."[39]

The fact that King uses three quite different arguments to explain what is just is illuminating. First, what is just is that which rests on moral law - or, as he goes on to add - eternal or natural law. This is an appeal to fundamental principles. Second, he suggests that what is just is that which upholds human personality. This is a sense of psychological justness. Finally, he goes on to argue about what is just in terms of the legislative process itself. This is justice through fair processes.

Why so many arguments? I suspect that this is a result of King's own awareness that no one argument is enough. The appeal to natural or moral law is one that makes great sense in a uniform culture. It made sense to argue on this basis to the eight Alabama clergymen who had written to King in jail: they would all have subscribed to a view that there is a fundamental moral law - in each case revealed to them through religion. What is tricky about this is there is no evident and unimpeachable source that is supported by everyone that also tells us exactly what constitutes the principles of moral or natural law. We can read each of the fundamental texts of various religions, and they are inconveniently opaque and contradictory. The first of King's justifications requires one unarguable statement of natural law. The existence of such a document would provide an impressive foundation for justice, but there is a problem here: we cannot agree on where to find this critical and basic source.

If there is no one certain statement of what is just, then our search for fairness requires looking elsewhere. One possible source is in seeing ourselves as the touchstone of what is fair - that justice is based on respecting our human-ness. As King says, justice may rest on uplifting human personality. That is a powerful, evocative statement - but it is not entirely clear what it means. It certainly implies that one criterion is that all people are equal. It also seems to suggest that difference is to be respected. The combination of those two statements seems to cover exactly the difference we noted before, between fairness as comparative equality, and fairness as getting just deserts.

Then King has one more argument to make: fairness comes from fair and reasonable processes (in his case he gave the examples of the scope of application of laws, and participation in their making). However, there is ample evidence that good processes can still result in outcomes that many will regard as 'unfair'. Ask any high-income earner about the fairness of the tax system, and he or she is likely to complain about special tax penalties for the very rich. Surely that is demonstrably unfair - the majority imposing an unfair rule on a minority?? Indeed, many would argue that the whole idea of progressive taxation is unfair - why should you have to pay a higher proportion of your income as tax simply because you earn more? Of course, we know in practice that many very rich people know how to minimise their tax, (which led Warren Buffet to ask why he was paying less tax than his secretary).

Is income inequality itself fair? Research has shown that many people are comfortable living in a country where there is income inequality, especially if they see that they have the same chance as anyone else to work hard and become rich. Inequality is only unfair if one is unable to do something about it. However, if one were able to work hard and become a high-income earner, why would one consider the system unjust? Work hard and get your just deserts: not the same level of income as everyone else, not that form of justice, but just in terms of getting higher rewards as a result of extra effort.

Of course, what people 'see' may not be what *is* the case. The US is unusual in that it appears many people believes that upward mobility measured by income and/or wealth is there for the taking. Anyone will be rewarded if he or she works hard, and anyone can become rich. From the outside, it is a sad but revealing to find that such a belief is confounded by the facts. The proportion of people experiencing significant upward income (or wealth or social) mobility in the US is no greater than in many other countries, and is among the worst for low-income earners. These are the people for whom opportunity is the most important, the young and the disadvantaged. You might believe in the 'American Dream', but it is just that.

So far we have explored fairness in terms of justice. However, there is another element to consider, happiness. When a daughter complains that she has not been treated fairly, the issue may be based on some legal sense of equivalence, but rather that she is unhappy. "I had to work hard to get this, and now you are giving it away to someone else without them having to do as much as I did" You can almost see the tears welling up in her eyes!

There has been a great deal of research on happiness. Levels of satisfaction with one's life seems to be tied up with such factors as income, marriage (and divorce), children, work, aspirations and health. It is also a function of comparison - the 'keeping up with the Joneses' phenomenon. What is interesting about such comparisons is that we tend to make them with people like us, not with those who are very different. Research has found that we are not as likely to feel the impact of envy when we compare ourselves with a Bill Gates (he represents more of an aspiration than a comparison point for many people). Rather, the relevant comparison is when we assess ourselves against a neighbour, work colleague or family member.

This first analysis of 'fair' seems to suggest it is one of those portmanteau terms, carrying a whole lot of elements within it, each of which is hard to isolate and consider alone. What is fair is what is just. What is fair is what is clearly applicable to everyone. What is fair is what others like us can do and have.

This leads to a rather interesting point. When someone proposes a new topic for legislation (unless it is in some very esoteric area of activity), we do seem to have a sense as to whether or not it is fair. We can't find the unarguable source that verifies that feeling, nor can we explain why this seems to bridge the gap between just deserts and treating everyone the same: however, we seem to just know that this is right. Our shared culture seems to do this for us, even if there are some areas of sharp distinctions between us. Is this a situation where we *want* an elephant on roller skates?

It may be that it is convenient to say that something is fair, or unfair, then not have to think about any further, rather than to examine it more carefully and in so doing expose our differences about the basis of justice and fair treatment. To avoid such a discussion may mean that we can get on with life by sliding past some difficult differences. That seems 'fair': don't ask why, but just accept that it is.

If we allow something to become an elephant running away from us, then should we look at where it may go? Identifying the elephant in the room, and then letting it escape means that we may be subject to some surprises when the errant elephant hits a tricky juncture!! Well, what I mean by that is that unexamined ideas will sometimes come back at us, precisely because we haven't continued to examine their consequences. If we choose to slide over an examination of what we mean by fair treatment, we may find we have unknowingly agreed to something that we should or could have challenged. It was great when the Supreme Court outlawed segregation in schools: it was much easier to feel that had addressed the issue (it was, after all, only fair), rather than to continue to examine what would be fair in practice, and confront all the uncomfortable business of bussing and teacher transfers that had to be undertaken make what was fair become fair in everyday life.

That intuitive sense of fairness that helps us agree with some proposed piece of legislation must rest on some fundamental principles, even if they are hard to define or source. Avoiding exploring what they are can also mean that we ignore or misunderstand that quite often those fuzzy underlying principles are far from consistent. The golden rule ('do as you would be done by') rubs up against 'do what the boss says' and 'the customer is always right'. Equality of opportunity for your children rubs up against 'don't waste money sending a child to college if he or she are not interested in study - encourage them to find an apprenticeship (education is no longer for its intrinsic worth, but for its value in finding a better job). Advertising a job so that anyone can apply rubs up against using your networks to get your son a position. It was the 'three witches' in Macbeth who said, "Fair is foul and foul is fair": things do change according to circumstances, and nothing is as it first appears. There are times when we are tempted to ask, "Is anything as straightforward as it seems?"

There is yet another facet to fairness and that is our sense of entitlement. When we consider something is fair, we are suggesting that it is something to which we are entitled, which we can expect to receive. This, after all is what Martin Luther King Jr. was saying when he used the concept of the promissory note - we expect our check from the bank of justice to be honoured, we are due our share of justice.

Why do we think we are entitled to anything? In Chapter 2 I suggested that there were a number of fundamental human rights to which everyone is entitled: sanctity of life, free speech, citizenship, and so on. These are rights that we claim simply on the basis that we are human beings. The International Declaration of Human Rights set out those entitlements clearly, and the great majority of countries have signed on to the Declaration (even if many fail to actually deliver the all rights that are included).

However, a continuing critique of the Declaration, and of the Amendments to the US Constitution, is that they cover only half of the situation at stake: surely rights need to be balanced against obligations. In recent years, some countries and states have started drawing up a slightly different form of declaration that covers both rights *and* requirements. In Victoria, Australia, the state government established the Charter of Rights and Responsibilities Act in 2006, and others are seeking to put something similar in place. With entitlement there should be an associated sense of duty. While that seems obvious - you cannot expect to be tried by a jury if you are not willing to serve on a jury - it still seems to be the case that many people feel entitlement takes precedence over obligation.

We first confronted this issue in looking at the ideology of the free market in Chapter 2. There we saw that some feel it is important that they have the right to do what they want, not have the government make choices for them. Similarly, in looking at what is meant by liberty we saw that true libertarians reject interventions that limit their freedoms. We have already explored the inadequacy of believing that freedom of choice can be exempt from some degree of respect for the choices of others - and their ability to make choices - a constraint that Mill included in his comments on liberty.

However, the sense of entitlement is more than that. It is also about the feeling that we are due recognition - in all its senses - because of who we are. This can be very general: we are due our rights because we are human beings. It can be far more specific: we have the right to choose and practice whatever religion we want to follow because that freedom of choice rests on our intrinsic right to liberty of thought. It turns out that exercising that liberty is rather more problematic in practice. While we feel free to choose our religion, we are concerned when others choose to follow religious principles that we feel are wrong - whether they be Seventh Day Adventists who refuse to allow blood transfusions, Moslems who allow a man to have several wives, or members of those many religions which clearly discriminate against women. The same challenge exists in relation to the belief that we should be free to follow the life style we choose. What I see as acceptable may be seen as unacceptable to others - ranging from allowing my garden to run wild to allowing my children to run wild!

There is a point where entitlement slips over into selfishness: that begins when I believe I am entitled to something irrespective of the cost to others. I want to listen to loud music: too bad if others around me don't want to listen to it also. I need to have my mobile telephone on so I can take calls at any time: too bad if the bride and groom getting married at the front of the church think they should be the focus of attention. The teacher asks me to do something but, too bad, I am not in the mood to do that today.

At the extreme, this becomes expressed in the phrase "it's my right to ...." as if no further justification is required. A culture that encourages individualism also encourages selfish entitlement. This is a pernicious elephant, self-justifying our sense of what is our right, and therefore without any need for reconsideration. I can do this because I want to do it: why would I need to reflect on my choice, as it is my right to do as I wish. This is an elephant that stretches the social fabric, pulling each person apart from others - pursuing what he or she wants to do without any need to take account of responsibility to others. When fairness slips into entitlement, the risk is that our obligations to others slip away to the periphery, and social cohesion becomes attenuated.

We will return to social cohesion later. Here we should simply acknowledge that many writers have argued against focussing on methods to promote social cohesion. They propose that entitlement and self-interest are the proper focus of our activities. They take their comfort from the argument ascribed to Adam Smith that the selfish behaviour of the industrialist or manufacturer is led, by the 'invisible hand of the market' to bring benefits to the wider community. In more recent times, the novelist and would-be philosopher Ayn Rand has returned to public attention with interest shown in her extreme view that "an individual's primary moral obligation is to achieve his own well-being". In other words, as we explored in Chapter 2, these writers claim that being selfish works, and that the free and open market is the best mechanism to allocate resources among all members of society.

However, Adam Smith's invisible hand ensures the successful operation of the market in terms of benefitting one another only if a number of conditions are met. Some of these we explored in Chapter 2, to do with transparency and reciprocity. Another condition is that participation in the market requires that we trust one another. There are a complex set of laws about contracts and agreements, of course, but they are merely the legal background to the more fundamental requirement that we have to be fair in our dealings, that we do not renege on our promises. Is this another issue that underlies that teenage daughter's complaint about her younger sister? It was not just that her sister was allowed to stay out late at a younger age, but that there was an implicit promise here: this is the rule that her father had established, a rule that she should be able to trust he will apply to each and every other child.

I would like to explore the notion of trust in more detail later. For now, trust can be seen as part of the necessary conditions that result from interdependence. We depend on one another, and we live in a society where interdependence is central to making things work. When we read Adam Smith talking about the 'invisible hand', he was really talking about interdependence, that we are unable to achieve what we want without the involvement of others. If that seems a little tricky to understand, just remember the trouble President Obama got into when he suggested that entrepreneurs were unable to create businesses alone! He was right, of course: the infrastructure of business, the education of staff, the legal system, and so much more is required as the context in which a new business can develop and grow. That is not to ignore the key role the entrepreneur plays, but simply to acknowledge their business skills are used in a context that provides a great deal of support (and sometimes some obstacles!).

The quote that is used to explain Adam Smith's 'invisible hand' is worth reading carefully:

"As every individual, therefore, endeavours as much as he can, both to employ his capital in the support of domestic industry, and so to direct that industry that its produce maybe of the greatest value; every individual necessarily labours to render the annual revenue of the society as great as he can. He generally, indeed, neither intends to promote the public interest, nor knows how much he is promoting it. By preferring the support of domestic to that of foreign industry, he intends only his own security; and by directing that industry in such a manner as its produce may be of the greatest value, he intends only his own gain; and he is in this, as in many other cases, led by an invisible hand to promote an end which was no part of his intention. Nor is it always the worse for the society that it was no part of it. By pursuing his own interest, he frequently promotes that of the society more effectually than when he really intends to promote it."[40]

What is Adam Smith actually saying? He is simply observing that industrialists seem to prefer to put their money into creating businesses at home rather than overseas, and that it is in the nature of pursuing their own self-interest that the capitalist benefits society through producing goods that are in demand, as cheaply as possible, and creating employment as well. Somehow, that has been changed into the belief that selfishness is a virtue, shaped by a hidden hand to promote the common good - and that, patently, is nonsense. Yes, the operations of the market *can* bring goods in demand to buyers at the best possible price, and they *can* create employment. However, that same driver can also lead to pollution, trickery, fraud, misuse of people, knowledge and resources, gross inequalities and the substitution of monetary value for any other form of value. The market acts to limit the consequences of the pursuit of selfishness, but it does not mean that selfishness is, in itself, a contributor to the benefit of society. When Gordon Gekko claimed "greed is good', we knew he was wrong: that *was* the point of *Wall Street*.

We live interdependently, and that interdependence rests on the requirement, among others, that we are fair in our dealings with one another. Being fair is a cost we have to bear in order to live effectively in a network of relationships.

In business, however, what is "fair" has some interesting nuances. The old saying was that all's fair in love and war, but perhaps a more accurate statement would be that "all's fair in love, war and business"! We don't consider it unfair for a business to try to siphon away your customers (we are a little more tetchy when someone tries to take away our boyfriend or girlfriend, of course!!). After all, we are trying to 'steal' customers from other businesses. 'Fair' is clearly contextual in meaning.

As is often the case, we might get a clearer perspective on this if we ask 'what is unfair in business practice'. Deceitful practice includes lying - about products, services or even competitors. It includes breaking the law. It includes reneging on deals, even if there was no formal contract signed. It does not include 'poaching' staff, but it does include using information that a member of staff brought over from a former employer: certainly if this information was confidential, but, even if that was not the case, using another's business data is problematic at the very least.

As in so many things, what is unfair is to be found in the contested territory around the edges of the law and normal practice.

The real estate practice of gazumping (allowing another buyer to put in a bid for a house when it was already under contract) was initially seen as "unfair", but now it seems it has become accepted practice in house buying, at least in some countries. At one extreme, some forms of business practice are not unfair; they are simply ways of being smart and showing business 'savvy'. At the other, other business practices are examples of 'sharp practice', and this easily slides into deceit and illegal behaviour. In practice, so complex is the issue of fair business practice we often don't think of talking about it in that way. Indeed, there are occasions when we are surprised to find a business has been really 'fair'.

Being fair and demanding justice, these are the processes by which we impose limitations on what we want to do. When we seek to be dealt with in the same way as everyone else, (that golden rule, again), we are assenting to a denial of our unique needs and concerns. To be more precise, we are making sure that whatever happens we are not being disadvantaged when compared with others. This implies that fairness is a levelling process, putting us all on the same footing. If this is the case, no wonder it is so hard to be fair. In many circumstances, we want more than just getting what everyone else is entitled to receive: we want a bit more. Our natural self-interest propels us past the sense of fairness in terms of equality to seeking some kind of advantage.

Perhaps that is what the daughter was up to in complaining about her sister being allowed out late. She was not just seeking equality of treatment, but was putting in place an ambit claim to get a better deal on the next area of negotiation. It wasn't fair that her sister could stay out later at an earlier age, so can't she, (the 'cheated' one), now get permission to stay at the beach with a few friends next weekend. Pointing out what is not fair may be a way of pushing your entitlements up, rather than dragging others down.

'To be fair' is a complex thing. At one extreme is the judicial sense of fairness, set out in laws and precedent. Even this is far from straightforward as we consider the application of fair in various circumstances. As Martin Luther King Jr. pointed out, laws can be unjust, and so can their implementation. However, this is an aspect of being fair that has some clarity about it. At the other extreme is selfish entitlement - what is fair is what I am due, whatever the implications for anyone else. In between are all the other senses of fair: fair in terms of ensuring equality; fair in terms of due processes; fair in terms of what you can get away with; and even fair as a base-level imposition to ensure that everyone works together with a reasonable level of confidence that promises will be kept, deals will be honoured.

Francis Cornford was concerned about promises being kept. Well, to be more precise, he noticed that others were concerned about the consequences of their actions - whether they were promises, decisions, or changes. You will recall that he explained the Principle of Dangerous Precedent was that you should "not do the right thing now for fear that it might be harder, require courage even, to do the right thing the next time around". This was a concern about change, since his colleagues were felt every new thing one does is either wrong, or, if it is right sets a dangerous precedent. As we said earlier, this is a basis for claiming that it is clearly better to do nothing for the first time! To be asked to be fair where things were previously judged to not be fair is to be asked to set a precedent. Francis Cornford was being humorous when he suggested this was a reason not to act. However, we know that people have refrained from being fair because they were worried as to 'where will this all lead?'

Examples abound: we could refer to freeing the slaves in the US, or later giving them the right to vote; or another example is giving women the right to vote. When Harriet Taylor Mill (perhaps with the assistance of J S Mill) wrote on 'The Enfranchisement of Women' in 1851, she could not have anticipated that she laid out exactly the issues that a cluster of academics would have used in preventing such a change using the Principle of the Dangerous Precedent. She argued that women have never had the vote as a result of centuries of outdated and unacceptable custom, so now we should cast this custom aside (*oh dear, whatever will be abandoned next?*). Or "there need be no fear that women will take out of the hands of men any occupation which men perform better than they" (*good lord, I hadn't even thought of such a terrible thing*). Or "we look in vain for abler or firmer rulers than Elizabeth; than Isabella of Castile; than Maria Teresa; than

Catherine of Russia; than Blanche, mother of Louis IX of France; than Jeanne d'Albret, mother of Henri Quatre. There are few kings on record who contended with more difficult circumstances, or overcame them more triumphantly, than these" (*so if we let them vote, next they will be our rulers!*).[41] You can imagine the conclusion - let us wait until a more timely opportunity arises to contemplate such a radical change. Martin Luther King addressed that point very clearly in his letter from Birmingham City Jail: "We know through painful experience that freedom is never voluntarily given by the oppressor; it must be demanded by the oppressed."[42]

If the counter to slippery slopes is political action, then reasoned analysis and shared logic are being set aside. Were Shakespeare's three harridans correct after all? Is it the case that "fair is foul and foul is fair"? How confusing. Fortunately, the issues of justice and fairness have been subjected to a very far-reaching analysis by John Rawls, generally regarded as the greatest philosopher of the 20th Century. Rawls came up with a very interesting thought experiment in thinking about what was fair, or just – which so far we have been considering a key part of morality.

His idea was to suppose that we sat down to design an ideal society, but that each one of us is completely ignorant about ourselves, our characteristics, or where we might be in society in terms of wealth, position or employment. We do not know our gender, ethnicity, capabilities, physical character, and so on. This 'veil of ignorance' leads to a rather different set of conclusions from those developed by Mill. Since we do not know where we will end up in the future, we are likely, Rawls argues, to come up with a view about how society should operate that minimizes the risk of disadvantage for everyone, irrespective of where they sit in society. After all, if you ended up with the least valued set of attributes, you would still want to be treated as well as everyone else: genetics is a lottery, but being human is something we share with everyone else.[43]

Suppose you were born with superior intelligence, or a strong and moral character, or extraordinary hand-eye coordination. Surely it would be reasonable to argue that such a person should receive reward for having such attributes? Doesn't he or she deserve it? Rawls argues that this is not the case. As a member of society, I am like everyone else. As an individual, I may possess certain attributes, but these are not things I deserve, they are simply the outcomes of that genetic lottery of birth. Society should be designed to treat everyone in the same way, and not be structured to treat variations in genetics differently (we accept that in relation to racial characteristics, but we find it hard to go as far as taking that on to other attributes we inherit). However, we can 'earn' difference, if we choose to work hard, undertake dangerous activities. Rawls wants us to distinguish between unearned (chance, if you like) characteristics, and reward for effort.[44]

We do not need to confront the details of all of Rawls' analysis: he is a deep and thoughtful writer who deserves a book of his own (actually, you should read him for yourself!). However, one of the critical outcomes of his analysis is that he concludes two very interesting things. First, that everyone should have the same set of rights as everyone else, and that among those rights, liberty is to be paramount. Actually his working thesis is that "all have the same adequate equal basic liberties" - those three words 'adequate', 'equal' and 'basic' carry a lot of weight.[45] Adequate and basic - well, like Mill, he sees liberty as being central to a fair society, and something we would want to ensure that the systems and structures of society enable and support.

Rawls does not see these liberties as moral considerations, however, but as principles that must be embedded in the way society is structured. Among those liberties and in addition to the liberty of the individual, we might want to specify some of the other rights we have mentioned before – to life, to freedom to congregate, to health, to education, to trail by jury – I am sure that we could take a number of items from the Universal Declaration of Human Rights and feel we have a good set of basic rights. Equal - yes, they must be available to everyone (whatever their genetic attributes).

However, Rawls then has a second point to make which – roughly simplified - argues that society should operate in such a way that equality is seen as the goal, and that measures should advantage the most disadvantaged. Again, his wording is very precise: "social and political inequalities are to satisfy two conditions: first, they are attached to offices and positions open to all under fair equality of opportunity; and second, they are to be of the greatest benefit to the least advantaged members of society" (this he calls the 'difference principle').[46] Here is where the 'veil of ignorance' shows its power. As a participant in designing this just society, I may end up at the bottom of the heap, and if that is the case, then I would want to make sure that there would be measures to reduce inequality, and ensure the most disadvantaged become less so.[47]

Rawls has moved the debate about fairness away from morality to a discussion about principles, and how they are to be implemented through social institutions. A just society is one where people are treated fairly - rewarded for effort, but not disadvantaged by the chance process of inheritance. To be fair is to balance what we do ourselves against the variations in 'unearned' attributes with which we were born. Rawls is not an individual libertarian in the sense that Mill proposed: he wants to reform society so that it is fair.

There has been a major debate following Rawl's work. He offers a strong argument against the benefits of the untrammelled free market, and shifts the debates about rights away from arguments about morality to an analysis of what makes a good society. We will return to some of that debate later, but for now we might want to look at one other element of the free market approach - and another sense of the notion of 'fair'. Surely there is at least one thing that we do know, free from debates about justice and our rights. When we are considering meeting our personal needs and desires, we are free, free to go out into the market and buy what we want (provided we have the money to do so). There are some questions that even this freedom raises, however. In the next chapter we will turn to examining the scope of our 'wants' and our desire for more. Is there a limit to the things we want? Can we ever have enough?

6. Entitlement, or can we ever have enough?

In understanding the nature of capitalism, John Locke played a central role. In his second treatise on government, written in 1690, Locke tackled the issue of property, and, in particular, why there should be a right to private property. He begins by declaring that the world was given to us for our benefit, and that there has to be a mechanism to allow an individual to acquire property to use for his or her own benefit:

> *"God, who has given the world to men in common, has also given them reason to make use of it to the best advantage of life and convenience. The earth and all that is therein is given to men for the support and comfort of their being. And though all the fruits it naturally produces and beasts it feeds belong to mankind in common, as they are produced by the spontaneous hand of nature; and nobody has originally a private dominion exclusive of the rest of mankind in any of them, as they are thus in their natural state; yet, being given for the use of men, there must of necessity be a means to appropriate them some way or other before they can be of any use or at all beneficial to any particular man."[48]*

How do we obtain property? The answer Locke gives is that we use our labour to take what is there and add value to it: *"Thus labour, in the beginning, gave a right of property, wherever any one was pleased to employ it upon what was common".* Locke imagines a world in which there was everything available 'in common', and then explains how out of labour a person could appropriate land and natural produce; having done so he or she could then increase their activities to develop more than was needed for personal use, and be able to sell the extra - for their benefit, as well as those to whom he sold his produce. That imagined state was, in his mind, when "all the world was America", when it was an unlimited commons.

To begin with, there was more than enough land, but Locke then went on to explain:

"Men, at first, for the most part, contented themselves with what unassisted nature offered to their necessities: and though afterwards, in some parts of the world, (where the increase of people and stock, with the use of money, had made land scarce, and so of some value) the several communities settled the bounds of their distinct territories, and by laws within themselves regulated the properties of the private men of their society, and so .... by positive agreement, settled a property amongst themselves, in distinct parts and parcels of the earth"

"This partage of things in an inequality of private possessions men have made practicable out of the bounds of society and without compact, only by putting a value on gold and silver, and tacitly agreeing in the use of money; for, in governments, the laws regulate the right of property, and the possession of land is determined by positive constitutions."[49]

In reflecting on Locke's analysis, the first issue that presses on us today - even if there was a time when all the world was America - is that the commons is long gone! If there is not enough land for each person to 'appropriate' his or her part, then does this mean we have to revisit the whole story about the right to own private property? Locke was basing his analysis on a physical resource: today, we would translate 'property' into 'capital', and while many people do have capital through owning their house or apartment, many do not. There are many ways to raise capital, of course, but generally capital flows to those that already have capital, and many are excluded from that process. If only some members of society can have access to capital, is it still the case that we have access 'to the world in common"? Do we need to rethink Locke's justification?

A good starting point is to look at 'property' today. As I write this, I am sitting in a small apartment in Italy – in the hills above Pistoia. My life here is simple – three rooms – a kitchen with a dining area, a lounge, and a bedroom, together with the usual bathroom facilities. Next week I go into a smaller apartment – no lounge. Did I say simple? I have a plethora of kitchen items, crockery, cutlery and glasses. I have a toaster and a coffee maker. There is a television in the lounge. The apartment has heating – it is still chilly at night here in June. I have money to buy what I need.

Yesterday I went to one of those huge supermarkets – Co-op – in Pistoia. The choice was almost overwhelming, and I wandered around with my trolley trying to remember what I really wanted. Vegetables, fruit, cereal, bread – and then I stumbled on the cheeses. There were cheeses from Italy, and France; there were cheeses from Germany and from the UK; there were wrapped cheeses, huge cheeses from which a slice could be cut for you; and, around the corner a cool cabinet with yet more cheeses. I thought that I might like a bottle of wine, too, so that could have a glass of wine with dinner. There were four long imposing rows of wines – hundreds of varieties. How to choose when you are a stranger? Price? Half remembered names and varieties from Italy are not enough to guide me. Did I say I was leading a simple life? The truth is very far from that; I was living surrounded by riches.

But here's the rub: we live in a world where some of us experience abundance. Compare our lives with the 800 million living in rural India, the 400 million in Western China, the 1 billion in Africa. Despite all that, we want more. We want to have the new iPhone or Samsung Galaxy III. Can we ever have enough?

I can still remember the first time that I was struck by this question. I was taking part in a seminar in Aspen, and a fellow participant invited everyone to his house for the evening. Unlike most of us, who had come from around the world, he was a local, and had a house in Snowmass. Or so I thought. The house was amazing. It was huge, beautifully decorated, and containing some stunning pieces of art. There was one room, which was described as 'the grandchildren's' room' and it contained six bunk beds. At the foot of each bed there was a television, and each television was personalized with the set of channels that child preferred. It turned out that my fellow participant was not a local, but this was one of his homes, and it was used for holidays: he was in the television industry, and thus the source of pride in the personalized TV's.

Altogether it was a house with about a dozen television sets. It was something I noticed because I had – just that year – decided to do without a television altogether. Little did I realize at the time, but there were two things that visit exemplified. The first was that there is always more that people can want: a personalized television set. The second has become more important over time, which is that having more and more can also be quite isolating: each child watching its own television, just as today you see people everywhere isolated from everyone around them as they concentrate on their smart phone, 'tethered', as Sherry Turkle describes it, but alone.[50]

I am sure you have friends and acquaintances like mine, whose desire for more is quite consuming. One person I know is always redecorating and reorganising his house. It is quite beautiful, but then he reads about some new idea – a new kind of door to open out into the garden, a new stove that has intelligent heating elements – and he is off again, refurbishing anew. I have another who hankers after the latest gadgets. There is a new iPhone, and he will be off to see if he can get one. There is a device that takes photographs from his camera and wirelessly puts them into a display on his television, and he will have it installed. And so it goes on.

Perhaps the example I should have given is cars. I have discovered that in the area where I live in the US, everyone in the household has a car – how else can you get anywhere? Even if you do not want to have a car, you have little choice, as the standard of public transport in most places is very poor. But once you have one, well perhaps you will need more than one car per person, because you might also want a car when you go on trips – something designed for mountain trails and beach driving.

Then there are all the other things it would be good to have: perhaps you would like new and better camera; or the latest kind of coffee maker; then again, you will also need a new season's coat; and so it goes on, ending up with a lovely golden collar for the dog – and a matching food bowl! There is always something more.

If you ask why this is so, one of the common explanations is that the marketers working in companies drive this constant desire which makes us want the latest thing. They keep offering these tempting options, manipulating our weak resistance, dragging us into shops and on to the Internet. As is so often the case when we try to place the blame on others, I doubt this is the case. There is a long history of writing about the way in which we are constantly adding to our list of wants, turning wants into needs, and always on the look-out for the next thing that might give us satisfaction. We don't need marketers; we can do this all by ourselves!

Plato wrote about this some 2,500 years ago, in a section in The Republic that is often called 'the city of pigs'. In it, Plato performs one of those philosopher's tricks, telling a simple story to ensure that we see what he wants us to see. In this case, he describes the emergence of society, the division of labour within a community, the ways in which our various basic needs are met, and then asks – through Socrates, his familiar spokesman – is this not an ideal, yet simple life? The response to the world he describes is quick and simple – "But surely we will want relish to go with the foods you have described". Socrates adds more to the simple life, but it is all too basic, fit only for a city of pigs, he is told. Even then, it seems, the never-ending desire for more was quite evident.

Why are we like this? What is this restless urge that drives us along, never quite satisfied, and yet never any more satisfied when we do get the next thing. No sooner have we bought something new, than a brief moment of pleasure is eclipsed by the desire to just have a bit more, do a bit more, see a bit more.

It is a disease that is predominantly characteristic of youth and middle age. People who are older seem to be less inclined to be driven by this need for more. Some go as far as to tell us that there are few things that really matter: family, friends, and good health. Some are able to slough off the material burdens of their earlier lives, and travel more lightly. Some even become itinerant monks, sadhus, unencumbered as they travel on. Does this mean that we only learn to stop wanting more when it is almost too late?

There is a long tradition of speculation that suggests that this desire for more is in large part a function of our 'human nature'. There is another section of Plato's Republic, where this is examined in another story, often called 'Gyges' ring'. The story centres on a magical ring, which, when worn, makes a person disappear – not just physically, but as if they had not been there before the ring was put on. This is much better than the ring Bilbo Baggins found in 'The Hobbit':

that ring made him disappear, but everyone knew he had just been there a moment before! The purpose of the story of Gyges' ring is to ask us to consider how people would behave if they had the ring. We are asked to imagine there are two such rings, and two people – one bad, a criminal, and the other good, almost like a saint. Clearly, the criminal would revel in having the ring, able to carry out more and more nefarious activities while being invisible. But what about the good person? Glaucon explains it in this way to Socrates:

> *"Suppose now that there were two such magic rings, and the just put on one of them and the unjust the other; no man can be imagined to be of such an iron nature that he would stand fast in justice. No man would keep his hands off what was not his own when he could safely take what he liked out of the market, or go into houses and lie with any one at his pleasure, or kill or release from prison whom he would, and in all respects be like a God among men. Then the actions of the just would be as the actions of the unjust; they would both come at last to the same point."*

This examination of what is meant by 'our human nature' is one contribution to a topic that has a long and complex history. While the story of Gyges Ring reveals that it intrigued at least one Greek philosopher 2,500 years ago (and probably many others both before and around then), it remains just as controversial and central today, hotly debated by psychologists of various persuasions, sociobiologists, behaviouralists, ethicists, theologians, psychiatrists and philosophers. As a view of human nature, not much has changed over the centuries.

Machiavelli, that dry-eyed empirical observer of princes and power at the beginning of the 16th Century had an equally very clear view of what he saw as human nature. In *The Prince*, in Section 17, he comments: "For it may be said of men in general that they are ungrateful, voluble, dissemblers, anxious to avoid danger, and covetous of gain" Are we all 'covetous of gain', always wanting more?

Why does this remain such a central issue? Perhaps it is because the term 'human nature' juxtaposes two possibilities - being human, and hence something special, outside of nature; and being a human animal, and therefore very much part of nature. It is precisely the tension between these two that makes human nature so important - it is a touchstone as to how we see ourselves, and what we see as the limits on how we behave and what we can aspire to do.

Human nature is usually defined as those behaviours that are independent of our cultural upbringing, that derive from humans as species within the animal kingdom. Establishing what is our human nature is a measure for discriminating between those attributes that make us unique, and those we share with other creatures on planet earth. In other words, our human nature is our animal nature.

There can be no doubt that we do some things at an animal, instinctual level. Our responses to sudden events, to being attacked, for example, demonstrate some fundamental instinctive or automatic responses - the so-called 'fight or flight' reaction. However, trying to pin down the borderline between what is 'animal' and what is not quickly becomes a messy area. We are capable of rational thought - but now it seems some other animals may be able to do the same. We have language, yet perhaps there are some other animals that have this capability: indeed our ability to use language appears to be a function of genetics rather than just socialisation, if Noam Chomsky and Steven Pinker are right. Clarity over this borderline is important - we want to be able to define what makes us unique, and to do so means that we have to be clear about what we do, and do not, share with other creatures.

Philosophers are tricky to deal with, as they often tell stories in order to sell a proposition that is important to the case they are developing. If our concern is with what constitutes our human nature, perhaps we should look elsewhere to answer this question. Is there some empirical evidence we can use?

We could start with young children. As all mothers note, to their chagrin, very young children are poor at playing with others. They want to keep what they have, and will take things away from the other children around them. They quickly learn the power of the word 'Mine!' So we begin the battle to help our child learn to share, mindful that there has to be give as well as take. At the same time as we are trying to introduce this lesson about life, we are often teaching another – sometimes less thoughtfully. We teach our children that they can get rewards if they do what we ask of them. Do this, and you will have a cookie. Do this, and maybe you will have two cookies!! The smart child soon learns that you can't just take what you want, but, if you do what is asked of you, you can get more.

Have we tamed the selfish child, or have we taken the natural desire to play with what is around us, and replaced that innocent skill with taking the first step on the path to get more? Perhaps a better question may be that it doesn't matter if it is nature or nurture that makes us selfish and always wanting more: however we got there, it soon becomes part of the way we live in the world.

As usual, that may be too simple. Is everyone selfish? Does everyone always want more? If we look at the people we know around us, it seems that the desire to want more and more if very differently allocated. Some people are just 'driven'. Others are less frenetic – they would like more, but it does not drive their lives. Yet others seem willing to always share, not so concerned about what they have: if there is a drive to want more, it has been held in check or restrained in some way.

Perhaps this is also a function of semantics. I have talked so far about a desire to always want more. If I reword that, and instead talk about us 'liking to improve where we live, or the car we own', where the drive is to have something that is a bit more reliable, something nicer, then that seems less uncomfortable. That no longer seems like an insatiable desire to have things, so much as a natural desire to try to improve our lot. I suspect that is just semantics, however. There does seem to be some driver that means we are never quite satisfied with what we have – except, perhaps, for some people as they get much older.

The key word in this is 'enough'. Can we ever have enough? Is the desire to improve, to add something more, to acquire - is this another 'elephant on roller skates', running away from us, and unable to be stopped? Perhaps there are some stopping points. Instead of one car, we might want two – one for work, one for leisure. However, eventually, there is no point to adding another. We can replace our car with a newer car, perhaps one that is more fuel-efficient. Once we have so many sets of cutlery – including a special set for visitors - there is no need for any more. It would be a waste of money. Does that mean there are limits to our desires, once what we have reaches the point that we actually cannot use more?

Even if that is true, there is another problem. Those of us living in the rich world already have so much. If the rest of the world is to have the same as we do, the demands on resources are going to be enormous. Alternatively, we may have to be satisfied with less, rather than more. This has been brought home in the past 50 years as another term has come into play – the need to do things that are sustainable. In a sustainable world, we cannot keep on having more, as there are limits to resources, limits to the levels of pollution we can tolerate.

There are two puzzles for you to consider at this point. The first is the development puzzle. Do we tell developing nations they cannot have what we have, because that level of activity is unsustainable? What right do we have to do that? Are we going to demonstrate how to live a better life than we do now, by having less? I think that most people in developing nations see what we have, and see no reason why they should not have the same. The only difference is that they may be able to get the things we have now, rather than going through the long process of innovation that has led to our current lifestyle.

That leads to the second puzzle. Is sustainability different, or is this also something 'more'? It turns out that people who invest in sustainability – better energy systems, sustainable homes – are themselves adding to their stock of having more than others. Sustainable homes get built in affluent suburbs, and increase the value of the homes in those areas. Being sustainable in practice seems to be about having more than others; not about declaring we have enough. Sustainability is just another path to identify something more that we can desire.

In case you are confused at this point, I am not saying that seeking to be sustainable is a bad idea, just the contrary. But I am pointing out that those who see it as another "addition" to make their home yet more desirable and expensive can subvert even such a laudable goal in the marketplace.

Some people have argued that the 'good life' would be one in which work would play a much smaller part in our lives because the economy as a whole is producing enough, and we would engage in other pursuits: leisure, dialogue with friends, even philosophical discussions. We would escape from the compulsions of work and the market, and enjoy the things in life that are meaningful, no longer constantly wanting more. Sadly, this seems a very weak argument. If you study the world of leisure, you will quickly see that this is also full of yet more things that we need, and there is never enough here, either.

You enjoy sport? There are shops full of goods to ensure your sporting experience is the most enjoyable it can be, and – just in case you miss the point – exemplars of the best in sport urging you to share with them in the joys of the latest running shoes, new weights to trim off excess fat more efficiently, and even a sweatshirt just like the one today's hero wears. Leisure? Perhaps you would like to be a photographer? There are innumerable camera bodies and lenses to choose from, an escalator of enhanced capabilities, able to take pictures at high speed, in poor lighting conditions with lenses that can focus on a single bird 500 yards away, filters that add fascinating effects. Your next camera can have a new system using 1000 lenses simultaneously, each combining with the others to take the perfect picture (until an ever better system comes along). It is not just about cameras, of course: now there are the many programs available for you to manipulate the digital images using your computer.

Perhaps you want to escape all this focus on toys and gadgets. You enjoy reading? There are hundreds of new books being published every month, magazines to help you make choices, book groups to join where you can share what you have read with others. You can read a book on an iPad or a Kindle (or any other kind of device). There are books to be read on your smart phone. There are books about books, and books about reading. There are on-line courses about reading and books. If all that is not enough, you can go on and write your own book, and even publish it yourself.

In any area of leisure, we find the same situation. Whatever you have is not enough. There is always more. In some areas, the more is almost unimaginable. The Internet provides us with an abundance of images, writings, films and videos – and there is always more being added. The World Wide Web has simply made more 'more' available.

Wanting more is not just about work and the desire to earn more. It is not just about material things as such. It is about something much deeper – about our desire to always want to explore beyond what we know, to do something that we haven't done before. It seems it is part of being human – having an inquisitive, exploratory, and competitive driver that never lets us rest, or at least not until we lack the energy to keep on pushing forward in this way. It is a driver that affects us all, but it is the curse of the affluent that having so much more than everyone else has no effect in limiting their desire to have yet more. One psychologist working with CEOs found this compulsion to achieve and have yet more led some to the edge of crisis. "I am working so hard, being paid so much, and still I am not satisfied"

There is another perspective, which might tip this 'elephant' of wanting more on its side. It is about the definition of 'more'. If you watch a craftsman, a potter for example, the more is about the richness of the experience, not the quantity or the novelty. Great potters often spend years working on the same basic shapes: they keep exploring different clays and glazes, testing the limits of shape and structure. Their 'more' can be one vase, twenty years later, which for them is a culmination of exploration and deep understanding. It is the same for some photographers: it is not about the tools of the trade, but the same old camera can provide the opportunity to take photographs that are the culmination of the skills of framing, exposure, and light, revealing the subject in a way that is richly illuminating. It is more through quality rather than quantity.

In the same way, for the reader, the goal can shift from reading more and more, and talking about the books they have read to going back and rediscovering – slowly and carefully – the richness of a writer they really like, allowing the words to seep in, to create a sense of satisfaction. In reading, too, there can be a rich experience, not a race to complete book after book.

This is the real lesson that some older and wiser people can teach us. It is not that they have lost the desire to have more, but that they have learnt that more can come through appreciating one thing in depth rather than many in terms of numbers. I have visited art galleries for much of my life, but only in more recent years have I found myself being held by a picture, and spent time enjoying that one work of art, rather than racing off to see what else is there. I used to notice people sitting and staring at a particular canvas and wondered if they realised what they were missing. Now I see it differently – it was I who was missing something, confusing seeing more pictures with really appreciating a work of art.

Is this a potential benefit of being better off? Is it that no longer having to work so hard to make enough money to live reasonably well allows you to shift the emphasis from wanting more in terms of quantity to more in terms of richness and intrinsic quality? There is a lot of evidence to suggest it is the other way round. People who are not necessarily affluent, but whose lives are less driven, seem to be quite capable of enjoying their situation: they can sit in a chair in the garden at the end of the day, and drink in the solitude, admire the scenery and the birds flitting about, or perhaps enjoy a conversation with an old friend. There are people like that just outside my apartment in the Tuscan hills. I am sure they wonder why I am so driven, typing away when I could be out there too, with a nice glass of Italian red wine, a bit of cheese, some fresh bread (I think I may be about to join them!). In fact, they and I are not so different. For me, the satisfaction of working out some ideas and writing them down is also a rich experience – I don't even care if what I write is never read, as the task is satisfying in itself.

As for those who are far more affluent, and are working hard, there are many I know who never seem to have time to enjoy what they have. They seem anxious about what they have achieved, and always concerned to ensure they have kept up to date. In a later chapter I will explore what we mean by 'keeping in touch'. There are many people who are so busy keeping in touch with what they believe is essential to do, that they lose sight of how to enjoy themselves. You can see that when you go to a concert: while some people are there to enjoy the music, there are many who are there because it is important to be seen there, important to look good when others see you there, and important to make sure you see and acknowledge others like you. It is easy to slide from expecting to be immersed in music to anticipating an evening of anxiety.

In an earlier chapter, we explored the ideology of libertarianism, and how this embraces the capitalist market economy. It is easy to say that the market serves our intrinsic motivations – greed and competition. In fact, this is just another elephant, ready to race off at a moment's notice. Human motivations are complex and confounding. Greed sits alongside altruism; competition has its complement in caring; acquisitiveness is balanced by wonder and enlightenment. Elephants are created by giving precedence to one aspect of ourselves and our lives, and then believing that is all there is: once we do that, the skates are on. We are not simple, and nor should we accept simple solutions.

Today, of course, we do live in a world driven by business, growth, and the production of more and more. That is the dynamic that is intrinsic to the capitalist market economy. It is a dynamic to which governments are increasingly bound: they are trapped on the one hand by fiscal pressures, trying to ensure the balance of payments remains positive, and the country is paying its way, and trapped also by social obligations as the cost of services tomorrow exceeds the money being saved for those purposes today. Only continued growth can sustain the economy.

A significant element of the capitalist free market story is that it is the engine of progress. It seems to me there are two challenges here. First, why have many societies before ours progressed and then failed? Second, is the way we live today an indication of progress?

When Jared Diamond's book *'Collapse'* was published in 2005, he unveiled an uncomfortable truth. There have been many civilisations before ours, and some of these have become rich and achieved very high standards of living and yet, over time, one after another has disappeared. How can this be? His account of how societies fail is telling. He identifies several critical issues. The first is that some societies collapse because they use up the natural resources on which they rely (non-renewable, and even renewable resources if they are not well managed). The second is population growth, as the number of people living in a society exceeds the capability of the land and resources to support them. The third factor has to do with destroying the resources that are necessary to survive, either through destroying habitats, typically by introducing alien species; land degradation through over-use; or chemically poisoning the land, the waterways or the oceans. Jared Diamond ties this into what is often called the tragedy of the commons - we used to care for what we held in common, but we no longer do so - through ignorance, greed, and a continuing belief that a new technology will come to the rescue.[51]

Concerns over limits to growth have been with us for some time, but particularly in the past sixty years. They are driven by the depletion of natural resources (especially non-renewable energy and water), by pollution (ever since the 1962 publication of Rachel Carson's frightening book *The Silent Spring*, and then more recently by concern over global warming). In the face of these concerns we seem to repeat exactly what Jared Diamond observed in his studies of past empires and countries - we simply seem to not notice, or to ignore what is going on; or, if we do take action, undertake so little to minimise the problems that they continue to grow, rapidly reaching the point where they cannot be easily addressed. To all this, the proponents of the free market approach have a quick and ready answer - technological innovation will continue to find new ways to do what we want to do, if not more. That has been the case since the industrial revolution, and surely it will continue to be the case into the future.

Here, then, is one really important challenge to the effectiveness of the market and its contribution to progress. If there are limits to growth, they seldom enter the pricing of goods and services. We may try to manage fluctuations in the value of currencies, and some countries are exploring the introduction of carbon taxes. However, by and large, the market does not price the future, focussing on what is happening today. Instead of acting as stewards of the world around us, the market encourages us to sell what we can now. Imperceptibly, as Jared Diamond's analysis of past great empires has shown, that process may be bringing a catastrophe upon us.

Back in the 1970's, Ernst Schumacher wrote *Small is Beautiful,* with the telling subtitle *Economics as if People Mattered.* Schumacher was concerned about the future, and the likelihood that we would run out of non-renewable resources. He was also concerned about the popular view that the "road to peace ...... is to follow the road to riches"[52] He foresaw a path towards catastrophe that was almost inevitable, and worried that the "foundations of peace cannot be laid by universal prosperity, in the modern sense, because such prosperity, if attainable at all, is attainable only by cultivating such drives of human nature as greed and envy, which destroy intelligence, happiness, serenity, and thereby the peacefulness of man"[53].

Schumacher believed that the only way to avoid the challenges that lay ahead was to strive for the 'economics of permanence'. This is another way of talking about the kind of 'stewardship' for the world around us that Jared Diamond has advocated, an approach that we would call sustainability today). His prescription was to get away from big business and big science, and seek instead to develop technologies that were cheap, small scale and therefore available to everyone, and, at the same time were consistent with "man's need for creativity".

So far, Schumacher's path has been largely ignored, even if there is a lot of talk about sustainable business models. As we noted earlier, sustainability has become part of the 'something more' that is available to the affluent - exactly what Schumacher was trying to avoid. The emergence of mini-fabrication may be one stepping stone along the path to the economics of permanence, and currently a great deal of interest has been shown in the 'makers' movement, where manufacturing returns to small scale activity undertaken by individuals.[54] However, while this may be a significant change in the scale of technology, so far its implications remain asserted rather than proven. To date it seems the world is still facing a future in which non-renewable resources are used up, and the costs of goods and services increase to the point where we are unable to sustain today's standard of living.

If that seems overly dramatic, perhaps we should return to the theme of the commons, when 'all the world was America'. There has been a pervasive myth, fuelled by an article in 1968 by Garrett Hardin, (on *The Tragedy of the Commons*), that greed made the sharing of resources 'in common' unsustainable, when he commented on what would happen to common pastureland. He observed, "The rational herdsman concludes that the only sensible course for him to pursue is to add another animal to his herd" as he seeks to maximise his advantage. As a result, things would quickly move to the point where every rational herdsman will do the same thing. The commons will be used beyond its carrying point, and will be overgrazed to the point where it is so degraded that it is unable to support any animals at all. In fact, a lot of economic history has shown that this is simply not true, that communities held the commons under a form of stewardship, each person being aware that they all had to share this resource - whether it was land, animals in a forest area, or fish in the rivers or sea.

Today the commons has largely disappeared (with the possible exception of ocean areas well away from the coastlines of countries). At the same time, a sense of stewardship over the lands and waters of countries has also largely disappeared (except for making sure that people from other countries do not acquire 'our' resources). Locke built up his story about the right to have individual property using a story about a time when there was more land than was needed by each person, what the early settlers saw as the empty lands of America.

Surely when there is not enough land - or other resources - it is essential that these resources are held in common, and that rights over private property are rapidly going to lead to an exhaustion of resources (or a very unequal access to them), and the end to progress? The very factor that allowed capitalism to flourish is now - slowly but surely - eating away at the system. Jared Diamond has argued that we need to redefine progress - perhaps we need to rethink how we relate to Locke's statement that "God, who has given the world to men in common, has also given them reason to make use of it to the best advantage of life and convenience". Are we making the best use of it to the advantage of life and convenience?

We can also ask the question as to whether or not 'progress' is creating a better life. There are some trite ways of exploring that question. Has the mobile telephone, tethering us 24 hours a day, seven days a week, improved the quality of our lives. For many people working in companies where that tether is held tight, the answer is 'no': you can never 'leave' work. Another answer is that my enjoyment of life is at the cost of people in China, Vietnam, Mexico, Nicaragua or Cambodia being paid miserably low wages to make the products and goods I consume. Of course it is better they have some work rather than none: however, is it right they should be exploited for my benefit? Am I not complicit in treating other people as means to my ends?

There may be a more illuminating answer to this question, and this requires that we delve somewhat deeper into what we define as a good or better life. Socrates suggested that the only life worth living is an 'examined life' - and perhaps we should spend more time examining what kind of world we would want to inhabit. Remarkably, we have a unique opportunity to do that right now: while the commons that Locke was describing is long gone, we now have another much vaster commons, seemingly inexhaustible in its ability to keep providing according to our needs. That commons is the digital commons, the World Wide Web, where each person can keep taking information, as much as he or she might want, and still it is there for everyone else to use. Its existence allows us to rethink how we make use of the resources we have. The story so far is instructive.

The World Wide Web (the 'web') was developed at the beginning of the 1990s; at first as a development sitting on the top of a data transfer system that had been established between military agencies, and later universities, in the years before. The web has grown incredibly in the past twenty years, and analysts claim there is something like 40 billion pages of information available today on open searching. When it was developed by Tim Berners Lee (who put in place the early software necessary to make it work) and others, it was assumed that it would be free. Since then, we have seen two decades of people seeking to make money through the web: entrepreneurial capitalists are always looking for opportunities.

So far, if your searches on the web lead you to a physical object, or a service you require that is delivered by a person or a machine in the physical world, the systems of the capitalist free market continue to operate. You pay for the item - provided it is at a price you consider acceptable - and the product or service is delivered to you. However, the web is much more interesting when it comes to digital products and services. Many advocates of the web want to keep everything that is digitised free: however, many companies - and individuals - want to charge for those same digitized products.

The case of recorded music is a telling one. Before the web, recorded music existed in the form of a physical medium on which the recording had been placed. For some time, this was a 'record' (originally a '78', and later a vinyl disc of which the 'LP' was the standard). Things began to change when the recording was placed on a cassette tape, as it suddenly became much easier to copy music from one cassette to another (something which the recorded music industry tried to prevent, as it undermined the copyright they had in the recording). The same problem arose with CDs.

However, the industry was turned upside down when music was converted into an MP3 format, entirely digital, and easily placed on the web for someone to copy. In 1999 Napster commenced a 'peer to peer' sharing system, allowing one person to copy music from another using the web using the MP3 format. This was seen as a direct attack on the recording companies copyright, and Napster only lasted for 2 years. However, it signaled a process that has continued to this day. Despite every effort to stop this happening, more and more recorded music is freely available on the web, and recording companies are seeing their business shifting from selling recordings to promoting live performances and selling merchandise (and we can see the same processes changing the movie and TV industries, where increasingly income for these companies comes from advertising, product placement and merchandising, while income from DVD's continues to slide).

Why is this happening? It seems as though the rules of capitalism and the open market do not apply in the same way in the digital world. How can you have capital in cyberspace? Some companies try to 'enclose' a part of the web, putting a barrier and a system of subscriptions and passwords, around their territory. When it comes to commercial information 'in confidence', that is seen as part of the ways in which the physical world operates. When it applies to digital products and services, smart programmers quickly unpick what has been put in place. Sony's XCP and MediaMax were digital copyright protection systems put on to CDs to prevent copying, and their discovery provoked an uproar, and they had to be withdrawn: "the design of DRM systems is only weakly connected to the contours of copyright law. The systems make no pretense of enforcing copyright law as written, but instead seek to enforce rules dictated by the label's and vendor's business models. These rules, and the technologies that try to enforce them, implicate other public policy concerns, such as privacy and security," noted two reviewers of the ensuing events.[55] It seems likely that, like it or not, digital media will not easily be covered by the intellectual property laws that were developed to cover physical objects, and music and videos will continue to be freely available. However, this is contested territory, and companies are unlikely to retreat from this fight for a long time.

The new commons, the digital world, allows us to step back and ask if this sphere of life should be freely available to all, as Locke thought might have been the case with land when all the world was America. Certainly, the fact that the digital commons has remained largely free has not stopped innovation - far from it. There has been a massive development of applications and systems to exploit the riches of the web, which we may put on our computers of smart telephones free or charge, or for a minor cost. Many have improved the ease of living in contemporary society, even creating a 'better life'. Is this not the way we should go - with a shared commons, which we will all ensure is not partitioned or encroached on by companies or government? Is this creating an alternative path to progress quite different from the approach that has dominated the past two centuries? As people in developing countries are able to access the web and develop their applications and ideas, so we are seeing another change taking place - progress is taking place in the disadvantaged parts of the world, and the lessons from those developments put back into the developed world. You don't have to be a traditional capitalist to be contributor in the digital world.

Fencing off the commons has a long history. Common land in the United Kingdom was slowly eroded as landowners, often relying on 'enclosure acts', gradually took over more and more of previously open fields. Causing riots in the sixteenth and seventeenth centuries, the process continued, enriching the landowners by disenfranchising the poor who lost rights that went back over the centuries. By the end of the nineteenth century, common land had all but disappeared. That commons is long gone. As we have seen, the digital commons is similarly under threat today, as companies seek to find ways to fence of their place on the Internet.

In observing the enclosure process, the question arises as to what should be "freely available to all"? This is really a question about the limits to private property. To date, we have agreed that at least ideas should be freely available. While copyright or a patent may protect the particular expression of an idea, intellectual property protection laws make it clear that ideas themselves should be disclosed to allow others to take them further. This was the reasoning that lay behind the rules of patenting: that you had protection for the technology your idea created, but not for the idea itself, which would be revealed in your patent documentation.

If companies cannot build enclosures round ideas, they do work hard to enclose in other ways. One approach is to ensure that copyright is extended for as long as possible. This is dramatically illustrated by Disney's bizarre yet continuingly successful efforts to extend copyright for some of their materials. Lobbying every time it appeared that Mickey Mouse might fall out of copyright, the most recent Congressional support came with the passing of the Copyright Term Extension Act of 1998 that extended copyright terms in the United States[56]. In 1976 the Copyright Act gave protection for the life of the author plus 50 years, (and 75 years for corporate copyright). The Copyright Term Extension Act extended this to the life of the author plus 70 years. At the same time protection for works published prior to January 1, 1978, was increased by 20 years to a total of 95 years from their publication date. Quite a lot more than the 14 years of protection that existed in Jefferson's time!

Did I say 'bizarre'? Well, one of the defences put forward by companies like Disney to extend copyright is that this will enhance their competitiveness: now, I always thought that innovation was the way to ensure competitiveness, and that we frowned on monopolies. Not surprisingly, concerns about copyright extension are not just mine, and the extension to copyright protection has provoked a great deal of discussion and calls for reform[57]

Another controversial area of 'fencing off' has to do with the patenting of genes. The United States Patent and Trademark Office has issued some 3-5,000 patents for genes, and one study suggests that as many as 20% of human genes may already be covered by such patents[58]. This is problematic in many ways, not just because of the implications for innovation and competitiveness. For example, the American Civil Liberties Union argues that gene patents violate the Federal patent statute, which says that products of nature and laws of nature are not patentable subject matter. Defenders of gene patents argue they are valid because they apply to genes in their "isolated and purified" state, but the ACLU and Public Patent Foundation argue that "[h]uman genes, even when removed from the body, are still products of nature, and their associations with diseases are laws of nature."[59] It seems business is not only keen to continue the process of fencing off the commons by taking on the digital world, but also extending their fences into hitherto protected territory. Can business ever have enough?

As I continue to think about what constitutes progress and what makes for a better life, I am struck by one final thought: is there something else wrong here? When I started writing this chapter, two people were seeking to be the next President of the US. As part of that process they met to set out what the US needed to ensure its financial stability over the next few years, and how they were going make sure those needs were met. A lot of the time seemed to be taken up with plans to cut costs, reduce services, and restore the economy to allow individual effort and entrepreneurial activity to flourish. Both candidates seemed focussed on sustaining the 'old model' in the face of growing problems (with minor differences in emphasis and approach!). Surely the questions we have just been exploring - about the benefits of capitalist free market system versus the benefits of redefining progress and seeking to establish the good society; about the nature of the digital world and how it should continue to be freely available to all - surely these questions should be central to the contrasting approaches being put forward by the two rivals for the presidency of the US? In a forum where debate was supposed to take place, these were the issues that needed to be addressed. Well, just in case you hadn't noticed, they weren't!

The goal of progress provides the dynamic that is intrinsic to commercial enterprises. Companies rely on growth, and this creates an environment where there is pressure to consume, playing on our latent motives of greed and one-upmanship. But they are not our only motivations. I have no idea when – or even if – we will ever be able to reconstruct the economic system so that it is sustainable and satisfying, rather than exploiting the motivations of acquisition and aggrandizement. Markets can and do corrupt how we see the world. There are alternatives.

Some twenty years ago, my eldest daughter went to live in a hilly region close to Melbourne. A group of young people there re-established a system of barter, trying to escape from those corrupting influences of the monetary economy, and to set aside the wild desire to have yet more. It was only half successful. They still depended on roads, cars, computers and utilities. It is very hard to step outside the current system. However, twenty years on, such experiments are looking more likely to succeed. Robots can do most production. Money as a physical object is disappearing, and, at the local level, can be treated more as a digitized medium of exchange rather than an end in itself. The Internet has transformed much of what we do. We can – and I believe we will – develop better ways to live in harmony with the world around us, and when we do so, we will be able to find so much more to enjoy than the chase for more possessions.

Like many of the issues I am exploring in this book, the initial questions are familiar, but they are also misleading. At the beginning of this chapter, I asked 'can we ever have enough?' I hope you can see that the answer to that question should be 'No!' We should always be striving to learn more, understand more and even do more. However, a lot of what we seek to achieve can be directed towards the intrinsic satisfactions of mastery, insight, satisfaction and enjoyment. The more we seek to achieve does not have to be in the form of more physical goods; some of the most desirable things we can obtain are knowledge and wisdom, and they just sit inside our heads.

Much has been written on the depletion of natural resources and the ever-increasing levels of pollution in the atmosphere, soil and waterways of the world. While there continue to be arguments as to the extent and effects of climate change, there is little doubt that there are very real limits to quantities of non-renewable resources that are available to us, ranging from oil to potable water. If we continue to demand more, and if the developing world demands as much as the developed world has, then those limits will begin to have a real impact. This is becoming a redistributive issue. If we are to ensure that people in the developing world have enough - in the sense of shelter, food, clothing, basic medical care, heat, etc. - then this can only be achieved by the developed world being satisfied with less.

So here is a conflict staring us in the face. We know the demographics of the world, on track to include more than nine billion people by 2020, with an increasing percentage aged over 60 years old (and a declining percentage less than 15 years old). We can see that there are some very real resource limitations that will constrain how much can be done to enhance the position of the bottom 80% of the world's population. To date, we can see only two conventional choices. The first of these is to allow resource prices - from food and water to oil and gas - to increase: this will penalise the developing world, but leave the developed world comfortable but frightened for the future. The second is to rely on science and technology to find new ways to replace non-renewable resources, and enhance the efficiency of agriculture, construction and service delivery.

There is a third approach. Rather than focussing on how to ensure that everyone has more, we could seriously examine how to live with less and adopt the kind of approach Schumacher was advocating 40 years ago. This would mean giving up some of the 'things' we have and accept a different style of living; it might also mean that governments would have to rethink and reduce the level of expenditure on security and defence, and reconsider the importance of ensuring there is more expenditure on health, welfare and education. Are we capable of standing back and undertaking such a task, getting the balance right at both a personal and a government level? How bad will things have to get before we agree that action is essential?

It is easy to be caught up by the elephant of more things. More dangerous is to believe that things are all there is to more. I am reminded of a very good friend of mine, someone who had been a

CEO of major companies, sat on the boards of major enterprises, and, as a result, had acquired many things in his life. However, when we talked about business and success, he always came back to the same point: material success is obtainable, but there is one thing that you can never buy, and once lost, can never get back – and that is your integrity.

Integrity is not something more; it is something we already have early on in life. You can't have enough integrity, and you can't have more integrity: you either have it, or you don't. We can have enough stuff. However, we can never have enough wisdom: wisdom helps you understand what really matters – like integrity. Wisdom allows us to see ourselves as we are; wisdom may lead us to want to change the way we are.

7. Can we change?

There is one example of an elephant on roller skates that is particularly hard to manage, which is where the elephant is the way we are now, and we want to be different. In this situation the elephant on roller skates is actually pulling us back in the opposite direction from where we want to go, back to living the way we used to live.

I first became aware of this challenge a few years ago, when I had taken on a new position as the CEO of an organisation. I loved my new job. It was the second time I had been a CEO. Now I had my new organisation to build and grow, and I sat in my office thinking about what I could do. I found the job surprisingly easy. People would come and see me, and discuss what they were doing. They would ask me questions, and I would answer them. It was deeply satisfying.

I had the habit of getting to work early. I was living well away from the office, and to avoid traffic, I would leave home at 6 am, and be sitting at my desk at 7 am. I had a routine: read the morning papers, and while doing so muse over the meetings, the issues and the tasks that I knew were waiting to be addressed. It was a quiet, reflective time.

One morning, there was a knock on the door, and in came one of my staff. I was a little surprised, and a little miffed. This was my quiet time, and this was not my favourite member of staff. Hardworking and good at her job, but always a little too direct for my comfort. She asked me to look at a letter she had written. I glanced at it quickly. It was brief and to the point, and it seemed to me that it was also very clear and appropriate. I told her it was fine, hoping that she would leave. She didn't, and asked me to read it more carefully. I did so, feeling a little more annoyed at having to spend time on this: there really wasn't a question I could answer, and all I had was a letter that looked fine.

I guess it took a few more minutes before I realised that the letter was really an excuse for this staff member to raise a topic with me. There was an issue behind the letter that needed to be addressed.

Realising this, we had a long talk about the issue, resulting in her identifying a better way to address her concerns. Through discussion she came to realise there was another approach to the issues, one that allowed her to send a letter that would really meet the requirements of the correspondent at the other end, and, at the same time, meet the concerns of our organisation.

It was just before nine that she left my office, and I sat and thought carefully about what had happened. All of a sudden, I had to question how I had been behaving, behaviour that had been based on the approach I had learnt in my previous position. I saw that if I was going to be an effective CEO, I had to stop answering questions, (doing other peoples' work for them, if you like), and start to help people answer questions for themselves. When someone came to see me, my role was to tease out the issues with them, and then take part in an exploration of the options, hopefully in such a way that the colleague, not just I, saw the best path to adopt. I also had to expect that sometimes the discussion might result in an answer that would be quite different from mine. I had to stop thinking that I was so clever I could deal with anything, and instead create an organisation full of people who could do many things well.

Sometimes change is like that. A small thing can trigger the realisation that a comfortable approach is the wrong one, and that there is a need to do things differently. Writing about it now makes it all sound so easy. It wasn't. Years of being "clever" had to be wound back, and I had to make myself stop and think before I launched into an exposition on what needed to be done. I had to practice keeping my mouth shut!!

Now I can see that I was stumbling into adopting an approach that some writers on leadership call servant leadership, and others call adaptive leadership. Academic descriptions are interesting, but it is lived experience that matters: I had to work out how to behave differently, exercising helpful leadership, rather than being a clever leader.

Was there an elephant trying to pull me back, as it went backwards on its roller skates. There certainly was. I was proud of the skills I had developed over the years, and I was suffering from at least a mild case of *hubris*. Pride does come before a fall, and I was lucky I hadn't made a big mistake. That elephant was about confidence in my abilities, and it was tugging away at me, wanting me to go back to behaving in a way based on my previous view of myself, as someone who was clever, capable, and in charge.

Not all change is like that, of course. Sometimes the desire to change comes upon us more slowly, seeping into the way we work. That happened to me some eight years later than the first incident. I was getting a little bored with myself and with the work I was doing. In part that attitude might have been self-fulfilling, reflecting my belief that a person can only be effective in a position for a limited time, precisely because he or she becomes convinced of his or her competence, and too easily see the "new" challenges that come forward, wrongly, as things that have been addressed and resolved before. Whatever the reasons, when I had the opportunity to go to Aspen, and take part in The Aspen Institute's Executive Seminar I jumped at the chance. In those days, the seminar comprised two weeks of facilitated discussion, using short extracts from famous philosophers, historians and political economists as the starting point for the conversations that took place around the table (now the Executive Seminar is only one week long).

The two weeks were magical. I loved reading and exploring the ideas we were asked to debate. Our moderator was a wise, well-read facilitator, who managed our discussions deftly, making sure we all took part on an equal basis. My fellow participants came from government, the private sector and business, and from different parts of the world. I came back determined to set up something similar in Australia, and with the help of several people The Cranlana Programme was established. However, the point of this story is about what I learnt, not what I did.

The seminar experience had re-awakened my love of teaching, a love that had been set aside some twenty years before when I had left the academic world to go into industry, and then on to various other jobs and experiences. I was never an academic researcher, determined to explore new areas, and discover new knowledge: this was not because of a lack of interest in new ideas, but because research topics always seemed so narrow and specific. I was a teacher at heart, and loved facilitating the learning of others. Slowly, I began to think that I should change careers again, and go back into some kind of teaching role. This was a much harder change. I had no track record as an academic, and knew I would find it hard to get back into the university world.

At the same time, I had become accustomed to the car, the Personal Assistant, and a whole organisation that could work on topics that I found interesting and which I saw would help further our objectives. You might say there was a very big elephant, on very well-oiled roller skates, very determined to pull me back in the wrong direction to a way of life that was familiar and comfortable. I am pleased to report that the elephant lost out: I did change what I did, and overcame my resistance to abandoning a lifestyle to which I had become accustomed

These two stories illustrate something very important about the elephants on roller skates that make it hard for us to change. We create these elephants ourselves, and they are close to us: familiar, friendly, loved even. Why would anyone resist the pull of that which is comfortable, satisfying, and deeply ingrained in our behaviour? Moreover, we quickly discover that our friends don't help, as they keep asking why on earth you would want to give up what you are doing successfully. Habits don't help, either, as they trick you back into following those well-worn routines that have made you what you are.

Change also takes time. While the decision to change can sometimes be made quickly, the process itself can extend over months, even years. Change has to work its way through, and it is easy to become impatient, to feel that nothing is being achieved, and give up. Anyone who has tried to change his or her eating habits can understand this. Perhaps you have decided to cut back on carbohydrates, give up on eating those lovely fruit muffins and chocolate cup cakes. For a day or so, it is really hard work. You find that breaking the habit of a eating a (small?) cake with morning coffee takes an effort, especially if your friends are still happily munching away. For much longer, there is a lingering taste shortfall: you would love to have just one piece of sweet cake, just one! Of course, just one cake is all it takes to waste all that hard work. All the while you are trying to resist cakes you are monitoring your weight. Has it gone down? A little to begin with, and that little bit of evidence reinforces your resolve. Then nothing seems to happen for a long time. Why bother with the withdrawal symptoms for no evident gain? Why were you doing this anyway: we all know that what is regarded as harmful one year is taken off the 'banned' list a year later!

It is easy to tell a story like this, which probably comes across as something of a parody. However, change really is hard work, and there are numerous reasons to abandon the attempt in the face of criticism, a lack of encouraging evidence, and a lack of will power. Even worse, change follows its own logic, and your expectations as to what will happen are not always borne out. I have always liked the phrase "like riding a tiger". Trying to change is like riding a tiger: it may be docile for a while, but suddenly it will race off, and it may take you to places you had not envisioned. Change can be a "wild ride".

The process of change clearly runs much deeper than that. We invest in the person we become, and that person becomes our "self". If that sounds rather odd, perhaps we can look at it this way. In order to take on a role in life, and to perform reasonably well in that role, we have to put in a lot of effort. Some of that effort is in learning skills, languages and practices that are necessary to accomplish the tasks we perform. Some of that effort is in how we learn to present ourselves, our public face. Some of that effort goes more deeply into how we see ourselves: we are the person in that position, and even though we indulge ourselves by thinking about the "real me" that sits somewhere inside our heads, that is just an indulgence. The person that exists is the one we, and everyone else, can see doing things. For all practical purposes we are how we behave, not how we imagine ourselves to be.

That means that the task of change is not just about doing something different, taking on a new job, moving to a new organisation. It is actually about work on your "self", about becoming a different person.

We can see this particularly clearly when we look at someone who has undergone involuntary change. An uncomfortable example that comes to mind is when a friend suddenly finds her partner has left her – a marriage, a major investment in how we see ourselves, falls apart. The process of recovery from an event like that is hard and slow. The facts are easy, but your friend quickly discovers that rethinking who she is is far from easy. Colleagues and acquaintances have to make choices, and sometimes they are unexpected: perhaps she discovers that one of her close friends decides to ally herself with the partner who left and not with her. Why? She is forced to ask herself what is it about me that made my previously close friend make that choice?

If you have observed a friend go through this experience, then you will know what a disconcerting and upsetting process this is. You can see there are so many reasons she might want to go back to the way things were. Sometimes well-meaning friends try to bring the partner back to encourage reconciliation, believing that the whole thing was just a mistake. This may be right some occasions, but on many occasions it simply exacerbates the problems and rekindles the sense of unhappiness that had resulted from the break-up in the first instance.

It is also hard to deal with the changes that result from a partner dying unexpectedly. However, there is a sense that in this case dealing with a partner dying is actually "easier" than having a partner leave (but I don't want to diminish how deeply distressing this situation is). The point I am making is that no elephant can pull you back with the same immediacy once your partner is no longer alive; elephants can be very tricky when your partner is still around, maybe even living close by, or working near to where you often go, constantly reminding you how things were before.

In the examples we have considered so far, the issue is that we *can* change when we want to or when we have to, even if the process is uncomfortable. Perhaps we should explore a more complex idea – that we might want to change for the sake of change, rather than because we need to so for some external reason. This is about wanting to change and become different for our own more personal reasons. How can we resist the elephant whose efforts are pulling us back from making changes in this case?

One example of this is to be seen in people who discover they have a calling. Many people find it hard to understand when a friend, unexpectedly, decides he has been called to become a priest. It is a convention to use the word 'calling' to refer to those who decide to enter the church, but actually someone may find he or she has a calling to become a nurse, a writer, or a comedian. It isn't that there is a position to apply for, but rather that there is a strong conviction that this is the path that his or her life must now take, even if it means abandoning a well paid job, a comfortable home, or even a happy partnership.

Callings are unpredictable: they can be sudden and unanticipated, and for that reason all the more challenging to those who felt they knew their friend well before they changed. On the other hand, the power of having experienced a calling is such that it may provide the determination necessary to make the changes that are required, even if those changes require years of training and practice before that new life can be fully undertaken.

To experience a calling is not common. To aspire to be different from the way you have been is a rather more common experience. But now we enter a particularly challenging process of change – this is no longer about an external demand (a new job, a partner abandoning you), nor is it about a sudden but unshakeable faith about a new direction (a calling). This is where there is a gnawing desire to do something different, often a change that is unclear and unfocussed, and where there is a great big elephant happily pulling you back to where you have been. Can you change when you don't *have* to change?

To answer that question, we have to look more closely at what change means. Obviously to change is to do things differently. The one key word there is *do*. Doing is about behaviour – about actions out there, not just in your head. To do something different poses three challenges that require hard work: they are about competence, context, and habit (and all the while there is this one big elephant nudging you back to the comfort of skills, habits and friends that are familiar!).

The first challenge is about competency. When we do what we have always done, we have a practiced competency, a set of skills and experiences on which we draw, sometimes almost intuitively. To do something different, to make a significant change, requires the development of new competencies, as well as learning how to apply them.

For example, if you have been a musician all your life, you have spent much of your time practicing, teaching, playing and learning new repertoire. To decide to change all that and become a visual artist, say, represents a major change in the skills you will now want to employ. The musical instrument disappears, and is replaced by a new set of tools, tools that do nothing of themselves, as they are all tools of potential. There are no familiar keys to press, but unwieldy mediums, brushes and palette knives, and alarmingly blank pieces of paper or canvas. Often in a very real sense, you realise you will have to go back to school.

To go back to school, to be taught again, can be embarrassing and confronting. Someone is pointing out your mistakes. The techniques you need to learn ("why do I have to learn this, in particular, you wonder?") expose your physical limitations. Although you may not remember with great clarity how hard it had been to learn your instrument, you are now going to go through all that again, possibly with less flexibility than before (but that might be balanced by greater patience). More to the point, the brush won't do what you want it to do, at least begin with, and it takes time (and a lot of frustration) to gain the mastery you need.

That is only the first challenge. The second is about the context of change. While you are trying to establish new competencies, you are not living in isolation – there are people around you who knew you when you were the musician. You find you have to manage a wholly new set of expectations, reactions and suggestions. They can range from those who inadvertently hold you back: "I know you are busy, but would you mind playing with this group for the next couple of weeks, as they've lost a key player"; to those who expect you to be running already, "I've always wanted a painting of my mother, and I was hoping you would be able to do something. She is getting pretty old now, and I don't want to leave it too long ……"

Partners, children and close friends can sometimes be the most difficult (and sometimes the most supportive, or course!). Even if they are wholeheartedly encouraging your process of transformation, they may fail to see that the change is not superficial, and still expect you to do things you always did. As a musician, your work was in the evening, practicing in the morning, and the afternoons were left for housework, reading and cooking. It turns out that art doesn't have that kind of timetable, and dinners may get forgotten, or appointments missed.

Learning new skills and dealing with the expectations of others are major challenges, but so is the third issue we listed above, in some ways the most difficult of all, which is managing your own ingrained habits and rituals. Before you *were* a musician, and that was part of the embedded self you had become. Now you have to throw off a deeply established part of yourself, and become a different you. That is a change that can have many consequences, from self-doubt ("will I ever be any good as an artist?") to self-reexamination ("do I want to live as I did before, do I still want to be with the same friends, or even the same partner?").

I deliberately picked a relatively easy change, of course. An artist and a musician probably share at least some attributes, both seem to be concerned with expressive and interpretive activities. Both are generally poorly paid, too!! However, if I had made my example of change going from being a musician to becoming a geologist, the whole process of change would probably have been a great deal more daunting.

My example is not just about degrees of difficulty, however. It is to make the point that our ability to change is in large part about how we see ourselves, and how we want to see ourselves differently. But to make that shift requires that others around you will work with you to make that change work, or the battle will be long and hard. There is a sense in which the best way to really change is to run away, to go somewhere where you are not known, so that all the stuff about the expectations of others, the habits by which you are known, even the way you have lived your life before, all these can be quickly sloughed off. In running away, you have escape from being pulled by an elephant. Unfortunately, most of the time it turns out that running away is not an option!

To describe the challenges is not to answer the question: "can we change?" It simply sets out a series of hurdles to overcome. Rather than focusing solely on the degrees of difficulty in making changes, it might also be helpful to examine the concept of "degrees of freedom" – the amount of "space" you have to make changes. Those degrees of freedom are partly external, and partly internal.

The external degrees of freedom are a function of what we are doing with our lives, and what obligations we have to those around us. For example, it is likely to be much easier to change when you are 22 years old than when you are 42 years old. Most young people have yet to settle in a career or future path. Indeed, it is often a time of experimentation, testing out alternatives, trying new ideas to see what seems to fit.

Twenty years later, you are more likely to be in a long-term relationship, and perhaps have responsibility for one or more children. Parents may be getting older, and you are thinking about what they will need in the future. The degrees of freedom seem somewhat reduced. Another twenty years later, they may have increased again. Children may have grown up (they will be older, but being 'grown-up' might be more than that!). You and your partner may be in a position to contemplate retirement, at least in the sense of no longer having to work full-time or continue to do what you have done before. Parents may need attention and care, but there is a good chance that the ways to do this have already been discussed, agreed and put into place.

These shifting degrees of freedom that sit around you are fateful (to use our running metaphor, the elephant can change in size and influence!!). They can stifle an emerging desire to change, or enable you to go on and do something quite different. They are not fixed, but they certainly play a central role influencing the ability to change.

The factors that shape our internal degrees of freedom are less easily categorised. We often talk about being "stuck in a rut", or just "stuck", and at other times being "ready to move on". Even though we are often poor judges of our own situation and our flexibility, these are the ways in which we judge our freedom to move. Anxiety about change makes us tentative, and even though we think we are ready to do something different, initial feedback can quickly stop us in our tracks. "You are thinking of doing *what*?" Someone has just put an elephant onto roller skates, and they have even taken the trouble to launch it off on its way, just for you! On the other hand someone may say, "Go for it" and push you into commencing a process of change for which you are ill prepared mentally, and you discover the degree of freedom was much smaller than you thought.

Of course, we are talking about non-trivial change. When we are thinking of living a very different life from that we led before, the dead weight of inertia can be very great, whether it comes from within or from those around you. However, inertia has a funny effect: once you start to change, then you begin to build up momentum, and then the weight shifts to pushing you forward, even if you are no longer so confident that this was what you wanted to do! It is like confronting one of those huge grinding wheels at a water mill. Try to move that stone (it may weigh a few tons), and it is almost impossible to shift it at all. Keep pushing it, fifty times, a hundred times, and it starts to move. Push some more and all of a sudden, the wheel is moving and it is almost impossible to stop. So it is with making changes. There are many obstacles to stop the process getting under way, but once you are a little way down the track, it becomes easier. You feel more confident, and those around you begin to see you in a new light. It may be impossible to go back!

Can we change? Yes, we can. If circumstances force change, or make it easy, the process is less difficult. Where the motivation is internal, so the barriers to change may be much greater. In all cases, the biggest issue is to fight the elephant trying to pull you back to where you were, as you start to move away, it gets on the roller skates and starts to move in the opposite direction.

To ask if we can change presumes that we have addressed another question, "Should we change?" Having the ability or opportunity to change is not the same as knowing that such a change is desirable. Involuntary change is one matter, as there is no choice. But when we are thinking about choosing to do something different, it might be a good idea to go back and ask, "Why?" While the last chapter of this book focuses on the importance of thinking and reflection, it might be worth having a preview at this point.

In examining whether we can turn into someone different, we realised that making a change is not a trivial business. If change means becoming another person, then it is clearly worth asking *why* we want to be a different person. If our motivations are negative, because we don't like the person we have been, or we don't want to keep leading the life we have led, there is every reason to think carefully about what will be different when we change. We might make some external changes in what we do, but we might leave a lot of our psychology intact. When we focus on performing a new set of tasks, developing new competencies, then there is a risk our other attributes will not change as much as we might have hoped. Was that what we wanted?

The other alternative is that you seek to make a change because there are new things to explore, to learn and to do. This is a positive driver, encouraging us to experiment, (bringing out the inner gypsy in you!). I can think of few things more exciting than changing for these reasons, so it seems almost churlish to add, "but be careful". When you change, it is not like putting on a new and different pair of shoes; the next day, you can go back to wearing the older pair you now realise you preferred. You can't go back, because you are no longer the same person you were.

That rather strange remark "you can't step into the same river twice" makes that point very clearly: things might look the same, but they are different, and they will never go back to the way they were before.

Actually, there are at least two ways of thinking about that image of stepping into the river twice. The first is that things change, and you can't go backwards. The other way is to think about the river: whether or not you step in it, it is never the same from one moment to the next. That is true of us, too, for we (just like the world around us) also keep changing, even if those changes are usually gradual and unremarkable. The issue for us then becomes whether we want to change consciously, redirect the flow of our lives, and end up in a different place. We can, even though it will be hard work. However, there is still that earlier question which is still worth asking, and that is whether we are prepared for where we might find ourselves.

Up to this point we have been talking about change as a personal matter. There is another perspective on change, which has to do with social or organisational change. Anyone who has worked in a large organisation knows that they are, in effect, systems to prevent change. Organisations develop policies, "standard operating procedures", rules and cultures, all of which reinforce the way things are done, and militate against innovation. They are analogous to those huge container ships and oil tankers that cross the oceans: huge, moving with massive momentum, and very hard to quickly turn or reverse. In same way, organisations are also rigid, they suffer from inertia, and they are slow to change (they are, after all, the exemplars of bureaucracy). Despite all this, they do have one important characteristic when it comes to making changes. Organisations are among the last bastions against democracy, they are centrally controlled and can be dictated to: they can be *made* to change!

To explore organisational change, we get a helpful perspective by going back to Machiavelli. Niccolo Machiavelli is one of those misunderstood figures in history that really deserves a better press. He was a political scientist, and was one of the leading analysts of his time: today we would also call him an empiricist, relying on observation and the analysis of facts to draw his conclusions. Somehow his dry-eyed observations have been turned back on him, and Machiavelli is now seen as some kind of evil schemer, seeking to grab power and hang on to it by any devious means. Actually, what he wrote was simply a description of what he saw! Ever pragmatic, he wanted to understand how people gain power, and how they keep it.

The Prince could well be described as a 'Dummies guide to Leadership', and just like many of those funny yellow books, his observations summarise what is now deeply ingrained in our beliefs, in this case the "accepted" model of how to run an organisation. When I was younger, it was called the '*ploc*' approach: management was about planning, leading, organising and controlling, and the emphasis was on the last word. In making his observations about princes and the ways they gained and kept their power, Machiavelli realised that a central issue was how you maintain control. In looking at what had to be done, he shared Glaucon's somewhat jaundiced view of the world: his view of humanity is encapsulated in this characteristically brief but pointed comment: "For it may be said of men in general that they are ungrateful, voluble, dissemblers, anxious to avoid danger, and covetous of gain".

Given his recognition of the importance of self-interest, so well expressed in the observation "*You gotta look after number one, right? It's a good idea to look out for number one. Who else will?*"[60] Machiavelli argued there was a need for leaders to cultivate obedience in their followers (this is the standard and universally recommended approach to dealing with the self-interested anti-social selfishness illustrated in the quotes we have just read). To ensure obedience, you need a carrot for encouragement, and a stick to keep them in line.

Actually, Machiavelli was very interesting on the subject of carrots and sticks. When he asked, "Is it better to be loved or feared?" the answer was clear, he suggested:

"The reply is, that one ought to be both feared and loved, but as it is difficult for the two to go together, it is much safer to be feared than loved, if one of the two has to be wanting. For it may be said of men in general that they are ungrateful, voluble, dissemblers, anxious to avoid danger, and covetous of gain; as long as you benefit them, they are entirely yours; they offer you their blood, their goods, their life, and their children, as I have before said, when the necessity is remote; but when it approaches, they revolt. And the prince who has relied solely on their words, without making other preparations, is ruined; for the friendship which is gained by purchase and not through grandeur and nobility of spirit is bought but not secured, and at a pinch is not to be expended in your service. And men have less scruple in offending one who makes himself loved than one who makes himself feared; for love is held by a chain of obligation which, men being selfish, is broken whenever it serves their purpose; but fear is maintained by a dread of punishment which never fails."[61]

Well, we can forget about love! Indeed, we can forget about trying to be nice. He has another set of acerbic comments to make on being generous, and, once again, I can do no better than quote:

"I say that it would be well to be considered liberal; nevertheless liberality such as the world understands it will injure you; because if used virtuously and in the proper way, it will not be known, and you will incur the disgrace of the contrary vice. But one who wishes to obtain the reputation of liberality among men, must not omit every kind of sumptuous display, and to such an extent that a prince of this character will consume by such means all his resources, and will be at last compelled, if he wishes to maintain his name for liberality, to impose heavy taxes on his people, become extortionate, and do everything possible to obtain money. This will make his subjects begin to hate him, and he will be little esteemed being poor, so that having by this liberality injured many and benefited but few, he will feel the first little disturbance and be endangered by every peril. If he recognizes this and wishes to change his system, he incurs at once the charge of niggardliness.

A prince, therefore, not being able to exercise this virtue of liberality without risk if it be known, must not, if he be prudent, object to be called miserly. In course of time he will be thought more liberal, when it is seen that by his parsimony his revenue is sufficient, that he can defend himself against those who make war on him, and undertake enterprises without burdening his people, so that he is really liberal to all those from whom he does not take, who are infinite in number, and niggardly to all to whom he does not give, who are few."[62]

Love and generosity seem to be out of the window, and Machiavelli's observations seem to suggest that our human nature *is* to be selfish, it *is* a given, and we have to address selfishness through *exercising control.* However, if Machiavelli is right in drawing these conclusions, does that mean change has to be forced on us?

History is on Machiavelli's side. Kings and emperors, CEO's and presidents, all have shown a predisposition for making change from the top, by fiat, laws, and the use of power. While I sometimes believe we have progressed little from Machiavelli's observations and conclusions (and organisations are much as they always were), there is at least one different strand in management today that places a focus on collaboration, enablement and the "servant leadership" approach I mentioned earlier.[63] A participative approach can mean that all voices are heard, and that change is brought about because everyone takes part in a discussion about what is required, using a collaborative approach to come to agreement. This is not an approach that denies our individual predisposition to self-interest, but rather argues, "the way to a better society lies in appealing to the rational self-interest of *all* concerned".[64]

What does this mean for organisational change? It suggests that rather telling people what they will do in the future and what the changes should be, a leader should set the agenda at a higher level. Having defined the principles and the goals to be achieved, the leader should then leave the operating areas of the organisation to agree on the necessary changes in their area that will best meet those higher order goals. Let those closest to the action work out how to deal with the local issues.

As Charles Handy suggested some years ago, the Roman Catholic Church advocated a good model for this. For many years, the church operated on the basis of subsidiarity: "It means that power belongs to the lowest possible point in the organisation. 'A higher order body should not take unto itself responsibilities which properly belong to a lower order body' is how a 1941 papal encyclical puts it, because subsidiarity has long been part of the doctrine (if not always the practice) of the Catholic Church".[65] This is, in effect, a system of multi-level governance, comparable to the democratic system used in Switzerland.

Both of these systems have their limitations, of course, and the Pope certainly promulgates principles that may overrule the preferences of parishioners; the Swiss system has several checks and balances, which limit the likelihood of radical change taking place. However, subsidiarity is a system that allows, at least to some degree, the resolution of what needs to be done through debate and the consideration of rational self-interest, finding solutions "from the ground up" (or at least at ground level), rather than from the top down.

Charles Handy also identified another issue central to change when we look at organisations, and that concerns how we treat employees. Companies were created at a time when the need for capital to undertake developments and build new areas of business exceeded the resources that an owner could provide. Through selling shares, a wide range of people could invest in a company and provide it with the capital needed to build its activities. Somehow, buying shares has become seen as "owning" an enterprise, as if the company and the people it employs were something you could possess. On that logic, not only can companies be bought and sold, but also so can the people who work in them. Intuitively, there is something wrong here.

Charles Handy saw two problems with the approach. First, owning shares is only a form of investment. As he put it, shareholders are "more akin to punters at the races, as the Economist once described them, placing their money on their financial runners."[66] Shareholders get a return on their investment if the company prospers, through dividends and the increasing value of their shares, and lose out if it does not. The only thing they clearly own is the share certificate, which they can trade on the share market!

Second, when equity funding was first developed, the money was largely used to acquire and build property, plant and equipment. The assets of many companies today largely comprise their staff, with relatively few physical assets and those mainly required to allow the staff to perform their tasks. Can anyone own the people in a company? The concept of owning people was largely set aside with the abolition of slavery in the 19th Century. As the 13th Amendment to the United States Constitution in 1865 stated: "Neither slavery nor involuntary servitude, except as a punishment for crime whereof the party shall have been duly convicted, shall exist within the United States, or any place subject to their jurisdiction."

Rather than seeing a company and its staff as a thing, to be owned, bought and sold, Handy suggests it is better seen as a "community" that has some common property. In this model, the staff of the company are best described as the members of the community. Not only would this approach ensure that we move away from the idea that shareholders own the company and its people, but it has other implications. Seeing yourself as a member of an organisation will inevitably change the way you see your role: as a member, you will be more concerned with acting as a steward for the company, seeking to ensure that the assets are used well and that the enterprise is sustainable, both in itself, and in its use of external resources[67].

Handy is a provocative writer, pushing us to re-examine things that have become so familiar that they have disappeared from real scrutiny. Our image of the corporation is another elephant on roller skates. To re-examine how we see companies and the financial system that surrounds them is a huge task, but the need exists, and we should not be held back by an unwillingness to scrutinise and even change the peculiar system that has developed from the need some two hundred years ago to raise funds for business activities.

Handy sparked a great deal of debate in asking "What is a company for?" and his lecture led to the formation of the Centre for Tomorrow's Company, which currently spearheads efforts to change the institutional structure of work and investment. The Centre's proposals have encountered a great deal of resistance, as there is a very weighty elephant trying to stop change in this area. Nonetheless, the Centre is building an agenda of which every businessperson should be aware.[68]

For both individuals and organisations, bringing about change is still a matter of compromise. We want to be free to do what we want, and escape the systems, rules and habits of the past. We also want to be fair, respecting the views, needs and concerns of others. In that sense, change is about the pragmatic balancing act when seeking to find the path that lies between the ideals of Mill's liberty and Rawls' justice. It is a difficult path, and for that reason we often choose to live with things the way they are, grumbling about the issues that annoy us, but unwilling to take on the real work of creating a better future.

Sometimes avoidance is not possible, however, when change is forced upon us. The heading of this chapter is "Can we change'", but it might have been more accurate to have worded it "We have to change". For the past 15 years I have been asking students in MBA courses and managers in executive programs to stand back and think about the changes that are taking place today. I have suggested that we are going through a period of major revolution, an information revolution comparable to the industrial revolution of 200 years ago, and the internal combustion engine revolution of 100 years ago. This is a revolution enabled by information and communications technologies, a revolution which is transforming every area of business, as well as financial services, education, medicine, entertainment and culture. Based on the history of previous such major revolutions, from printing onwards, the changes that result will play out over decades, and we are probably only now in the middle stages of the current revolution and its consequences.

The scale of these changes was well captured in a recent popular article, *Prancing on a volcano*, which caught some of the magnitude of what is happening in stating:

"When Ronald Reagan was sworn in for his second term, in 1985, the Human Genome Project was still years away, but the era of genetic engineering would soon be upon us, bringing capabilities we may not want but cannot forestall. Cell phones in the Reagan era were bigger than bananas (if not breadboxes)—it's impossible to watch the movie Wall Street today without laughing—and the Internet was in an embryonic state, known to few and used by fewer. The rise of the Internet has been the biggest leap forward in communications since Gutenberg; it has changed the nature of information, made privacy obsolete, put vast new power in the hands of corporations and government agencies, and become a weapon of war that anyone can deploy. Money ricochets around the world like so many charged electrons, making a mockery of national borders and undermining the very idea of the nation-state. (China owns two-thirds as much of the U.S. debt as the Federal Reserve itself does.) At home and abroad the availability of sophisticated weaponry has the same destabilizing effect. The migration of peoples from one place to another sparks conflict and violence but also establishes new realities on the ground. When Reagan took office, the United States was 83 percent white; last year, for the first time, more than half of American children under one year of age belonged to a minority group. Meanwhile, the world is run by a new, multi-national global elite that is educated and affluent and owes loyalty mainly to itself, rather than to any cause or country. The

Financial Times is its constitution. The "Ambassador" lounges at airports are its embassies."[69]

Allowing for a certain amount of journalistic hyperbole, these are amazing times. The writers went on to quote from Abraham Lincoln, who said in 1862, "The dogmas of the quiet past are inadequate to the stormy present. The occasion is piled high with difficulty, and we must rise with the occasion. As our case is new, so we must think anew and act anew. We must disenthrall ourselves, and then we shall save our country."[70]

They could also have referred to Albert Einstein, who is reputed to have said, "The significant problems we have cannot be solved at the same level of thinking with which we created them." If we are going through a process of transformation into a "new world" as many commentators and researchers suggest, then we will *have* to change. Experience should tell us that the changes that are required are profound, not just about what we do, but they are also about how we see ourselves, our relationship with others, and the world around us. They will require us to rethink, and set aside ways of thinking that are becoming less and less well suited to the world around us.

There is one simple but clear illustration of that rethinking process. In the late 19th Century, a number of measures were developed to protect 'intellectual property'. Today, there are a whole set of such forms of protection, ranging from patents to various forms of copyright. The logic of intellectual property (IP) protection was clear: innovative ideas should be made available to everyone, but an inventor should have the means to realise some benefits from having come up with a new idea, a new process or product. The key point in this was that protection was extended to the physical manifestation of thinking - the book, the machine - but not to the thinking itself. Until recently, the distinction between the physical object and the idea has been clear: I can buy the object, the manifestation of someone's thinking, but I can't buy the idea (although I can buy someone's time to generate ideas for me, which can then result in a book or a new product or service, which is exactly what companies do in hiring research and development staff).

All this has begun to fall apart in the 21st Century as more and more of what is valuable is knowledge, and that is available in digitised form on the Internet. In many ways, the World Wide Web is like a vast, free copying machine: the same piece of digitised information can be copied a million times, and yet it still sits there waiting to be copied again. If I sell a car, then I no longer possess it. If one of my knowledge products sits on the Web, it can be copied, but it is still available to me - and anyone else. The World Wide Web was established on the basis that everything that sat there was free. If I try to sell my ideas on the Web, you can be sure there are plenty of people who will seek to make what I have done freely available, as this is seen to be the purpose of establishing the Internet. In this world, the rules of IP are harder and harder to align with what is happening. They worked well in a world of tangible things, but not well in a world of digital products and services. We will return to this topic in a later chapter.

For now, here is a powerful illustration of Einstein's comment. Today, companies around the world are trying hard to keep the same control over their property as they did in the past, refusing to acknowledge that the world is changing around them. Some are moving forward. Companies that used to sell recorded music on CDs are slowly changing to adapt to a world in which most recorded music will be free (perhaps all will be eventually?), and so are transferring their business to selling other products in the physical world - concerts and merchandise. They are thinking differently.

Change is always taking place, but there are times when the pace and nature of change seem to reach a crescendo. That appears to be the case right now. Or so it seems. There is another perspective on what has been happening, however, which is to suggest that the reality of change is not as great as it might appear. Essentially, what we are witnessing is, in large part, the consequences of better technologies to collect and use data. After all, that is exactly and yet all that Google does: it collects data from users, analyses that data, and then uses it to better target each user's interests and concerns. In effect, it is simply streamlining customer responsiveness. Streamlining is certainly nothing new: that was something the Japanese realised when they developed 'just in time' manufacturing. While the world of big data and faster transfer and analysis of data is changing things, perhaps the only change is in the speed with which this can be done. Is a speeded up world a different world? Maybe it is just a more market efficient world, and we have already explored the challenges that arise if we allow the market too much space.

In situation of rapid change, it is easy for people to be left behind. Some of the most interesting writing on leadership recognises that part of leadership is helping people adapt to change as it takes place. The role of the leader is to understand what is taking place and seek to use foresight and intuition to anticipate where change is leading, and then help others by articulating a framework that makes sense of what is happening. This is often described as the role of the servant leader.[71]

A leader with foresight today will be trying to understand what is really taking place. There is a lot of rapid change, but much of it may be superficial, just things being done more quickly than they were before. Some industries are being affected by digitisation, but in many cases that may lead to redefining how the business operates: this may be what we can learn from the music industry, where selling recorded music is becoming a smaller part of their business, and becoming event promoters and merchandisers is becoming larger. An "internet of things" may make communication between devices, monitors and computers take place seamlessly and efficiently: this could transform medical care, for example. As I try to makes sense of what I see, I am torn between accepting that the "digital information revolution" will change our world, or concluding that the only important shift is to make the market economy even more dominant.

We have to change? Perhaps the rhetoric hides the reality that we are being changed, being pushed closer to participants in a world where everything has its price, and the only measure of value is the dollar. Certainly change is taking place, and the task today is trying to assess where those changes are taking us. We need to be aware of the obvious differences that come from smartphones and their apps, intelligent software in various products, and the pervasive world of the Internet.

At the same time, we need to subject the heralds of a new emerging world to careful scrutiny, both technology commentators and enthusiastic business builders alike. There is a much-cited quote attributed to Petronius:

> *"We trained hard . . . but it seemed that every time we were beginning to form up into teams we would be reorganized. I was to learn later in life that we tend to meet any new situation by reorganizing; and a wonderful method it can be for creating the illusion of progress while producing confusion, inefficiency, and demoralization."*

It seems he never said this, but the sentiment is still worth remembering: we should beware the "illusion of progress", especially as it may be masking changes much worse than merely "confusion, inefficiency and demoralization". If this exploration of the dangers of elephants on roller skates does anything, I hope it encourages you to keep questioning and keep thinking!

Understanding the nature of change, using foresight and working with others to adapt to new circumstances is not just a matter of leadership, of course. Change at a personal level also impacts on how we relate to other people, how we keep in touch with them, and how we take the trouble to really understand them. Keeping in touch is the topic to which we now turn, in the following chapter.

8. Keeping in touch

In your circle of friends, do you have one or two who you know will always be there when you want them, and who don't demand long explanations as to why you haven't been in contact recently? This category of "true friends" is a very interesting one, because their friendship does not depend on your constantly "keeping in touch". What makes the situation all the more interesting is that when you do go and see them, it is as if you had been there yesterday. You just sit down and talk as usual, as if there had never been an interruption from the last meeting that took place days, weeks, months or even years ago.

Perhaps I can put this observation a different way round. Why is it that we feel obliged to "keep in touch" with some people, and yet others we are close to do not expect the same frequent contact from us? What is this business of keeping in touch? Is "keeping in touch" the same thing when we are talking about close family members as it is when we are referring to our wider circle of friends? There is yet another sense in which keeping in touch which is important and to which we will refer later in this chapter, and and that refers to the task of keeping in touch with what is happening, and even with events in the world more broadly.

If we start at the personal level, we often describe keeping in touch another way, we talk about "staying in contact". Both these phrases – "keeping in *touch*" and "staying in *contact*" – use a physical word and that betrays something very important about this process at the personal level: it is not just about facts, it is about feelings, emotion, or, if you like, the whole person. All this makes a great deal more sense when we are physically together.

Keeping in touch at the personal level is a relatively easy task when we can see the other person, (as long as we are paying attention, of course!) We know our close friends, partners, and children well, and we are quick to pick up the nuances of behaviour that suggest something out of the ordinary.

Of course, this is a two-way street. Those same people in these close personal relationships know us, too. While they may be being themselves, there are times when they choose to "present" themselves to us, so that we respond in the way that they want. Children are past masters at this art. They know their parents well, and can quickly encourage the response they want. Adept in the subtleties of communication, they draw us in, by a little flicker of the lower lip, an imperceptible drop in the eyes. Unseen by others, and subconsciously read by us, we are guided to support, to agree, to change our minds. Often we do not realise what we are doing, but we are always pleased to see we have said the right thing. Reinforcement is everything!

This alerts us to something else that is important about keeping in touch at the personal level: it is easy to slip from paying attention to following learnt responses. The rituals of a relationship can take over from the reality. We respond as we have learnt to respond. It is like watching the courtship ritual of birds: the patterns of behaviour are well established, automatic, instinctive even, and it all works. Well, it works at one level at least some of the time.

Sometimes the choreography of practiced interactions goes off course. We may want to communicate something that is out of the ordinary, to be really heard: we signal, "This is serious". On the other hand, we are encouraged to become alert when a personal friend does not respond as he or she usually does. These breaks in the normal flow of interaction are easy to see when the behaviour is very different; it is as if a warning bell has rung. However, there are times when we see only the usual response: the shift may be too subtle, and we fail to pick up on what was being said. Without paying attention, we may glide over our friend's signals, allowing the familiarity of everyday rituals of interaction of "just keeping us in touch" to ignore something that should have been seen, passing over a topic that needed to be addressed.

Over time, then, as familiarity can dull our sensitivity so the risk increases that we fail to focus on really paying attention in personal relationships, a failure that can lead to shocks. The partner you knew so well suddenly is no longer there. The child you thought you understood so well does something "out of character". Sudden changes like these quickly make us realise that we were not really staying in touch. We have allowed an elephant to get away from us, one based on habit and confidence, which pulls our eyes away from focussing on what is happening. This is not an easy elephant to restrain: there is always so much more to be done than to be working on our personal relationships. Do we have the time to sit back, reflect, and talk openly with a close personal friend, or with our partner? After all, not only is there a lot that needs to be done, but also there is a risk he or she may say something we do not like!!

We sometimes hear that a couple has 'drifted apart'. It sounds like a slow process, each incrementally paying less and less attention to the other. While the analogy is helpful, it does not alert us to the fact that diminishing attention may have resulted from the habits and rituals of interaction having become stronger. Building walls that are more than just comfortable conventions, we cease to "see" the other person. We would do a better job of keeping in touch with people we care about if, every so often, we sat down and just reflected on what *we* have been doing, allowing each to talk about issues of mutual concern *and* giving permission to say what has been on his or her mind. Perhaps this is a way of bringing the elephant back in the room, making sure it is both addressed, and no longer able to run away from us. This is a theme to which I will return in the last chapter of this book, where I want to explore the ways we can stop elephants getting away from us: then, as here, I will emphasise the value of making sure we set aside time for reflection.

What makes someone a close friend? Part of it seems to be history, a friend who was around when you were at school, at the birth of your first child, or who worked with you on a project. If you sense empathy and interest, then that initial link seems to get stronger over time: you share a history, and a set of stories, confidences and events. However, a close friend may also be quite unlike you in some respects. Just as serendipity may have brought you together, suddenly a close link can become fragile as the strands you share weaken in the face of other differences. The best friend becomes an acquaintance, and then more distant, finally forgotten.

Close friendships matter, because they are the people with whom you can set aside the barriers that you put up to keep most people away from the 'real' you. For that reason we expect our close friends to be circumspect, keeping secrets, but willing to tell us exactly what they think. Keeping in touch with a close friend is a bit like a dance. You want to give, and you want to respond, but it is a matter of timing and pacing. Even with the closest of the people around you, you have to judge if the time is right: perhaps he or she needs you to listen to what has been happening, rather than you spending time talking about your latest worries and hopes. If friendship requires attention, just as it does when you dance, so you are conscious of the edge of the dance floor: today you are close enough that you can talk about anything, but tomorrow that freedom may be gone. It is as if being with a best friend allows you to stop thinking about 'being someone', and in so doing your natural self is allowed some space. To be someone's close friend is a privilege, and like all privileges it can be lost quite easily: you stop paying attention, you fail to be a good confidante, or you simply lose touch.

Some friendships just are. If you are lucky, your relationship with your partner is like that. It may be the case with a friend who, over the years, is always just there, not needing support, contact, or being kept in touch. Such friendships do not require a lot of work, but such friendships are rare. Apart from these very special relationships, most of the time friends are demanding. To sustain a friendship, we may have to set aside some of our preferences, concerns or views in order to meet some of our friend's needs and expectations. The cost of friendships may be that you have to give up a little of yourself to fit in with the other person. You accept that this is the way *they* are, which means that you also accept that this is the way *you* have to be for them. Keeping in touch is about monitoring the way they are as much as talking about what you have been doing: without friends our lives are shallow, but having friends is real work.

If keeping in touch with a personal friend is a challenge, so the difficulties of keeping in touch with the wider circle of friends and acquaintances also present us with a number of hurdles. There are some interesting practices here. Do you know someone who writes one of those Christmas newsletters, telling everyone to whom it is sent what they have been doing, where they have been, and what has happened to their close family? How do you respond to these newsletters? I know that some simply irritate me! They seem to be a minor hymn of praise to what this person has done, a list of achievements, betraying more about their desire to be seen as important than any real desire to keep in touch. Sometimes what you would like – at the very least – is a personal handwritten comment at the end of the circulated update.

There are some other newsletters I receive where I find the facts are helpful. Oh, so that is where they are. Oh, he has got a new job now, that's good. Perhaps this is a defensive comment – I used to send out a newsletter of this second kind to a small circle of family and friends back in Australia. I tried to make it factual. It was keeping in touch at the level of information, but the 'touch' was almost non-existent. I also decided to have a page on Facebook: my motivation was quite simple, that way I could see what my children and grandchildren were up to, especially now when I live a long way away from them!

After a year, I dropped the regular newsletter because I felt it was becoming a ritual, something that I did because I did it! Now I feel that I should go back to the way I used to behave, and remember to write letters (well, emails today). I am not a good correspondent, but if there is something I would like to say to someone, it should be personal, really keeping in touch and not just fulfilling an obligation. The trouble with that approach is that I am also aware that my family and friends know me well. They know I am not a good correspondent, but they also know I *will* get in touch every now and then. Even better, they know I will try to see them when I can. Does that mean I can forego the updating email?

I still use Facebook, and I post an occasional set of photographs. One the whole, though, I continue to use Facebook as a voyeur: keeping an eye on a small circle of friends. A significant part of what I used to do was simply ensuring I was sharing and obtaining information, knowing the facts. If I really want to be in touch, I used to feel I could only do that face-to-face, but recently I have discovered that even here technology can help. At the simplest level, when I talk to someone living far away from where I am staying, I have become a user of Skype. "Skyping" allows me to *see* and talk to someone, and its immediacy gives a real sense of contact.

Is the on-line network of connections a good way of keeping in touch in a broader sense? Surprisingly, I think it is: surprisingly, because the idea of posting all that stuff on line seems both time wasting and also too revealing. However, the more I read the posts of family and friends, follow the links, and see the photographs, the more I sense this is an extremely effective way of keeping in touch. It doesn't just allow information to be shared, but it can be used as a forum to discuss concerns, explore emotions and resolve differences. In fact, the very manner of it being "on-line" contributes to its effectiveness in keeping people in touch. You can say things on-line that may be hard to say face to face. What seems to be a very impersonal form of contact enables very personal interactions.

This brings us back to another theme in keeping in touch with personal friends and the broader circle of acquaintances. It is often hard to reveal face to face what we think or feel about something. We seek to find the proper time and place, and in so doing, push it back, making it even harder to eventually disclose something important that might have been on our minds for days, weeks even. Keeping in touch with other people is as much about ourselves as it is about those with whom we want to keep in touch. Who do we want to be when we relate to another person? How open are we willing to be? Perhaps keeping in touch is often one step removed from real intimacy, close enough to touch, but not so close as having to embrace the other person (the English handshake rather than the continental hugging of friends). How strange that the impersonal medium of the Internet may in some ways allow us to be more intimate than we can face to face!

If this is all so tricky, it raises yet another question: why do we want to keep in touch? At one level, human beings are social beings, and we are nothing by ourselves, living in isolation. Part of what makes us whole is the fact that we are embedded in a network of relationships. We have no choice but to keep in contact, because not to do so is to diminish ourselves, to make us incomplete. We are what we are because we are part of a web of relationships, connected to others. Keeping in contact is what keeps us involved in life. Losing the ability to really keep in touch diminishes us; falling into rituals in relationships takes us one step away from what makes us really human. Stiff and proper English boys – I was one once – live on the margins of life, protected but removed from intimacy and a life worth living. I know!!

The step away from family and close friends to other acquaintances and friends is to take us into the hardest area in which to find the right level of "keeping in touch". These are people we know, people we may see often, at work, in our neighbourhood or community, or when we go to a concert, a football game, the cinema or an art gallery. We do not want to be constantly "in touch", but nor do we want to be distant. These are neither impersonal relationships, nor are they intimate.

Life inside an organisation provides us with a compelling window on how to manage friends and acquaintances. There are occasional lunches, a birthday cake at morning tea, and once a year the 'office party'. Each one of these social activities can bring us close to peril: being seen as putting someone outside the charmed circle by forgetting to invite them to a lunch; being close to one colleague, creating jealousy and back-biting; becoming too close, and creating an intimate relationship that destroys the manageable level of impersonality that allow the organisation to run smoothly. It is for this reason we are fascinated by "affairs" at work, as they cross a boundary we prefer to see kept safe, yet tantalise us precisely because they do cross that boundary.

Each one of us is within a web of relationships, some held together by strong ties with many overlapping elements. Other parts of that web have ties that are less strong, less complex. Each time we put the web under stress, building a new and strong link where before was one that was weak means that the web as a whole begins to distort. Under pressure it may even break apart. Managing that web of relationships is not an easy task. Like the real spider's web, the network of relationships is both strong and yet easily broken, as a thousand novels and movies so clearly depict!

So far we have explored keeping in touch as if it was about personal relationships, the task of staying in contact with family, friends and colleagues. There is another dimension to keeping in touch, and this is paying attention to the broader world around us.

I was thinking about the importance of this other area when, for a couple of weeks, I was based in a tiny village near Pistoia. It was the summer of 2012, and the Italian community around me was pretty much focused on one small bit of the broader world – the European Nations Soccer Championship in Poland! One night while I was there Italy won a match, and was through to the quarterfinals, and right across Tuscany there was sigh of relief. A scrappy game against the Republic of Ireland, marked out only by an extraordinary second goal in the dying minutes of the game: Mario Balotelli's athletic brilliance was almost matched by his demeanour as he walked away from kicking what might prove to have been the goal of the tournament. The bad boy had come good – although it seemed likely he would continue to follow his own idiosyncratic ways, as well as continuing to be subjected to racial abuse. A complex young man, to whom I suspect a lot of Italy was paying attention that night. As for the broader world for those around me that day in Pistoia, well it was pretty small!

However, the theme I want to explore is rather more demanding than following the ups and downs of a national soccer team (even though that can seem overwhelmingly important at the time!). It can be put in the form of a question: "Do we really keep in touch with the world around us?" At the same time as Balotelli was scoring that memorable goal, an ex-journalist in Baltimore, David Simon, posted his latest blog, a commentary on the topic of "Dirt under the rug"[72]. There could not have been a better example of the importance of paying attention to what was going on around him.

David Simon is an ex-crime reporter for the Baltimore Sun, and still keeps his hand in by keeping an eye on interesting reports from the crime beat in his city. His attention was caught by a statistic: in 2011 the Baltimore Police Department had charged 70 people with murder or manslaughter, as compared to 130 the year before, and 150 the year before that. The murder rate was down in Baltimore (memorable to many non-residents as the city where the *The Wire* had been set), and there must have been a sigh of relief in Baltimore comparable to that across Italy.

Simon was not convinced by what he had read, and decided to do some digging. His article is well worth reading, but in summary, what he found out was that there had been a change in policy about how cases were pursued, which had led to a change in reporting. I do not want to go into all the details that Simon explores, but just emphasis his key finding – that in 2011:

> *"the new State's Attorney in Baltimore — who, notably, had campaigned for office on a claim that he would be more aggressive than his predecessor in pursuing violent criminals — managed to quietly prevail on the police commissioner to change the long-standing policy. Going forward, the prosecutor's office alone would decide when to charge a murder or manslaughter case. .... Now, the state's attorney — acting unilaterally and without any possible contradiction by police commanders — was free to charge only those cases he was absolutely sure he could win in court. Now, police had not only been prevented from charging murders in which they had weak evidence, but also from charging those cases in which evidence was substantive, but not necessarily ironclad......... the State's Attorney for Baltimore .... lives by his conviction rate, and by his high-profile successes. He fears nothing so much as to, say, lose a murder case in court, or be obliged to drop the charges publicly, after indictment, when, say, a witness backs out — and then, a year or two later have the same defendant commit another crime. And why was the defendant on the street able to commit another crime? Because the prosecutor failed to convict that defendant in court. Those are the headlines from an elected prosecutor's worst nightmare"*[73]

This was a story that could have come from Season 6 of *The Wire*, another example of the ongoing manipulations, half-truths and evasions that fictional series so brilliantly explored (there was no sixth season, of course). Why have I taken the trouble to highlight this particular piece of journalism? Because it deals with a theme close to my heart, which is that much of the time we do *not* pay close attention to the world around us.

Let me take that point a bit further. It is commonplace to say that we live in a world awash with information (not quite as much knowledge, but a fair bit of that, too). It is also commonplace to say that this leads to a problem of 'objectivity': how do we know what we read is actually true? It is a real challenge. We deal with the flood of information by ignoring most of it, just paying attention to what we read in our favourite newspaper or see on the television news program. Given this, we are unlikely to spend much time on trying to sift the facts from the assertions and speculations that accompany stories – especially on those news and commentary programs, where discussion of what has happened often runs far ahead of understanding the real facts of what had taken place.

However, not only is that a major problem, but there is another. In addition to the difficulty of knowing what had happened, we are also stuck on the "surface" of events, without investing the time and attention to discover what has been going on beneath. After many years as a journalist, David Simon had become an investigative reporter, digging beneath the stories about current events and discovering that the superficial story was often quite different from what lay beneath. Once clearly examined, the events that we first notice may fail to make clear – or even mask – the more important underlying trends, the very things that are only revealed through doing some of the hard work of investigative excavation. When we explore some perceptions of China in the next chapter, I hope you will find it is a case study that makes my point.

As I see it, we are paying less attention today, because it takes time and perseverance to look carefully at the world around us. Keeping in touch with what is happening is time consuming. It requires a willingness to suspend certainty. It requires us to sift through data and try to make sense of what is there, not accept what we are told. David Simon has done a good job of exactly that, digging down to find the dirt under the rug.

Surely the skills he used are not unfamiliar skills? These are the very techniques we learnt in school, to analyse, think, assess, and conclude. One of the most exhilarating phases in my development was going to university, and being left to find out things for myself. I had to go away, research, analyse, draw conclusions and be prepared to argue what I had presented, rather than memorising what the teacher told me. These are the skills that we learn as we go on from high school to study at a university. It is not the facts that we learn that are important, but the skills that help us identify what matters and what the evidence means: surely, then, these are the skills we need to really keep in touch with the world around us. These are the skills we set out to develop in our students.

When I talk to my colleagues in various universities, I find that it is not always as simple as that. Some of the students we see in class are bright, inquisitive and keen to learn. Many are smart, quick to see what is required, and find out how to answer questions, but I am not sure they all learn in the same way. Certainly teachers often find they have many students whose goal is to pass their courses, preferably with high marks. "Tell me what I need to know, and I will reproduce it for you in my assignments and examinations". If that is the approach that many students show us, then it is not surprising that those same ways of doing things continue on into later life. As they get older, they will still expect to be told what they need to know, and they will use the intermediaries of modern life, the bloggers, television news reporters, commentators and 'aggregators' to do the work of analysis for them.

If this sounds a bit like the world of George Orwell's *1984*, it is because that is what actually seems to be happening. We are no longer keeping in touch; we are being kept in touch. We are kept in touch with what is important to know, and, curiously, we are also being kept in touch with what might happen. Indeed, the borderline between the two is often blurred, and it is not clear as to whether something has happened, or is in the process of taking place, or will likely take place in the future. Add to that the penchant that sources of information and news have to make things seem slightly frightening, and so we live in an anxious world of possibilities and unfolding events, brought to us continuously, reinforcing that this is the way things are.

It is hard to keep in touch – at the personal level, and at the global level. Is David Simon's analysis of what has happened in Baltimore correct? He is a blogger, and I am relying on him to tell me what is happening. Isn't that exactly what I was criticising others for doing? Perhaps it is reassuring to read the comments that followed his blog: some wrote in to corroborate his analysis, some to add to it, and some to question points and ask him to explain more, and even to elaborate his initial analysis.

Keeping in touch, paying attention, requires work and time, and these seem to be commodities that are in short supply. Just because there is such an industry to keep us in touch, so it is less easy for us to carve out time to find out things for ourselves. Heidi's story was as interesting for the fact that she went out of her way to find out what had happened as it was for the complex situation it revealed. Many people are too busy to question why some boxes have been sent to the business that need not be opened. So what?

As you can see, I find this area of keeping in touch with what is going on as hard as anyone else does. I try to find sources of information that seem reliable and well researched. I try to 'triangulate' what I find out – getting corroboration from a range other sources. I certainly have to rely on a lot of secondary information. All I can say is that I try never to rely on one source of information, and I constantly look for data that seems reasonably objective. I have certainly learnt one "trick" well: if there is something interesting I read, I try to find another source on the same topic, where the writer has a very different point of view. Allowing for a little bit of hyperbole, it is like balancing articles from *The Economist* (the magazine of the capitalist free market economy) with those from *The New Internationalist* (the magazine of revolutionary students and Trotskyite commentators).

Do we need to keep in touch with what is going on? When we look at science and technology, there is an argument that is advanced from time to time that most change is superficial, and we would be well advised to avoid being caught up in the hype surrounding the pace of change and innovation. It is easy to put forward examples. Aeroplanes were invented at the beginning of the 20th Century, with a significant push in the 1940's when the jet engine was developed, and they made a major change in speed and the movement of people and goods. However, since then, there has been little progress, just a lot of continuous improvement. The internal combustion engine was developed in the last decade of the 19th Century, and while its efficiency has been improved, it is still the major form of power for land vehicles. Improved sanitation and the development of penicillin and similar drugs pushed the average life expectancy in the western world from under fifty years at the beginning of the 20th Century to around 75 years by the 1970's. Since then, despite so much investment in medicine and medical technologies, it has hardly improved.

Technologies that completely change our world are unlikely to occur frequently, and the bursts of major change that heralded the Industrial Revolution, and then the beginning of the 20th Century seem to have reached the point of marginal improvements. There is some evidence to suggest that technological revolutions go through 'boom and bust' cycles[74]. We can be overly cynical, and the invention of the computer, and the transistor, both in the 1950's, laid the ground for massive changes in telecommunications and information processing, of which the World Wide Web is the outstanding example. This may be the next revolution, but the consequences of these particular changes are far from clear. It seems each new technological revolution takes decades to reveal its broader implications. However, while there do seem to be some really important changes taking place, many technologies have simply improved and not changed in a radical fashion. We are bombarded with the results of research and development, and it is hard to discern what is important in the flood of ideas, commentary and claims. Much of what is said to be groundbreaking, or a major step forward, quickly slips into the background.

Is it important to keep in touch with geopolitics and economics? It seems clear that we are moving into an era when one country no longer dominates the world, as was the case with Britain in the 19th Century, and the US in the 20th Century. It will be interesting to see what it is like to inhabit a multipolar world, balanced between the 'old empires' of the UK, Europe and the US, and the re-emerging giants of India, China and Japan. It may mean that we are no longer hostages to one view of the world, but it is likely to be decades before it becomes clear as to what such a new order might comprise. We can be sure that most commentators today will get that story completely wrong: the only thing we can confidently predict about the future is that it is impossible to predict the future! At least we know that predictions are unreliable.

Beyond that, what really seems to matter is the fate of people whose lives are destroyed or damaged by wars, tyranny, famine and despotic rulers. For many of us, it is almost impossible to comprehend the pain that others experience. If we are to take Peter Singer seriously we need to seek to understand what is happening to our fellow human beings, wherever they may be. We should ask what we can do to alleviate the lot of others, and how we can support those agencies and individuals who work to reduce suffering, directly or through resources and donations. Perhaps this is another reason to suggest that it is keeping in touch with people that is important, especially, but not only, those who are close to us, such as our neighbours and our community. However, Singer's call to take on a wider view is compelling, and a strong argument that it is worth investing time to understand what is really taking place around us.

What is this elephant that pulls us away from looking at things closely, that inhibits us from keeping in touch? Is it indifference? Is it ignorance? I fear it is something more alarming, a tendency to expect that someone else will answer questions, tell us what we need to know, and then we can just get on and enjoy life. We should never give up the desire to dig, to find out what has been swept under the carpet. Socrates said, "an unexamined life is a life not worth living". I think he was right, and still is. I am not sure that everyone around me agrees.

9. Respecting others

I lived in Australia for over 35 years, and in that time had relatively little contact with Aboriginal Australians. The staff in most of the places where I was employed mainly comprised migrants, some recent, and some from several generations back. The great majority were Caucasians. That was not particularly surprising, as I worked in a major city, and for a large part of the time for multinational or national organisations. However, after ten years in Australia, I had the opportunity to go and visit aboriginal communities in the central and northern regions of the country. At that stage my work was concerned with ethnic communities, first generation migrants from different parts of the world, and the structure of the Australian Government at the time excluded my agency having anything to do with the indigenous people of Australia. However, it was agreed that I should, at the very least, have some understanding of their world.

It was a trip I will never forget, accompanied as I was by a very senior churchman who, too, had much to learn. We started in Alice Springs. I saw the typical visitor's view of the local people: drunk men and women shouting in the street, dozing on the pavement, sleeping under the bridges of the Todd River. Dogs in the street, and children running around, just loosely under the control of their parents. No one seemed to be working; some were begging. Then we went on to visit a modern high school that had been built for aboriginal children, just outside the town. It had a chain link fence all around it, and on the outside were parents and relatives living in their ramshackle humpies, waiting for their children to finish their education. It was easy to see that this was the basis for the stereotypical view of the aboriginal communities of Australia: feckless and living on drugs.

However, we next visited CAAMA (the Central Australia Aboriginal Media Association), which had just won, to almost universal astonishment, a commercial television license to broadcast television in the central and eastern satellite footprint of the country: a footprint that embraces most of the Northern Territory, Queensland and South Australia: while it does not cover any major cities, with the exception of Darwin, it does cover most rural aboriginal communities, and today has an audience of nearly 450,000 people. At the time of our visit, CAAMA was planning the establishment of Imparja Television, a station that has been broadcasting since 1988, a date that is, symbolically, exactly 200 years after the British landed in Botany Bay and set up the colony of New South Wales, the beginnings of the country now known as Australia.

CAAMA realised that the traditional broadcasting format for television would not work for aboriginal communities, many of whom spoke very different languages from one another. As they put it, they had to "re-invent television in central Australia". It was a mind-flipping experience: these people were like me, and the conversations and ideas we debated were exhilarating. Of course they were like me – we are all humans! I had seen those who had been abused and self-abused in the streets of Alice Springs (and one throwing rocks at the windows of CAAMA when we were meeting); but I had seen similar people before, those who lived on the margin of society, among the Caucasians of Sydney and Melbourne. It was just that the balance was very different: here there were many, and in Melbourne and Sydney there were relatively few.

We went on to Darwin, and went out to visit a number of communities outside the city. It was exciting and sobering to see people trying to establish their communities, empowering their own people rather than being directed by the various government agencies, and trying to deal with the insidious problems of petrol sniffing and alcohol abuse. The pull of our common humanity quickly got rid of whatever stereotyped prejudice I might have begun to develop on my first day in Alice Springs.

Nearly 30 years later, I went with my wife to see a highly recommended film, *Samson and Delilah*. It nearly broke my heart, and even now, as I type these words, there are tears in my eyes. Why? Because it seemed to me that nothing had changed: the lives, the problems, the wreckage of aboriginal society seemed indistinguishable from that which I have seen on that earlier visit to the Northern Territory. I saw the film as a brilliant yet terrible indictment of our inability to respect others.

I am not going to set out an agenda for what should be done in Australia. I am not living there right now, not am I competent to do so: all I can say is that I believe that it is self-determination that is central to whatever needs to be put in place. There are people like Noel Pearson who are bringing about much needed change, and they are the people who should address this issue. Rather, I am telling this story about myself because it is an introduction to a theme I see as very important and yet very difficult: respecting others. How can we respect others? What is the elephant on roller skates that drags us away from doing this well?

It is commonplace to say that we do not know what goes on in another person's mind. I think it is interesting to examine what goes on in our *own* mind as we think about another person. Sometimes I think we treat other people as vessels, waiting to be filled up, and we do that filling up. We may fill them up with our prejudices and stereotypes; we may fill them up with our expectations and hopes; and we may fill them up with our fantasies and desires.

Sometimes they may resist what we have 'seen' in them. In some cases, we are able to ignore that resistance, and still maintain our view of what they are really like. Sometimes, we are forced into a reappraisal. After all, I was close to accepting some rather stereotyped assumptions about aboriginals when I first arrived in Alice Springs and before I went to CAAMA. It was only when I started listening and thinking that I realised that I had been 'filling in' with a rather unconsidered view of the people I was seeing.

Can we escape that huge runaway elephant called stereotyping? As I was editing this chapter, two examples suddenly leapt out at me. The first was the screening of a documentary on PBS television, The Central Park Five.[75] It dealt with the violent assault on a young white female jogger in Central Park in 1989, so violent that it was assumed she would never recover. She did, but had no recollection of the events of that night. Five young people, four African Americans and one Hispanic, were tried and convicted of the crime - convicted in the press long before the case went to court. Many years later a serial rapist who had been imprisoned for other crimes, admitted that he, alone, was responsible. How had the five youngsters ended up being convicted? They were the "ideal" victims, young, wild, and from ethnically suspect groups living in the marginal areas of New York. Their "confessions" were coerced, and the trial was based on that evidence alone, ignoring the major inconsistencies between the evidence each gave, the fact that DNA found on the victim did not match any of the suspects (it was from the serial rapist), and that even the timeline for their suspected role was inconsistent with what had taken place.

Perhaps you feel we can discount this example as it is a story from our regrettable past. On the same day that the documentary was being shown, a small story emerged in the immediate aftermath of the two bombs that had caused carnage at the Boston Marathon two days earlier. There were more than a hundred wounded, but just one of them, while in hospital, had his apartment searched, and his belongings taken out. The reason for this was that police noticed he was trying to get away from the bomb scene, was fearful there might be another bomb (and there was), and smelled of explosives (perhaps not surprisingly!). There were many others like him, but he drew attention, for whatever reason, and subsequently turned out to be a Saudi Arabian national. In no time at all the media were talking about a suspect, someone claimed to be under arrest, a "person of interest", and so it went on with no evidence at all to support these comments. By the next day, it was all over, and he was "cleared".[76] Within a few days, the real perpetrators had been identified and found. At the time, however, I would say that the police actions seemed sensible and precautionary. On the other hand, the media reactions were inflammatory and outrageous, stereotyping and filling in at its worst.

Filling in is not just a process we apply to people who come from cultures very different from our own. When we first meet someone who becomes our partner, we often do not see him or her clearly to begin with (often our image of them is more than a little clouded by a certain degree of "lust"!). However, it is more than that. We want our partner to be a certain way, and so that is the way we tend to treat them and make sense of them. In time, as a relationship progresses, the person often turns out to be not quite the same as we first saw. Love grows as we accept our partner as he or she really is, although some people find it hard to make the transition to loving acceptance: they continue to want their partner to be the person they saw or expected to begin with. Sometimes this leads to divorce, sometimes just to a quiet but continuing pressure to make them change. A lack of respect for the person as he or she is leads many people into having less than satisfying relationships, which they manage by investing part of themselves in other relationships and activities, with friends, with leisure groups, with work colleagues. It is "easy" to live with a number of incomplete relationships, as they are less demanding, and often really superficial.

Our children offer another challenge to our ability to respect others. We want our children to be happy, to be successful, perhaps to achieve what we did not achieve. Our children often confound us. They succeed in areas where we didn't expect. They disappoint in areas where we had high expectations (and we can disappoint them in similar ways). They choose friendships that we think are wrong. They pursue interests that we think are wasteful and unworthy. They achieve things in spite of our expectations. It would seem to be easy to respect our children, but since they begin life with us as almost empty vessels, it is very easy to fill them up in such a way that our views and their reality are hard to align.

Often our failures in really understanding and respecting our partners or our children create tensions and distances that start a process of separation. Our mistaken image of them (and theirs of us) turns them into images that gain their own momentum. We have started the process of turning the people we thought we loved into the creatures of elephants on roller skates, and we forget to keep chasing after them, in order to seek to retrieve the respect that we were complicit in denying.

To respect others is to be willing to really listen to and make sense of the way they are, not the way we wish they were. Just recently I read two series of books that were very popular (by the time you read this, they will probably be consigned to the remainder tables of bookshops, no longer in favour!), and they both turned out to offer interesting reflections on the theme of understanding and respecting others. You may find it odd that I am using popular fiction rather than some of the great novels to make a point, but that is the point: even popular fiction touches on important themes, and often does so in a very accessible way.

The first was a series of books called *The Hunger Games Trilogy* by Susanne Collins (the name of the series is also the name of the first book). Aimed at teenagers, the books tell a story set in a dystopian future, concerned with events that lead to the overthrow of a dictatorship, and the gradual emergence of a more democratic world (somewhat timely, I now realise, as they started to become very popular just as the so-called "Arab spring" was flowering and then falling into confusion).

The books centre on a young woman, Katniss Everard, who plays an important role in some of the critical events that take place. I suspect that for many of the readers, she is a heroine, acting bravely, taking tough decisions, and spearheading revolutionary activity. However, there is a different reading of the books, one that sees her as an almost accidental participant in a series of events that she does not really understand, surviving by luck and the support of others, and committing acts that are often foolish, and sometimes contrary to the broader goal of overthrowing the dictatorship. The stories are told first person, and we are exposed, if we choose to read it so, to seeing the real confusions and inadequacies of this heroine as events shape what she does, and as she grows older. Certainly, at the end of the third book many readers must wonder "what was that last chapter all about" (just as some felt the last section of the final Harry Potter book seemed to be bent on tidying up matters in a very adult way, quite out of kilter with the underlying themes of the series of books as a whole).

I really enjoyed the Hunger Games series (I seem to have a penchant for teenage novels – best not to think why!), and I found the role of Katniss as an accidental agent a really fascinating one. I learnt to respect Katniss much more for what she wasn't, rather than seeing her as a colourful heroine changing the world for the better. Perhaps because I am older (and not a girl) I did not need to invest Katniss with attributes that I did not find in the books: I accepted and respected her for the character and the role she played, not the ideal she might have been. (Incidentally, I have not seen the film of the first book yet, and will be interested to see what reading is given of her character there – well, I should confess I have read that she is portrayed as heroic, and that some of the horror of the story is nicely left to be dealt with 'off-screen'). Katniss is like one of Jane Austen's leading ladies – intelligent, but sometimes somewhat confused, tentative, uncertain, and yet ever hopeful, even if for the wrong reasons.

Perhaps the close examination of a teenage novel is not enough to make my points. Let us turn to something quite different – though it may be equally unsatisfactory. At the same time as the Hunger Games books were high on the bestseller lists, so was another trilogy, *Fifty Shades of Grey* by E L James. This series of popular books centres on the relationship between a masochistic man, Christian Grey, and the slightly younger woman, Anastasia (Ana) Steele, he takes on as his next victim ("submissive" is the term he uses). The books comprise a traditional popular romance (a rich but damaged man saved by younger, beautiful innocent young woman), but added to the mix is a series of frequent and eventually overly long scenes of soft-core pornography (I guess it is hard to make bondage and sexual intercourse endlessly fascinating). However, like the Hunger Games trilogy, this is also a story about understanding and respecting others.

While the books are far from deep, they are easily accessible to readers who want to be entertained. The underlying form of the story is the eventual revealing the "true self " of the two key characters that lies behind their everyday façade. This is true for both of them. Christian discovers over the course of events that he is unable to see Ana as he wants to, but rather that the real person becomes more important than his fantasy. As he stops seeking to dominate and hurt, so his respect grows: he sees her as she really is, and through that respect for the real person begins to love her. Ana is equally fascinating, as she has created an image of what Christian is like that fits what she sees. However, she also believes that there is another person there, despite the way he behaves, and so actually holds two images in her mind, resolutely refusing to accept the person Christian appears to be, and holding on to a view of him that is true to the real person, but hidden under the surface of his observable self. She responds to both Christians, believing that in the end, the "hidden but real" self will prevail.

I am not suggesting you should read Fifty Shades of Grey any more than the Hunger Games. Certainly there are many more subtle and insightful novels for adults. Rather I am reminding you that a theme in many novels, popular or more thoughtful, is that respect comes from really "seeing" the other person, rather than accepting the stereotype, the "front" as it were. They also help us understand that if we are unable to see and respect the person as they are, then we are likely to end up attached to runaway image, an elephant on a roller skate. When you eventually let go, the landing can be quite bumpy, as we learn is the case with Christian's previous submissives.

So much for setting the scene. The question to be addressed here is "How can we respect another person?" While that sounds easy, just get on and do it, the illustrations I have given are all concerned with a simple but very challenging task: respecting another is about accepting another, and that means accepting "not like me". Being not like me is to be different, and we often demonise or stereotype people who are not like us. It is as if we live in a world of them and us: if you are not "us", then you must be "them", and you are to be treated with great suspicion. I find this particular elephant on roller skates a very dangerous one: it almost seems to be invisible; gently tugging at us to remind us that another person is different. It does so many times a day, but not all the time. How does this elephant diminish our respect for so many people, and yet sometimes allows us to respect, or even adulate, others?

One of the ways in which we assess other people is through being offered a 'filter', which throws some aspect of that person into high relief, and in so doing colours our whole understanding. In everyday life, gossip is one such filter, and a very powerful one. At work, with friends, there is a tendency we all share to talk about other people we know. Almost without noticing, such conversations often include some information that immediately changes or shifts our perception of the person. "Did you know that ......" is the opening line of a comment or statement that will almost certainly convey some details of an attribute or action that demeans or diminishes the person being described. Even a positive comment can become the basis of suspicion about what this person is really like: "Did you know that Jane gives 20% of her salary to charity every month?" "Why? Is she one of those Scientologists?" "No, I think it is a guilt thing. I have heard stories about her and heavy drinking" – and so it goes on. Why do we want to pull people down, to show that we are better than they are?

Stereotypes serve the same function, as my experiences in central Australia made clear. They provide a framework that already starts to colour our perceptions. I can give some silly examples to make my point. "She's a single mother" "Did her husband die?" "No, I don't believe she was ever married" Hmm, sounds like casual sex. Or perhaps the opening piece of information is this: "He plays football for one of the leading teams" Hmm, don't need to ask much more – he'll be big, a drinker, and abuses women.

Yes, they are silly examples, but there are other more powerful stereotypes that sit behind these. When I opened this chapter I didn't go into some of the details of the stereotype that many Australians hold: in that view, being an aboriginal means being a person who is lazy, a user of addictive substances, living off handouts, abusive, dangerous. Not everyone sees aboriginals in this way, of course, but it is a stereotype that runs deep.

The point is that stereotypes can be sufficiently powerful that they shape the way we see the person in front of us, as exemplifying "what we know" before we even think about it. That overweight, badly dressed woman shouting at her child in the street, she is "trailer trash". That well-dressed woman, cashmere jumper, pearl necklace, drinking tea in a nice restaurant, she is a snob. It is easy, really. You just look for the clues, and then your work is done.

What we don't see, because it requires us to really look and seek to understand the other person, is what is actually the case. That overweight woman, well, she is a social worker trying to help homeless children in the city, and the child is not hers, but a street kid, scared to be helped. That well-dressed woman drinking tea is a recently abandoned wife, left by her husband because she has cancer, trying to reassure herself that she can hang on to a decent life, even though she has lost income and respect.

Situations, gossip and stereotypes can sometimes pile on top of each other in frightening ways. Australia recently witnessed the fourth coroner's inquest into the death of a young child, presenting its finding in June 2012. Nine-week-old Azaria Chamberlain disappeared in August 1980 from her parent's tent at a camping ground near Uluru in the Northern Territory, nearly 32 years earlier. At the time, her mother, Lindy Chamberlain, told everyone a dingo had taken her baby. It seemed improbable, but an aboriginal tracker found evidence of a dingo having dragged something away from the tent.

However, the evidence that was there was soon swamped by gossip, fueled by the fact that Lindy Chamberlain did not conform to the expected stereotype of a grieving mother. She was seen at the inquest wearing dark glasses, showing no emotion, and appeared to be associated with some kind of religious sect rather than a mainstream church: clearly, something else had happened. She went to prison on the flimsiest of evidence of a crime.

Eventually Lindy Chamberlain was acquitted. However, it took all those years; many recorded dingo attacks in that area and in the Northern Territory generally; and the forceful presentation of relevant evidence before a coroner could hand down the finding that Azaria had been taken by a dingo. Lindy Chamberlain did not fit the stereotype the situation demanded. Indeed, there have been many more cases over the years where, despite the evidence, a mother is held, at least in the court of popular opinion, to have murdered and disposed of a child, just because the mother did not fit the image that was expected (not sad enough, caught up in a "weird" religious life style, uncaring, or simply just "not like us").

So far we have been exploring the way in which we see people in terms of negatives: we see them through stereotypes and on the basis of attributes which make them "unlike us" in a bad sense of the term. This can, and does, go in the opposite direction. These are people who are not like us, unattainable in some sense, and yet representing the person we desire to be: again, this is looking at the stereotypes, not someone we really know well but still someone we want to emulate. This is the world of sports stars, popular singers, and television and film personalities.

Is there anything wrong with admiring and wanting to be like one of these people? The relevant question is, perhaps, do we know what it is we wish to be? There is nothing wrong, and much to commend, about wanting to be an outstanding athlete. Perhaps we want to excel at soccer. Here is our idol, talented and successful, married to a beautiful wife. Just a minute, is this the same person who sleeps around, unfaithful to his wife, and who fathered a child with another woman? Do you respect this person, or is it rather that you want to have the same success, the same income, the same recognition, and, in the case of many men who want to be like this star, to have such sex appeal that you are constantly having to brush women aside (and perhaps satisfy just a few)? Adulation is not respect.

The business of adulation is so great today that there are magazines and journals devoted to keeping the credulous up to date with the real (did I say real?) and imagined activities of the stars that swirl around their heads. Who is being unfaithful to whom? Read about how this person managed to retain her figure; this person, his athletic prowess. What your favourite star eats, reads, and does in his or her leisure time. Here is a moment to savour, this stars brief moment of poor dress sense. This one was in a car crash – and my, look at the car he was driving at the time!

I fear there is another danger in being too enamoured of the successful. The story of Lance Armstrong, which was being played out as I was writing, illustrated how easy it is to become so caught up with admiration that we begin to lose perspective. Lance Armstrong was an amazingly successful cyclist, even returning to winning after beating cancer. There *is* much to admire there. Then we learn that he used drugs to enhance his performance, and even bullied his teammates into doing the same, and bullied others to stop them from exposing what he had been doing. As a result we can see that there was another side to him, where his behaviour was appalling. Now there is discussion taking place as to whether he should be given "a second chance". The message in such a view is clear: if you are famous and do something wrong, perhaps you can be excused. If that is true for the rich and famous, perhaps it should be true for the rest of us!

Paparazzi are criticised for invading the lives of the rich and famous, but they do it because we want to see what has been going on: not what these people are really like or do, of course, but the exciting, titillating and silly activities of the rich and famous that amaze us and make us admire them even more. Perhaps there is no harm in this. It is no different in some sense than reading a novel or watching a film. It is enjoying an imagined world. However, it is not the way to respect others. Living a life as a voyeur is a way to harden stereotypes and avoid seeing the real person. It creates elephants on roller skates, which pull our perceptions away from reality into a world of fantasies.

A discussion about how we see other people may seem rather superficial, but we can address a rather more serious element of this in talking about behaviour, and in particular how we treat others. This takes us back to the chapter on being fair (chapter 4). There we explored the very demanding analysis by John Rawls, and his views as to how society should be constructed. One part of that analysis concerned the distinction between the attributes with which we are born, and the efforts we make to contribute to society. Rawls argued that we should not be rewarded for our attributes because they are the result of what is, in effect, a genetic lottery; reward for effort, however, is earned and therefore a just desert.

In other words, a discussion about how we see others has to move beyond rewards and entitlements to also talk about responsibilities. Some have argued that in recognising the need to move beyond respect to appropriate action there is real value in the concept of "responsibility-sensitive egalitarianism". This has two elements.

First, people should be compensated for "undeserved misfortunes" and that compensation should be the responsibility of those who have "undeserved good fortune", that the able should be required to contribute to the ensuring a better life for the unable. Second, people should be rewarded for the outcomes they achieve through their choices and actions, in other words what they deserve through their endeavours.[77] This is a justification for progressive income tax and many other measures. It is also a statement that respect is not a matter of feelings and morals alone, but should be backed up by real behaviour.

Peter Singer has advocated this approach for many years, and we read about his views when we were exploring liberty in Chapter 3. Respect requires action, and in Singer's view, respect for our fellow humans requires that we take on our responsibilities seriously. For those of us who are fortunate, it may not be enough to make a donation to a worthy charity, or deliver meals on wheels once a week. Christopher Lasch once wrote on the "revolt of the elites", and forcefully argued that the emerging meritocracy that characterises many advanced economies:

> *"turns out to be a contradiction in terms: the talented retain many of the vices of aristocracy without its virtues. Their snobbery lacks any acknowledgment of reciprocal obligations between the favoured few and the multitude. Although they are full of "compassion" for the poor, they cannot be said to subscribe to a theory of noblesse oblige, which would imply a willingness to make a direct and personal contribution to the public good."[78]*

If respecting others is about seeing others as they are, it is also about responding to them as they are.

In discussing Christopher Lasch's views about the revolt of the elites at a roundtable of friends, I was forced to confront another dimension of respecting others. As we grow up, move into a career (or at least a succession of interesting jobs) and meet and mix with new colleagues and business partners, it is easy to slip away from remembering the people who had brought you to that stage in your life.

I used to pride myself on my ability to mix and talk with anyone, from the night security guard who looked after building where I worked through to the CEOs of the leading companies in Australia. Now I can see that was just a skill, a capability. It was useful, but it ignored the question as to whom it was I wanted to interact. I had left behind family and friends from the past, and forgotten the communities in which I had lived for years. It is easy to be successful and forget people who, at different stages in one's life, had been friends, supporters, and guides. Lasch's description of the elite of symbolic analysts refers to people more skilled than I, but when he described that meritocracy as being complicit in a "revolt of the elites against time-honoured traditions of locality, obligation, and restraint"[79] I felt some guilt, too.

There is one final theme in relation to respecting others, and that has to do with markets. Here I am talking about real markets, physical places where people come together to buy and sell. There are relatively few of these markets today, but two of them stand out in my mind.

The first of these was in Mount Hagen, in Papua New Guinea, some 30 or more years ago. This was a fascinating place. People came to the market from villages around Mount Hagen, many wearing traditional dress, some looking more like warriors than traders! Each person who was selling put out their goods in front of them - anything from roots or fruit through to wooden bowls and masks. Almost all the trading was actually barter. People went from one spot to another, exchanging their goods for another. Most people knew each other, if not by name by the reputation of their tribe or village. Bartering was open and clear: one person would consider another's yams to be inferior; another person's bananas were considered especially desirable.

In this market, respect and reputation were woven together. Both were earned by delivering on what you promised, and each week you knew the same people would be back. There were some underlying conventions concerning each person's space on the ground, and allowing adequate space for walkways, but no more than that, and no government controls at all.

I used to think that Mount Hagen was a unique place, the last vestige of the way the world had been. However, living in Melbourne, I eventually came to realise that the local Sunday 'trash and treasure' market was also close to the way markets used to be. Again, it was a place milling with buyers and sellers. As I went more often (I was collecting books at the time), I realised that the great majority of people there were regulars. This was not a place for bartering, money was used as the medium of exchange. However, in many ways the same issues of respect and reputation underpinned the way that market worked. You knew the sellers, and knew they would be back next week. They knew many of their customers. There were indicative prices, but bargaining was assumed at many stalls: buyer and seller made their points, and eventually a sale price was agreed upon. What little regulation that existed was in terms of renting a place in the car park that was used, with a fee schedule according to the space that was booked, run by a voluntary organisation, the Rotary Club of a nearby suburb. In later years, there was an entry fee that Rotary collected, used mainly, I think, to ensure the car park was cleaned up at the end of the day.

Unlike the theoretical free market we discussed in Chapter 2, these were real markets. In many ways they did meet the model presented by Friedman: exchanges were free and voluntary; participants were equal; and information was generally available about the item in which you had an interest. What Friedman did not recognise was that those requirements of his were sustained, not by rules and government controls but by the values of respect and reputation. They were the factors that made the real face-to-face market work, and Friedman's criteria were secondary to them. In real markets, you have to deal with the person in front of you, and many of the imperfections of the theoretical "free market" in practice disappear.

The discussion so far has focused on individuals, but now I want to shift the focus to a much more challenging area. This is one in which my own uncertainties are considerable, and I can only address this through revealing what I do not know.

The topic I want to explore here is respect for nations. In particular, I want to look at China (the People's Republic of China, or "mainland China" as it is often called.). I have found it interesting, and at times challenging, to have moved to live in the US for a while, and heard the demonisation of China. The challenge I face is to square up my perceptions of China with those of others, and, at the same time, make sense of Chinese perceptions of countries like the United States. Incidentally, I should explain that most of the times I have been to China I was living in Australia, an Australian citizen. As Australia has never been at war with China they seem to have a generally positive view of that country: it makes for easier conversations.

China is a country I have visited at least twenty times. Most of my time there has been in Tianjin (the city I have visited most often), Shanghai and Beijing. However, I have also been to Guangdong and Hangzhou, Qingdao and Xian, and several smaller cities (small cities in China, of course, may have more than a million people living in them). Some of the time, I have been sightseeing: the terracotta warriors of Emperor Qin's tomb, and the walled city of Xian; the Forbidden City and Heavenly Temple in Beijing, as well as wandering around the 798 Art District; the World Expo in Shanghai, and so much more. Some of the time has been taken up with my meeting government officials and university teachers, and some of the time giving talks, or running programs for business people. A year after it happened, I was able to visit one of the towns that disappeared during the terrible earthquake in May 2008, and to meet local people, see how they lived, and how they were dealing with tragedy and destruction. If all that sounds like a lot, well I have to confess I know so little about the country.

When I am asked about China, I answer with respect. It is a vast nation, more than 1.3 billion people, extending across some very different regions, from the affluent cities of the East coast to the poor rural areas of the West. It is changing fast, very fast, and cities that were run down ten or fifteen years ago are transformed within a decade. I find it hard to remember Qingdao as it was, for now it is a city of modern roads, modern buildings, and modern shops; when I first went there, it was still emerging from the run down state that followed occupation during and after the Second World War, the decaying German concession full of incongruous European mansions. China's leading universities are certainly world class. They have research centres working at the forefront of such activities as medicine, biotechnology, avionics and aerospace, telecommunications, and alternative energy. China will soon be producing world standard aircraft and cars. It has an emerging high-speed rail network that will rival Europe's in the next few years.

It is also a country facing challenges. The one child policy combined with a traditional preference for a boy is leading to a huge demographic imbalance (simply, a shortage of women compared to men) that will colour the lives of a generation of people, and of men in particular, for many years. Better health, education and welfare are growing the percentage of older people at a phenomenal rate. It is a country that has grown through the stage of being the world's manufacturer, and is now trying to grow its economy internally, seeking to increase the level of domestic demand and free up the savings that, true to tradition, people still keep safe at home. It has made remarkable strides in reducing poverty, and yet still many people live in terrible conditions.

At the same time, the country faces other challenges. It continues to be governed by an autocratic, semi-meritocratic system that ensures the Communist Party's unchallenged rule. It has slowly moved into fuller engagement with the world economy, but it is still trying to work out how to create a socialist market economy, an economy that reaps the benefits of the free market, but does so without creating inequalities and imbalances. Poverty has decreased, but there are still huge (and growing) income disparities between those at the top of the system and everyone else. Overall the standard of living is increasing, but vast swathes of the country still lack access to adequate clean running water, electricity and safe sewage systems. It controls its citizens and the media, practices censorship (often including forms of self-censorship practiced by commentators and writers themselves), and prevents access to sections of the World Wide Web by controlling the Internet. It is a country characterised by contradictions, a combination of amazing achievements and continuing problems.

I try to understand China by comparing it to the USA. Not the USA of today, but the USA of eighty years ago (about where China is now in terms of development). America then was also a place of contradictions: rising wealth was also accompanied by growing income disparity. Improved infrastructure was compounded by pollution and poor living conditions for many people. Corruption, lawlessness and crime were all common. Philanthropists were creating the beginnings of some great institutions, while shady business people continued to work with gangs and trade in the black market. This was the time of prohibition, glamour and patriotism. The US was a federal system, uniting very different States and temperaments. It was a country characterised by contradictions, amazing achievements and continuing problems.

The Chinese often discussed the United States with me, even though I was an Australian visitor. They asked me interesting questions. "Does the US have capital punishment?" "In many states, yes" "Then why do they criticise us for having the same?" I wonder if I should point out that capital punishment extends over a far wider range of crimes in China when compared with the United States; I don't, because I cannot imagine what it is like to try and govern a country of so many people, and how important the threat and use of severe punishment may be.

"Why does the US have so many people in prison – and why are so many black people in prison – much more than they are a percentage of the population?" History, marginalization and slavery: they understand that, and wonder why they are criticised for dealing with similar problems in relation to Tibet, Mongolia, and above all Xinjiang, Gansu and Ningxia provinces, where they have some 20 million practicing Muslims (and maybe as many as 50 million more of Muslim background). Surely the US can understand that challenge?

They are fascinated by geo-politics and the world economy, with good reason. In the next ten years or so, China will be a firmly established major player on the world stage in both political and economic terms, at least as strong as the USA, Japan, or Europe. They look at those parts of the world and ask questions, again. "Why does the US still want to dominate the world?"

It is a hard question to answer, because China appears to see the world differently. It has a long history, and it has never seen itself as an empire building power trying to control the whole world. Rather China's history seems to have been more about wanting to control its own territory (and it is patiently waiting to get some 'bits' back, like Taiwan), and then trade with the rest of the world. Will that change? Will China be one player in a multi-polar world, with a balance between the US, Europe, China, maybe Japan, and eventually India?

They are as fascinated as I am about the long-term future of Russia, of Brazil, and of Africa. Will their desire for resources become like that of the US, no longer satisfied to trade, but wanting to own and control, especially in places like Myanmar, South East Asia and Africa? The evidence is contradictory and unclear.

On the other side, when I think about US perceptions of China, I am reminded of the views we used to hold in Australia (and in Europe). China was the "yellow peril" that was going to come down from the north, and eventually take over Malaysia, Singapore, Indonesia, Papua New Guinea, and then Australia itself. Of course, it wasn't China. The scare was about communism. That was the real "peril". Today that seems so quaint. The bastions of so-called communism – China, Russia and Cuba – have all given way to the open market. Russia is an autocracy (as it has been for the last 100 years). China is a one party state, flirting with democracy around the edges (not that different, it seems to me, from Singapore, which is a democracy, but a one party state in practice!). Cuba is slowly moving into the world's market economy.

Americans fear China, and play up the atrocities to justify that fear. China certainly does quell rebellions and breakouts with an iron fist (especially in the last year of every ten year cycle when a new President and Premier are going to be appointed: they like to make the transition smooth and unchallenged). Dissidents are treated harshly, especially in physical terms. The US is more humane, although I would not want to be Bradley Manning right now, no more than I would have liked to have been a person on one of Senator McCarthy's lists in the early 1950's.

China, as a manufacturer, is loathed and appreciated. My iPhone is great, and I am delighted that it has been made so well. However, China has made toys using lead paint, China has put melamine into milk. Many Chinese products have been cheap and shoddy.

Actually, let me put it like this – "'their' economy has grown on the back of cheap manufacturing, poor quality goods, and battles over stolen IP". The only problem with this last sentence is that I am describing views of Japan in the 1950's, (they are the "their" in that sentence). This was when Japan was the world's cheap manufacturer, and Texas Instruments was fighting Japanese calculator manufacturers over patents TI owned.

In other words, it is always helpful to present things in an alternative perspective: China is not the first economy to have grown from being a cheap source of labour, a manufacturer that makes goods for the rest of the world, and starts off doing it "cheap and nasty". Today, China manufactures high quality goods, much of its production is of its own elaborately engineered goods, and it outsources a lot of the actual assembly to cheaper countries in the Asian region. We might be able to respect China better if we look at it in terms of the developmental path most countries seem to follow.

The things we fear the most are the ones that are closest to ourselves – other strong, growing economies, run by people who look different, but might actually be very similar. It seems it is hard to respect those we fear.

One more set of questions that Chinese friends ask me. "Why is the US increasing its presence in Asia, putting more military personnel and installations into Australia? What is the meaning of a US-Japan-Australia alliance? Who is the enemy?" I am sure that the United States would answer that it is 'protecting the balance of power'. What balance? Taiwan? China sees Taiwan as part of China, and is quite confident it will return. So do most Taiwanese, it is just a matter of time. North Korea? Does China want North Korea run by a willful leader armed with nuclear weapons? Of course not. Perhaps it believes that soft diplomacy will turn North Korea around, and end the decades of poverty, hatred and the politics of the cult.

In case it is not transparent by now, I know very little. I am probably seeing China through rose tinted glasses. I am certainly aware of the tensions, corruption, reliance on Keynesian economics and ruthlessness of those in power. I often talk about the threat of a property bubble bursting. But, for all that, China is still a developing nation. What I can see is that a lack of respect for China is simply inflaming prejudice, stereotyping and tension. China has many faults. So does the United States. The future of the world rests on rapprochement between great powers, not on escalating tensions and differences. Respect comes from trying to understand things as they really are. Respect does not come from prejudice, exaggeration and willful misunderstanding. Right now, I see the United States has a huge China elephant on roller skates, warping its view of the world, and pulling it into trade wars and economic challenges that are more likely to hasten the decline of the US, not China, as an economic power. I admire those Americans who try to reach through the mists of confusion and smokescreens of misperception to try to understand the real China, long may they prevail.

Respecting and understanding others is hard work. This leads into the next chapter, which is all about how we manage to live together, and some of the hazards that are becoming apparent there, as well.

10. How can we live together?

Several years ago, an academic researcher tackled the question of why different regions of Italy showed very different patterns of economic growth. Among the things he observed as he compared one region with another was that economic prosperity seemed to be associated with higher levels of civic engagement and density of social relationships. This led him to develop the term social capital (deliberately counter-posed to financial capital), a term which he summarized as referring to "features of social organisation such as networks, norms, and social trust that facilitate coordination and cooperation for mutual benefit."[80] It was an important observation, and has been the source of much academic analysis since that time.

That researcher, Robert Putnam, suggested that his data indicated social capital facilitates and even creates the conditions for both social and economic development, through supporting trust, collaboration and a sense of being part of a community, and not independent of it. The level of social capital is a measure of how well people in that society live together. The development of a rich set of social networks provides a very different framework from that of Milton Friedman. Putnam's thesis is that it is the level of social engagement, not the impersonal rules of the market, which creates a strong economy (as well as a strong polity and social system).

Putnam later applied the concept of social capital to looking at what was happening in the US, research that led to a memorable article, and later a book, called 'Bowling alone'. While we will not pursue in detail the link between social capital and economic development that Putnam's research suggested, his observations provide an excellent starting point for looking at how well we live together.

Putnam's findings, looking at the development of the US over the latter part of the 20th Century, were both illuminating and concerning. They were illuminating because they showed that the patterns of social interaction had definitely changed over that time. There was a lot of evidence of a reduced level of social and civic engagement. It was nicely captured in his analysis of bowling. Some decades ago, bowling was popular as a team sport. You joined a team, played in a league, and competed to push your team up the league ladder. Teams were drawn from the local community. Your team, together with members' partners, children and friends, would socialize together. It created a dense and strong network of social engagement. By the time of his research, bowling was still popular: in terms of the numbers playing, slightly more people were bowling than had been twenty years before. The more interesting observation was that the whole structure of teams, leagues and all that went with that had largely fallen away. People still went bowling, but the focus had shifted to a leisure pursuit with friends: the continuing interaction with teams and their supporters has dropped (and so had the revenue for the bowling alleys in terms of sales of food and drink!). Social engagement had narrowed.[81]

The example is, perhaps, a somewhat trivial one. However, Putnam's findings as a whole were not just illuminating, they were concerning. In discovering, in a number of areas, that social capital seems to be declining in the US, Putnam's findings also suggested this decline was associated with a fall in the level of civic engagement and civic trust. Such a drop has a number of dimensions. It would suggest that people would be less engaged with, and less trusting in, the structures of democracy and government. Voting trends would seem to support this, as would the low levels of trust in the politics of the nation that are increasingly evident today. Indeed, on this dimension, twenty years after Putnam's research, things seem to be even worse.

While the attitude of people towards government is clearly a matter of concern, there is a potentially much deeper malaise here, which may require even more of our attention. This is that the sense of community itself is eroding. If we don't know and fail to engage with the community around us, then neighbourly trust and support decline. If we do not spend time with the people who live near us then anxiety, a feeling of relative deprivation and a sense of isolation increase. Isolation can breed intolerance, and intolerance can itself spark a greater sense of deprivation and lead to aggressive behaviour. That in turn creates greater anxiety.

Just look around a typical suburb in the US: in the evening everyone has gone inside, and doors are locked. In Italy, where I have been writing, the evening is the time everyone comes outside, talk about what has been happening, the politics and the trivia of the day: if there is football to be watched (that European Nations cup again), then the television is brought outside, too. It might be noisy, as children run around, and political discussions get heated, but it is a community!

The question at the beginning of this chapter was "can we live together?" So far we have been looking at this from the other side: the evidence seems to suggest that we are living together less than used to be the case. Indeed, we seem to be living separately (and for many people this means alone, as the largest and growing type of household in many nations now is not a family, not even a couple, but a person living alone).

If social capital has been declining, it is worth thinking about the reasons. Putnam and others have placed a lot of emphasis on external factors. Social mobility, which is strongly linked to occupational mobility, is seen as one factor. People can and sometimes have to move for work, and often are uprooted from places in which they have lived for years. Settling in a new area can encourage a sense of isolation, and might even initiate an unwillingness to go out and make new friends (especially when you can keep in touch with your former friends and neighbours, a topic to which we will return in a moment). At the same time as mobility has increased, demographic changes mean that families are smaller, and more often both parents work, a change that has almost certainly contributed to a decline in the availability of people to participate in some of organisations that are a core part civic engagement, such as women's voluntary welfare organisations, and PTAs.

Some of the other factors that reduce the likely level of interaction with neighbours and the local community are more to do with technology. First and foremost, the increased level of car ownership has changed the patterns of shopping and leisure. For years the impersonal supermarket, the department store and the shopping centre have all pulled us away from the local corner shop. More recently, there is another development taking place: increasingly, people are seeking out specialist shops rather than supermarkets and hypermarkets. However, these are not the corner stores of old, but rather these boutique shops are located inside the shopping mall. Shopping in the neighbourhood remains a brief experience, driven by necessity: significant time on shopping seems to be undertaken in malls and centres.

A second, and equally important technology has been the television, closely followed by the computer. We can stay at home, and receive our entertainment there. Even the family does not have to sit and watch together. Parents in one room, a child in another, a television for each. Moreover, as we noted in an earlier chapter, many children do not even use a television: why would they when it is possible to schedule the entertainment they want on a computer or an iPhone, and at the time they would prefer?

It would be wrong to conclude from this that we are turning into social isolates. Far from it. Rather the technologies of today allow different kinds of social engagement. As we discussed earlier in looking at how we keep in touch with other people, Facebook, email, IM and all the other computer-based technologies of today allow us to keep close contact with the family and friends important to us, even if they are living overseas, on the other side of the globe. School children today have high levels of peer engagement, keeping in touch with the classroom friends seamlessly as they move between school and home. Within these IT-enabled networks trust and support are sustained. Even the game playing computer user quickly finds that success in on-line games comes from collaboration and cooperation (most young people playing on their computers in their room are far from the social isolates the popular media likes to depict).

Staff in organisations are equally strongly linked to their workplaces, to their colleagues and their boss. In an earlier chapter we described how the smartphone is a "tether", holding the contact between the company and the worker unbroken, 24 hours a day, seven days a week. Of course, there are still areas of face-to-face connection, and some of that is still with the local community. For example, there are still strong church communities, even if church going has declined significantly in the US (and much more so in other parts of the world). We are strongly connected. It is just the sphere of connections is generally very different, and so are the ways in which we maintain them.

In the past, when most social engagement was face to face, the local community was stronger. Like them or not, we met neighbours and families at the bowling alley as much as at the local shop or at church on Sunday. Today we can pick and choose. We can keep contact with family and the friends we like, and ignore the others around us. But by ignoring some of those around us, we set in motion the processes that lead to splitting the world into "them" and "us". From that it is just a short step, driven by anxiety, into stereotyping and discrimination. When you notice there are a lot of "them" around you, it is a good sign that an elephant is on skates and pulling you along: you are disengaged from the community. We are no longer living together, but living apart together.

Recently "living apart together" has taken on a new meaning, not just about living in a community without knowing the people who live next door. It refers to the practice of a couple living in two homes, one for each. The justification for this is that it provides "the optimum balance of time alone and time together. It is the social and personal quest that transcends marriage, family status, age, race and just about every other demographic characteristic". Perhaps this is the newest "more": being able to live a separate life, and just engage when it suits, and available only to those affluent people who can afford to have two houses rather than one. Even if this were only true of a privileged few, it is certainly another step away from building networks of strong social engagement.

There is another facet to the shift from physical communities to networks sustained on-line. When our community was around us, and social engagement was face to face, we had to practice a particular form of tolerance, which including accepting everyone around us, even those with very different views. Our neighbour, or the partner of a shopkeeper, might well have a very different political or religious philosophy. Once the closeness that communities used to provide disappears, so differences are less likely to be tolerated. Groups can be excluded, as was the case with Jim Crow laws and practices in the south of the US, or gang wars can develop, as has happened in many cities. We have explored some of the dimensions of different worldviews earlier, when we explored what it means to do the right thing, what it is to be moral, and what it is to be 'free'.

Of course, the extent of tolerance was relatively low. Before social mobility increased, it was very likely that most of those around you would have fairly similar worldviews: now, those chances of living near people with very different views are much higher. You might be a Democrat, your neighbour a Republican. You might be a Christian, you neighbour a Buddhist. Of course, your on-line network might be far more compatible in terms of their preferences and priorities compared to yours. Even is this is not the case, on-line communities also allow you to 'hide' some of your views and affiliations. When you are linked to another person through the Internet, you may not know how different they are on a number of dimensions.

As we have said, when the level of social interaction was much higher differences of opinion were evident, and, largely, respected. Some colleagues or neighbours might tease you about your views; they might even attempt to suggest you are wrong about some critical issues. However, proximity breeds tolerance. Around a barbecue in the evening, you can hold a robust discussion, and everyone still leaves as friends. Perhaps the beer at the barbecue helps, but there is something about conversations between people in the same place that allows you to say to yourself "Jack has some odd ideas, but he's OK really".

As social engagement declines, so too does tolerance. The more you can avoid having to engage in discussion with people who have different views to those you hold, the more likely you are to become a little more close-minded. There were some excellent examples of that during the Republican presidential primaries. Candidates spoke to audiences that were largely self-selected. When the audience was predominantly from the conservative end of the party (offering the "tea party" perspective), the candidates reinforced messages that suited the audiences' viewpoint. Participants left feeling comfortable with the comments they had heard, as they were their views. This was not real interaction, but a show, and a show that encouraged less tolerance and more certainty about what was 'right'. Little did the attendees realise how much had been tailored to their point of view, and that what was said to them could be wiped clean (like an etch-a-sketch as one advisor put it) so that a more palatable presentation could be assured for the next audience. If this example seems partisan, that is only because it was among the Republicans that a candidate was being sought – if the Democrats had been holding primaries at the same time, then I am sure we would have been able to make the same observations.

The underlying theme here seems quite clear. If you engage with the people around you frequently, because you and they are part of the same local (physical) community, you will learn to see them as people first, and their views as just one part of their character. If meetings are less frequent, political showpieces or a quick "social" chat with a neighbour as you leave for work, then the views take precedence over the person. The bonds forming social networks in the community are weak, the development of social capital limited, and we are quicker to judge, less willing to be tolerant. This is self-reinforcing. If you have little contact with your neighbours, and the little contact you have suggests they are "not like you", then your willingness to interact, to engage, will be less. You will avoid differences, and look to sustain links with those you know have similar views to your own.

This is the paradox of living together. If you really live in a community, you will have to live with difference and disagreement: people seldom share the same views on most topics. In an engaged community, that is good: it is good for democracy, because you learn to accept and live with difference, and respect the processes by which agreements have to be reached; and it is good for you because it prevents entrenched views, stereotypes and ideologies as we described them earlier, becoming so embedded that you are no longer aware they are there, even though they shape and influence what you do and think. Living together discourages some types of runaway elephants; living alone together provides a great environment for elephants to slip away from you. Social interaction and civic engagement keeps us in touch with the way people really are.

Just as the reduction of social interaction and engagement at the face-to-face level have their consequences, so do the new technologies of social engagement. Relying on keeping in touch through email and social networking sites can lead to a narrowing of contacts. We pay attention to those whose views we support, those in our network we see as important, at a cost to our willingness to engage with the broader community.

All this raises another issue about how we live together, and this has to do with the way we treat people with whom we do "live together", even if that living together takes place largely through on-line interactions. This is the dimension of obligation. There are some people in our network of relationships to whom we are loyal, and there are others whom we treat "like everyone else". This is the contrast between loyalty and impartiality. A good way to think about loyalty and impartiality is to see them as alternatives, rather than as extremes on a continuum. You are either loyal to someone, or not. Loyalty is specific and personal. We are loyal to our partners, our children and our family. We are loyal to our close friends. We know them as unique individuals, and we try to deal with them as their special relationship to us requires. We care for the people to whom we are loyal; we do things for them we would not do for others. Harking back to an earlier chapter, we even tell them white lies to preserve their feelings. For each person to whom we are loyal, there are things we will do we would not do that for others.

Then there is the realm of people we do not know well – the shopkeeper we met in the store, the person in front of us in the queue – and these people we try to treat without specific and personal considerations, but impartially. Impartially means without distinction. These people we do not know so well, we treat them all in the same way. Well, that is too simple, of course. There are at least two categories of people we do not know well, who are outside the sphere of loyalty. There are those who are like us, and we treat them impartially and fairly – these are the people to whom that golden rule applies (do not do unto others what you would not have them do unto you). There are those who are not like us: they are the people who are different (through where they live, their socio-economic or educational backgrounds, their religious preferences, their ethnicity, their race – whatever grounds of distinction we choose to apply): we treat them impartially, but we may not be as likely to treat them wholly fairly.

This business of loyalty makes the whole issue of living together even more difficult. Loyalty is a demanding principle. It drags you into doing things that you may resent, or fear. It coerces you into giving special consideration to some people, and then exposes your loyalty, which others may see as favouritism, blind love, or even deceitfulness. In some ways, it is easier to live with people who do not require your loyalty, where your biases and preferences will not be exposed.

One of the arenas where loyalty and impartiality come into sharp conflict is inside organisations. We didn't use the word there, but we saw that Heidi felt loyalty to some of the people she knew in her organisation. It was that loyalty that was one of the stumbling blocks to her simply saying "we must tell the truth about what has happened". Organisations are meant to be burcaucratic (in the good sense of the word), places where there are fair rules, regulations and processes, applied to all without any partiality. Of course, if we think about it, organisations in practice are hotbeds of politics, favours, deals, backstabbing, gossip and deceit: if that sounds exaggerated, then look more carefully! The politics of the organisation require that we become adept at sensing out those who have influence, whose views are compatible with your own, to whom you should be loyal, and to whom a little dissembling would be appropriate. No wonder that some organisations end up with senior managers who do not appear to be particularly capable. They were probably good at "office politics", and knew how to use their loyalties to advantage.

In many respects, organisations are a microcosm of society more generally. In the local community, loyalty is also expected. As a member of the local church, you are expected to stand by the priest and the other officers of the organisation. You might gossip about what happens, but your loyalty has to be clearly evident. If you know your neighbor, and if you are close to your neighbor, then you are expected to be loyal to your neighbor.

Loyalty is more than just a demanding principle, as it can also be blind and dangerous. Loyalty pulls us to do things that – in our more rational moments – we would never consider. Loyalty demands, and does not wait for a more reasoned analysis. It is our capacity for loyalty that takes us beyond behaving like a rational and logical analyst, that expects us to care, passionately at times, for (some) others. Loyalty is a lovely, smiling elephant, cute, loveable, and is just about to skate off as fast as it can go.

In Chapter 5 we examined one factor that seems to impact our capacity to live together, and that is the existence of an innate selfishness. If loyalty can be an elephant on roller skates, the same could be said about the role of self-interest. Adam Smith had noted that self-interest could lead to benefits to the wider community, and some have taken that to mean that 'greed is good'. As we argued in that chapter, surely cooperation is good, whereas greed may lead to some positive outcomes. Of course, cooperation may lead to the satisfaction of individual self-interest by achieving outcomes we cannot realise by ourselves alone. However, it is equally likely that cooperation bring its own rewards in terms of living in a 'good society'

Back in the 1960's, Ernest Becker wrote one of those multidisciplinary books that sought to draw various threads together to explain what is distinctive about humans.[82] Commenting on how he saw the relationship between humans and animals, and in how humans transcend instinctive reactions through the use of the mind, he wrote that: "The development of Mind, then, is a progressive freedom of reactivity. The reactive process which is inherent in the organism not only arrives a freedom from the intrinsic properties of things but also proceeds from there to assign *its own stimulus meanings*. Mind culminates in the organism's ability to *choose* what it will react to"[83]. Becker was antagonistic to the 'medical model' of illness: today, such views are less controversial, and one dominant strand in psychiatry is to seek to mold that process of choosing, replacing self-interest (or even, at its extreme, narcissism or selfishness) with respect, obedience, generosity and self-denial[84].

If Ernest Becker might seem a little 'out there', a similar perspective was recently advocated from a business writer. Dylan Evans, the author of a recent book on 'Risk Intelligence: how to live with uncertainty'[85] asked, "How can our competitive instincts and our innate desire for status be channelled in ways that favour a more equal society? The answer lies in our capacity for instrumental reasoning and our ability to respond intelligently to incentives." In speculating that self-interest and a desire for status is an innate attribute, Evans suggested:

"Left to their own devices, people will find ways to check the most extreme inequalities without eliminating all incentives to work. The spread of norms about sharing seems to bear this out. Norms that govern sharing and negotiating with strangers are a cultural invention, not an innate part of human nature. It seems likely that they began to develop only with the emergence of long-range trading between unrelated groups, around 35,000BC. From there, it was a long, slow journey to the merchant bankers who financed grain trading in medieval Italy, and on to the complex mechanisms of today's global economy. The gradual development of market mechanisms would have been impossible without the co-evolution of norms about what constitutes a fair exchange. And this gives rise to a paradox: markets are both the cause of great inequality, and the source of ideas about what constitutes fair exchange. Perhaps Marx was on to something when he suggested that capitalism would sow the seeds of its own destruction. Or perhaps it has simply provided the mechanisms for softening its worst excesses".[86]

As Evan's remarks suggest, while our human nature may be one driving force on our aspirations, the desire to be fair (and treated fairly) is integral to a life guided by moral considerations. We would like to lead a life where rationality, our intellect, and our values are the drivers of what we do. There is, however, a slippery slope here. To be fair is challenging enough. However, it easily slips into loyalty, and loyalty, like a lack of social engagement, is another of those factors that stop us thinking clearly. It can pull us along in directions we did not mean to travel, and does so without us even seeing we have a choice. Is loyalty a value? Or is it a description of blindness to values? Certainly the phrase "blind loyalty" reminds us that loyalty often takes us along without time for thought or reconsideration of what is best to do.

Our track record on living with others is not particularly good. Whenever unfamiliar people come to settle, in your street, or in your country, there is always a tendency to regard the newcomers as outsiders, who have to earn their membership of the community, a process that can take years rather than months. Living for many years in Australia, I noticed that we always viewed the newest group of immigrants with suspicion. They were not like us, and had to be held at a distance. However, the group that was most keenly aware of the differences between themselves and the newest group of immigrants was the group that had just preceded them! It was almost as if they had to prove they were now insiders, and the group just arriving were outsiders. Often, the group that was the most tolerant of new groups in the community was those who had lived in Australia for generations.

I recently watched an old documentary made in 1944 about the Japanese who were living in the United States when it joined the allies during the Second World War. The great majority of them were American citizens, but people of Japanese background were moved out from their homes into guarded camps, not described as prisoners, but still kept away from everyone and under the eyes of the authorities. The reasons for this action was the fear that there might be a Japanese invasion, and those of Japanese background might assist the invaders in these circumstances. As the commentary revealed, these Japanese Americans were taken out of their communities, and apart from clothes and other items they could carry, their possessions were put into store. Arriving in an unfamiliar (and for many hostile) environment, they were moved into barracks, each family provided with a single room, a single light, beds and a cupboard. Some put up signs on their former shops declaring their love for and commitment to the US, but the very people who had embraced them before were led to now believe they represented a (potential?) security risk.

What would happen today if we found ourselves at war with a country that had supplied immigrants in the past? Would we feel obliged to move them away from their homes and lives in the city, and put them in a guarded camp? Inter-marriage, business partnerships and membership of voluntary organisations and sports teams - all these things could be torn apart, facing those who were not to be moved with tricky decisions about where their loyalties lay. The events of seventy years ago revealed the fragility of living together.

The documentary also showed what happened to the families in the camps. People of different professions and experiences suddenly found themselves pushed together. Within the confines of the camp, they re-established the very distinctions that had grown up before. Those who were more affluent, and could bring and use some money immediately made the single rooms attractive - and some even partitioned off a bedroom area from the main living area (all in a small space). Standards and styles of dress differed, and the need for doctors, lawyers and teachers quickly emerged, again starting to build social hierarchies and distinctions between the residents of the camps.

People worked in while they were in the camps, principally farming. However, this meant that all sorts of ancillary occupations were needed. People with no experience in engineering, maintenance of equipment and lathe work suddenly learnt new skills. Strangely enough, as the war progressed some of these newly trained people were needed outside the camps, and they went back into the wider community. Some served in the United States Army, and left the sequestered life they experienced. We were not told what challenges these "returnees" faced when they took up their new tasks in the American community. Did they find it difficult to live together with the very people from who they had been separated just a year of so before? It must have been a real exercise in tolerance for many, both Japanese and American.

Living together requires a great deal of flexibility, as the American Japanese learnt as they moved into the camps and back out again. We dull the sensitivity to being tolerant of others by building strong links of loyalty with those in our 'inner circle'. We avoid the stresses of really living with others by retreating into living alone together. How can we avoid the dangers of loyalty, or the risks of living alone together? Appreciating the consequences of allowing these particular elephants to get on their roller skates, as in all the other topics we have explored, takes us back to those skills of thinking, analysis and reflection I have mentioned in some of the chapters before this one.

At the end of several chapters, I seem to have asked a question of the form "Do we want to …?" Well, "Do we want to live together?" Living together is not an easy business. Married couples often report that it is easier when at least one of them is working full-time, and then it all goes wrong when the former full-time worker retires: "I can't get him (or her) out of the house!" Parents seem conflicted over their children: they love to have them living with them, and yet wish they would move out and move on with their own lives.

As we commented earlier, we are social animals, but perhaps we are unusual in that we also want to have some time alone, or at least time where others do not control or interfere with the pattern of our lives. One curious part of this is "solitude". In a crowded world, solitude is becoming a rare commodity, and many live with lives always surrounded by (man made) noises. Without solitude, can we really sit back and think? I am sure, what ever you might feel about solitude, there are a lot of fast moving elephants out there delighted that we do not have the clear thinking time to wonder what is happening to us.

In the next chapter we will look at one significant change that has taken place since the end of the Second World War, often described as the advent of "postmodernism". This was a critique of how things were described, of "representation", and led, in turn to an acceptance of relativism and the idea that one person's perspective was as valid as another's. This will be our last foray into elephant hunting, and following this, the final chapter will look more closely at the skills that we should be employing to live a better life, skills that may help us stop elephants getting on roller skates, running away from us, and dragging us along in the process.

11. Anything goes?

In 1934 Broadway awoke to the sounds of a new musical, Anything Goes. Set on an ocean liner, it was another of those improbable stories mixing sentimentality with lots of fun, and acting as the backdrop for some memorable lyrics. Loosely based on a book by Guy Bolton and P G Wodehouse, it has been revived many times, and is one of the favourites for high schools' annual shows. Almost everyone will know the eponymous and delightful Cole Porter song at the core of the show. You may remember some of the lines:

> *"In olden days, a glimpse of stocking*
> *Was looked on as something shocking.*
> *But now, God knows,*
> *Anything goes"* [87]

At the time, the song was about changing standards and the breakdown of traditions and conventions in the 1930's. However, the changes were about morals, dress and behaviour. Alongside the freedoms and fun of the flapper era, the "Great Books' project was under way, setting a basis for liberal arts courses in leading universities. This major project led, in due course, to the publication of the "Great Books of the Western World" in 1952 (amended once since then, the series includes some 517 works by 130 authors). In literature, it seems, many things didn't "go' and the project identified the works of mainly western DWEMs (Dead White European Males) that were claimed to constitute the corpus of great ideas that defined civilisation.

Today, Cole Porter's lyrics seem almost prescient, as we live in the aftermath of post-modernism and the legitimacy of alternative and competing narratives. Since the 1930's we have witnessed further social revolutions, especially during the 1960's; we have accepted the importance of recognising thinkers' ideas from every civilisation; and, slowly, we are coming to terms with the rejection of any belief in a privileged position for western thought. The "Great Books" project has been largely discounted, with the concession that many of the books listed are worth study as works of literature and as examples of a particular (male and western) narrative, but, in most cases, only insofar as they are read alongside other works from other traditions and perspectives. Does all that mean today anything goes?

Clearly, we do not live in a world where *anything* goes. One cannot with impunity go around stealing, killing people, or destroying other peoples' property. However, having conceded there are some limits on the things we can do, there is a generally accepted view that "anyone is entitled to his or her point of view". After some time spent on spotting elephants on roller skates, I am sure you have already realised that we have just identified another: this is moral relativism, the corollary of which is an unwillingness to give priority to one person's values over another, or even to suggest that one viewpoint might be preferable to another.

We first commented that issue early on in Chapter 2, where we asked whether there is a moral code, or even a set of standards, that applies to everyone in a society. We briefly discussed how this related to the relationship between the government's role in relation to the recognition of forms of marriage, and the views held by people of different religious persuasions. It seemed that we could draw a distinction between political decisions and moral decisions: the recognition of a union between two or more people and the legal obligations that such a union entails are a matter of political jurisdiction; the moral constraints placed on the form of such unions are a matter of religious belief. The two can be separated. The state can recognise unions for the purposes of taxation, ownership of property, and so on; religions can prescribed what types of "marriage" are acceptable for their members. This implies a clear division between those matters that are the business of government and those that are the business of the "communities' to which we belong.

In fact, the "anything goes" elephant can cause us trouble in two different ways. If we fail to play close attention, we can fall into the trap of denying almost any constraints on what we can do, and find ourselves drawn closer and closer to an anarchical world. At the same time, we can also allow it to persuade us that the domains of the political (the realm of government) and the moral (the realm of religion and other "communities with values") can be clearly separated, pushing us towards world in which political power operates without any moral reference.

If we accept, for the moment, that the domain of government can be clearly identified and circumscribed, what does it comprise? For some, the central role of government is the protection of private property. There is a long history supporting that view. Critical in that history was John Locke, who sought to refute the divine right of kings, and to explain the emergence of private property and the role of government. Early in his Second Treatise of Government, he summarised the core of his argument concerning the role of government:

> "Political power, *then, I take to be a* right *of making laws with penalties of death, and consequently all less penalties, for the regulating and preserving of property, and of employing the force of the community, in the execution of such laws, and in the defence of the common-wealth from foreign injury; and all this only for the public good.*"

This, then, is one extreme, that the role of government is solely concerned with exercising power to ensure two objectives: that private property is regulated and protected (and hence all those rules about contracts, the operations of the market, etc.), and that the country is defended (and, obviously, this too can be argued as a further extension to the task of ensuring the protection of private property).

We have already explored the other side of this view, well articulated by Mill, whereby anything to do with personal values, behaviour and activity is a matter for individuals, and that the only constraint on individual liberty is the prevention of actions that would impact on the liberty of another person. Government's role in relation to liberty is to make sure we are free to exercise our liberties, and therefore it should "keep out" of our lives.

If we accept Locke and Mill at face value, then anything goes, except for interfering with either private property or the liberty of others.

Looking at "anything goes" in such extreme terms is easy, and misleading. If we want to explore this in a less "black and white" framework, there are a number of issues at stake. We know that there are many things that influence behaviour, outside of these two themes of individual liberty and government protection of private property. One example has already been referred to, and this is the domain of habits and customs. In the 1930's, the flappers and their friends were simply setting aside a number of social conventions that had become established over time: the stiff and restricted public world of the Victorian era was over.

More broadly, there are at least three ways in which we might want to think about the limits we place on a world where otherwise anything goes, and the rest of this chapter explores these in some detail. The first area for discussion concerns the place of morals in society, their relationship to individual values, and the 'ownership' of moral codes. Following that, I would like to turn attention to our right to disagree and the limits to dissent. The final section of this chapter will explore the topic of standards and how we made judgements about value. Some of the discussion on these three areas that follows may appear to overlap with topics we have covered earlier chapters, but the focus here is on the balancing act between emphasising individual freedom and following the constraints of broader rules and conventions. To use an earlier term, this is about the *trade-off* between liberty and regulation

In Chapter 2 we explored the question, "What do we mean by moral?" That chapter focussed on the challenges of following moral principles. Now the focus is on a different issue, which can be summarised as, "Who owns morals?" In terms of the extreme position that opened this chapter, there was a clear answer: morals belong to the individual, and government is about the exercise of power and control. When the government undertakes to protect private property, regulate the activities of the market, or defend the country, it does not do so on moral grounds. Locke may have said that these activities are "only for the public good", but perhaps he meant this in an instrumental sense, not as a statement of moral purpose.

To claim that the government acts in an amoral fashion seems patently absurd. The government introduces regulations and laws which it intends to be just: our way of determining what is just is to scrutinise what is being put in place to ensure that the outcomes appear to be fair, that we are all treated in the same way. Surely "fair" is a moral value. Even if we were to replace "fair' by "equal", there is still an underlying moral basis. However, this is mere quibbling. In practice we expect government to do more than just ensure that there is a fair legal code and rules of practice: we expect it to pursue the public good in a far more explicit fashion. We expect that roads will be built and maintained; that hospitals will be built and operated; that foods will be subjected to health standards; and much, much more. We expect that we our government will pursue the objectives of "life, liberty and happiness", and that happiness comes from creating a good society.

Here then is the first of the limits on "anything goes". Morals do have a place in society, and they are not the exclusive preserve of individuals and their specific values. How do we get from individual values to morals? One answer comes from considering the consequences of the fact that we do not live alone, but rather we live in communities. Communities have many characteristics: among these one is of particular interest, which is that each member shares, to some degree or other, a common set of values with all the other members of the community. That shared set of values is what we refer to when we talk about morals, and communities are characterised by a moral "code" that is part of makes them more than just a loose association or a random crowd. Further, there is a range from very clear and specific codes that all their members are required to follow, which define a person as being Jewish (a member of the Jewish community), say; through to much looser codes, less rigorously enforced, which we associate with being an architect (a member of the architectural profession), for example.

Today, we live in a number of "communities". We may reside in a physical community, although seeing yourself as part of a community based on local geography is increasingly uncommon (in many cases we know few, if any, of our neighbours, and even if we do the sense of community with them is usually rather weak). We may belong to a religious community, where the acceptance of a moral code is much stronger. We are likely to belong to one or more "communities of interest", groups that share an interest in such activities as painting, hiking, model railways, or Japanese manga: they, too, have a moral code, even if it is lightly understood and usually undocumented. Finally, it is also topical today to talk about belonging to a "community of practice" (which is simply a rather modern term for belonging to a guild): such communities comprise people who share an area of work or practical action, and can range from the very formal, like medical practitioners specialist colleges through to informal networks linking programmers or quilters.

There may be several other categories of community that we could add to my initial list. However, one more is of particular concern: do we also belong to a "broader community"? Surely we also see ourselves as being members of a nation, as American, or Canadian, or French. This last sense category of community is important. If we do see ourselves as belonging to a national community, then, at the very least, we must share a moral code with each other, including members of our government, all of us accepting and following the same general moral precepts.

This is not a game in logic. It really is the case that we do expect our government to act morally, and we also expect it to accept the same moral values that we support. At the same time, we also know there is a puzzle about all of this: there seems to be considerable disagreement as to what comprises the content of that broad moral code. In a modern, complex democracy like the United States, this is not at all surprising. We have Christians, Moslems, Jews and Buddhists living in America, as well as Native Americans, migrants and the descendants of settlers of many generations ago, and yet we expect everyone to "be like us" in the sense that they subscribe to the same core values as ourselves, the ones that define the "American way of life".

We do have some processes that seek to establish a degree of commonality in values and morals. Schools include civic education subjects designed to develop American values. When migrants to

America seek to be accepted as citizens, they have to meet some probationary requirements, as well as demonstrating their understanding and to American values. However, schooling and the citizenship process can only touch on some aspects of individual values, and people of different backgrounds may still hold a wide variety of attitudes and moral principles. To add to that diversity, people develop and hold quite opposed views on what makes a good society and how it should operate. The platforms of the Democrats and Republicans are good examples of these different views: each side claims to represent the "American way of life". Given all this, it is hard to imagine there could be any unifying national moral code: it doesn't appear to make sense.

It does make sense some of the time. After a national disaster like Hurricane Katrina, or a terrorist act like the bombings of September 11 2011, or at a time of war, at times like these we do all come together and act with similar values in mind. Outside of disasters and emergencies, however, these moments of national unanimity are rare. As we saw in Chapter 2, the American nation today is characterised by sharp, and at times bitter, differences of opinion as to what the government should do and what values are most important.

Acknowledging and debating differences is important, of course. We should always be on guard, unless we let slip an elephant on roller skates, an ideology that shapes our lives unquestioned. However, what we see today is that positions are stated, but discussions to build consensus are seldom held, and most of the few debates that are initiated remain unresolved. As a result, differences become hardened: north versus south, Democrats versus Republicans, states versus the federal government. They become stereotyped views. If these oppositions are familiar, they also remind us that 150 years ago America split into two warring parts along similar lines: once more the tensions of today make the model of "one nation" hard to sustain. This is not to suggest that we are moving towards a civil war. It is to make it clear that moral differences in society run all the way from local communities right up to being an American.

The public good that Locke saw driving government is more than an instrumental issue, (even if this is the sense in which he used the term). It is the result of our ability to find a moral framework that makes our complex society today work efficiently, a framework we all share that enables us to work together effectively and happily. That also means that we do expect the government to do more than look after private property, the rules of the market and national defence. While we might accept that the most effective way to coordinate the economic affairs of the nation is through the free market, we still expect to live in a moral nation. Given all the sources of difference we have outlined, however, it is hard to see how we are going to agree on the values that should define a "good" government.

We know that there are some areas of disagreement that seem unlikely to be resolved. Egalitarianism is pitted against meritocracy, each of these two approaches is supported by principles that appear incommensurate. Some argue that everyone should have the same opportunity to be successful and lead a good life, and at the same time others argue that each person should be responsible for his or her own destiny. We seek free choice and liberty, and at the same time we expect support and nurture. Despite all these conflicting expectations, often based on the different political and social philosophies, we still manage to get on with each other most of the time. If we are able to live together, there must be some areas where the differences between us are not so stark and immovable, areas where the details may be contested but still with specific issues on which we *are* able to make compromises and agreements. Are these the core components of a national set of morals, and if so, what are they?

One way to identify what sits inside a national moral code is to examine behaviour rather than words. Following that approach, we can see that one of the most important values in practice is "caring for others". When I was writing this chapter, there was a graphic and powerful illustration in the news from Australia. An old brick wall collapsed in strong winds in Melbourne, hurling hundreds of bricks on to three pedestrians. Within moments there was a chain gang of people, pulling the bricks away from them. By the time an ambulance arrived, all three had been uncovered, too late for two, but in time for the third to be given medical treatment on the spot, and then taken off to hospital (where, sadly, she subsequently died). No one knew the three people, but forty people sprang into action.

This small incident is repeated on a larger scale in the all too familiar similar scenes in the aftermath of landslides, earthquakes, tsunami and accidents: people do care for others, and sometimes at considerable personal risk to themselves. Indeed, the evidence from studies of reactions to disasters shows that it is often the people in the immediate community that are the most effective in providing help, and that the strength of local communities is critical factor in responding to needs[88].

Is this just an instinctual response? You will recall in Chapter 3 we considered the suggestion that humans have a "collaboration gene". Whatever the genetic basis of such behaviour, there is no doubt that there is a social expectation that we act to help others in desperate need. Almost every part of the world seems to subscribe to some variation of the golden rule: "do unto others as you would have them do unto you". That same expectation extends to governments: we expect them to show compassion and care. We only disagree as to how far and in what ways that compassion should be provided, not over the importance of compassion itself. We argue about the rights that immigrants should have as compared to citizens born in the country; we disagree about what level of support should be provided to the old, the handicapped, the poor and the unexpectedly unemployed; and we dispute what level of medical services should be provided free of charge, what educational provisions should be made for children. These are contested areas, but the points of difference are almost always about "how much" and "by what means", not about the importance of caring.

The development of a moral society and a moral framework for government is an always unfinished task. Attitudes shift as different philosophies gain prominence in society. A country that was persuaded of utilitarianism at one stage can see the focus shifting towards a more supportive role for everyone. The sense of living in a "nanny state' can lead to the value of individual effort and personal responsibility taking a stronger hold. If there is progress, it is by the slow but steady addition of more individual rights and a stronger sense of appropriate government responsibilities. These may be subject to review, but governments today seem to have accepted a greater scope for their responsibilities to everyone, even if they continue to disagree on the best way to meet them. Government is not just about power and control, and ensuring property rights and individual liberty.

If the broader moral framework of society is open to continuing review, this leads us on to a second issue, which is the importance of dissent. Using the example of the distinctive values held by religious groups, Stephen Carter examined "The dissent of the governed" in his William Massey lectures in 1995.[89]

His starting point was the Declaration of Independence, and that critical justification for action against the British King and government: "Our repeated petitions have been answered only by repeated injury". He argued that the force of this protest remains as strong today: if a government continues to ignore petitions, it ceases to sustain its legitimacy because it ceases to show "it cares". Carter's analysis of the importance of responding to "repeated petitions" is subtle and important, questioning conventional wisdom about the role of courts and the responsibility of government. It deserves close reading.

However, rather than pursuing all the implications of dissent and the desire for redress which are Carter's focus, there is a "balancing act" issue among them which is particularly relevant to our analysis. If we accept that there is a framework of morals, a national moral code, that informs government, then how do we deal with communities that have quite clear and different moral codes of their own? Carter chose to examine this by looking at issues to do with religious communities, as their moral differences are often quite clear; moreover, the Constitution in the United States makes it explicit that the federal government has no role in religion. There is a strict separation there. It is a good example to consider.

Some examples concerning the differences between religious groups have already been presented. There are alternative views about the nature of marriage (when some religions allow a man to have more than one wife), or about the sanctity of life (with implications for views about the termination of pregnancies). Stephen Carter explores two further examples that really pit the views of a religious group against broader moral values and the principle of caring for others: these concern views about non-adherents, and the nature of knowledge.

The first example rests on the distinctions that many religions draw between their followers and those on the outside. Often those who do not follow the precepts of a religion are not merely "outsiders" but they are described as "heathens" or even "infidels". An infidel ("one without faith") is seen as rejecting the central beliefs of a religion, and regarded as an enemy. Can we feel comfortable with having a religious community instructing its members that other people, living close by, are enemies? It seems close to inspiring violence. If a religion promotes a rather more evangelical aim, seeking to convert others to their beliefs, that seems quite acceptable: it is their way of "caring' for outsiders, even if it requires persuading them to abandon the moral framework and beliefs they had held before. But to talk about infidels within the country seems more like a direct challenge to the political authority of the state. It is claiming the right to power over others.

How should a government respond? Perhaps it should require, on the grounds of protecting individual liberty, that no group (no religious group in this case) should promote or instruct people to draw distinctions based on inequality: the underlying premise being "equal liberties for all" (John Rawls would be pleased with that approach!). This raises the question as to whether or not we have the right to say that some part of a religious group's philosophy is wrong. It seems to be one of those situations where neither side can be satisfied. If the government decides what is right, then those who dissent are oppressed; if each group decides what is right for them, we live in a world of inequality, verging on anarchy. Is there a middle ground?

The same problem emerges when we look at the second example, the nature of knowledge (in a sense, this is simply the first example writ large). In many religions (and, again, drawing on Carter, I am using religious groups to provide an example of a broader theme), knowledge is achieved by revelation. A religious text or the teachings of a religious leader tell us the way the world is, and any other source of knowledge is, quite simply, wrong. This is a problem both within and between religions, as the fights over "creationism" versus evolution reveal in disputes both within and between the Christian churches.

Governments tend to respond to issues of this kind by ruling on what is "right", as has been the case in the United States. There the government has made it clear that science provides the right methods to answer questions, and so that is the way in which we should make sense of the world around us. We can acknowledge that there are some challenges in accepting that science is the right approach, of course: after all, it also requires a degree of faith, and we know that today's scientific "paradigm" can be overthrown by a new set of internally coherent theories at some time in the future. Leaving these concerns to one side, by endorsing the central place of science in education the government is, in effect, directly intervening in religion: scientific truths trump religious revelations. However, the Establishment and Free Exercise clauses of the Constitution state, "Congress shall make no law respecting an establishment of religion or prohibiting the free exercise thereof". On first glance, it would seem that determining all children should be taught science would clearly be limiting the free exercise of a religion that holds to views contradictory to the findings of geology, biology, physics and chemistry.

Debates over the alternative views of various religious groups have been continuous in the United Sates since Independence. Many of the topics of dissent, like those outlined above, are not amenable to a clear and determinative answer. Rather there is a continuing process of accommodation and adjustment. Those debates and the processes to find compromise make it quite clear, however, that it is not the case that anything goes. Rather, we are constantly trying to find the right balancing point as to where there should be constraints over what we can do and say.

Religious groups have been used as an example, but there are many other areas of our lives in which constraints are put in place. To give a familiar but rather different example, in an environment where "political correctness" has become embedded in our interactions, we are far more careful about the language we use to describe other people, especially those whose backgrounds are very different from our own. We use the correct terms out of politeness and good manners, or perhaps out of a fear of being rude. Whatever the motive, we watch our language carefully: indeed, we feel the quiet ear of the government listening in and monitoring how we behave.

All the debates and controversies over conflicting values suggest that we do not want to live in a society where anything goes. There are values we hold dear, and we engage, sometimes vigorously, in discussions to find an area of compromise or a way to find a balance between our values and those of others. Those discussions are inevitable in any complex society, and are a means to ensure that there are no elephants surreptitiously pulling some of us away from what we care about, to find ourselves subject to a moral code with values we do not support.

There was a third topic mentioned at the beginning of this chapter that deserves attention, and that concerns standards. Defining standards takes us away from the contentious area of conflicting values and moral principles into a much "safer" territory. Standard define the way tasks should be performed. Moreover, when the government establishes standards over building safety, food handling, or infection controls, we are generally happy. Such standards fit comfortably within the framework of property rights and personal liberty, as they provide another regulatory framework to protect us.

Not all standards are concerned with the instrumental performance of tasks. In education, as one example, students and teachers will both agree that standards are a rather more fraught issue. A student writes an essay. The teacher can legitimately comment on the use of language, following the rules of spelling, grammar and syntax (even though that is becoming harder today as some of the rules of spelling come under challenge). However, when it comes to content, standards are less easy to apply. Each student can claim some legitimacy for his or her point of view. Teachers have to be wary of imposing patriarchal, authoritarian or racial narratives (and these are just examples, there are many more). One person's standard is another's oppression.

A particularly revealing topic is the assessment of art. One hundred years ago or more, there was a body of aesthetic standards against which paintings or sculptures were assessed. The various academies of art judged artists' work: they set the standards. Inevitably, their determination of the quality of a work was essentially conservative: necessarily so, as new genres and styles would sit outside what had been accepted to date, and the processes to bring about acceptance would be slow. Impressionism, cubism and surrealism were first rejected and then gradually accepted and included. Throughout the long history of art, however, there were many periods where the academy (either a real body, or in the sense of the recognised authorities of the time) had such a sway over what was being done that innovation was rare, and discordant artists shunned or even abused.

In the immediate post Second World War period something changed. After the attacks on existing standards that came from modernism and abstract art, next came post-modernism. Post-modernism was a critique of privileged viewpoints, a justification of "other' standards and criteria, and a direct attack on the authority of the academies. It was an invitation to artists allowing them to believe "anything goes". Many new approaches emerged, of which conceptual art represents an extreme where the emphasis in understanding the art is on the idea and not the expression of the idea.

While this was upsetting all the previous views as to the quality of art, art as investment was skyrocketing. The "value" of works of art saw a dramatic change as a new phase in the development of the art market emerged: art became a traded good. Masterpieces from previous eras suddenly gained great value, auctions witnessing every increasing sale prices. With a limited corpus of "old masters", attention was paid to new and emerging artists, and the business of art was transformed. Today buyers trade pictures in the marketplace, and artists' reputations can grow, or shrink, as the market shifts. Clever investors keep prices high for artist whose work they hold, and the place of aesthetic judgements about "quality" have become increasingly divergent from market judgements of "value".

Where has this left the judgement of quality in art? By and large, the pace of change has left the academies behind. Despite this, art critics, academics and museum curators still develop and practice their skills in assessing art. There is no single standard for quality to compare with the dollar for value, nor was there such a standard in the past. Rather there are a number of criteria used in judging quality. These include such matters are originality, the level of craftsmanship, and then the "character" of the piece determined by such attributes as confidence, coherence and memorability.[90] Even in a world where we might think just about anything is possible, there are criteria to judge works of art and to assess their quality (even though it may be the case that these standards still represent the conservative views that have characterised the academies in the past).

Our examples have been students' essay and works of art, but they could have been toasters or gardens. In all the varieties of products and services around us, there are standards that can be applied. Some are purely instrumental: is the toaster safe, and unlikely to give an electric shock; is the garden planted with flowers, shrubs and trees that can live in this climate? Others are about quality: the design of the toaster or the garden. Charlatans or poorly trained practitioners may try to sell us something that is "below standard", and sometimes that is all we can afford. However, standards do exist, and they are as powerful a limit on the world of anything goes as are government laws and regulations, and carefully crafted compromises between contradictory values.

We began this chapter with Cole Porter's song and lyrics, and the 1930's preference to cast aside conventions - well, at least by the affluent and dashing young things of the time. Are standards the same thing as conventions? Standards are about measures; conventions are more about habits and routines. We still live in a world hemmed in by conventions. I go to a restaurant, and I expect to pay a tip - even if the service is not particularly good. Why? Well, it is established convention. The justification for that convention is that waiters are poorly paid, and that the tips are a significant part of their income. If the service is really poor, then I might reduce the tip or even pay none at all. It is just a convention, a cultural expectation about how we behave. It is certainly cultural. Some research suggests that African Americans see the situation in a different fashion. If service is good, they may tip. If it is poor, they are very unlikely to do so: nor do they see the waiter's income as a critical factor to the same extent as others do.

We are a long way from living in a world in which anything goes. Some aspects of our lives may be freer than they were in the 1930's, others less free. The liberty to do as we please is as much shaped and limited by moral precepts and social conventions as it is by the laws and regulations of government. Why do we allow so many things to slip past us when we happily say, "anything goes" to a child, a student or a colleague? Despite all the issues canvassed in this chapter, we seem willing to accept the mediocre and even praise the inadequate. This elephant is a very trying one. By ignoring the consequences of letting things go we are complicit in throwing away many rules and agreements that underpin a good society. Why? Is it because it is hard work to keep a focus on standards and on enforcing rules and expectations? As is the case with all out elephants on roller skates, we suffer because we stop paying attention.

12. It ain't necessarily so

We began the last chapter with a reference to the Cole Porter 1934 musical Anything Goes. A year later there was a rather more controversial premiere, that of George and Ira Gershwin's opera, Porgy and Bess. First in Boston, and then later at Carnegie Hall in New York that year, many in the audience found it hard to accept a "folk music opera" with a classically trained and entirely African-American cast. Perhaps Ira Gershwin's lyrics to the song "It ain't necessarily so" were unfortunately prophetic: it took 41 years for Porgy and Bess to be accepted as an opera, and in the intervening period it was performed in a shortened musical theatre version, with a reduced cast and orchestra, and the recitatives turned into spoken dialogue.

In the opera, Sportin' Life, a drug dealer, sings about his doubts as to the truthfulness of statements in The Bible, with the opening verse:

> *It ain't necessarily so*
> *It ain't necessarily so*
> *The t'ings dat yo' li'ble*
> *To read in de Bible,*
> *It ain't necessarily so.*

That could be song for anyone who wants to remain alert and questioning about the world around him or her, a song for elephant spotters! Well, with apologies to Ira Gershwin, I suppose you would have to change the last three lines to:

> The t'ings dat yo' li'ble
> To take as reli'ble,
> It ain't necessarily so!

It is hard to think of a more apt warning for the 21st Century. On the one hand, we are likely to accept without question the effectiveness of the free and open market, or the necessity to tell the truth. At the same time, we are bombarded with advice, every day of our lives, on what to wear, how to manage our finances, look after our health, where to go for our holidays, and even how to make sense of gun massacres or why China will (or will not) becomes the world's largest economic power in 20 years time.

It is certainly an apt warning for me. As I look back over the chapters of this book, I see a degree of anxiety, negativity even, in the things I write. Looking at "doing the right thing", I am concerned about the consequences of moral absolutes. When I explore the importance of liberty, I am happy to explain all sorts of constraints on that freedom. I am certainly concerned that those of us who live in a world of plenty always seem to want more. Moreover, when it comes to discussing change I appear preoccupied with describing all the reasons we are unlikely to change. Enough already!

All this came home to me very clearly when discussing the operations of the free market with some students. While I was thinking about the dangers of people being left behind and the extent to which the market embodied "the survival of the fittest", I was taken up short by one student who commented: "Just look at how the operations of the market have transformed the lives of people over the past 100 years". I was about to comment on the poor in the United States, and then go on to the lot of rural Indians or those living on the margin in other developing and underdeveloped nations, when I paused to think. The quality of life for many, probably most, people has been transformed in the last 100 years. It has been greatly enhanced just in the last 30 years. While there are still people who are living on the edge and barely getting enough food to eat, the quality and availability of food is vastly better than it was 30 years ago.

That thought led to another, which was about the impact of science. There are many genetically modified crops that have increased yields and quality, even though there are others where the genetic manipulation has proved less successful. On balance and right now we are benefitting enormously from the positive side of these interventions. Even where there are problems, scientists are working hard to overcome them, backed by governments and industries keen to exploit new and better technologies. Shareholders may reap the benefits of companies' growth, but we will all reap the benefits of better and safer foods. My student was doing an excellent job in making sure that I kept on thinking!

"It ain't necessarily so" is a warning against falling into an easy acceptance of ideologies, principles and everyday advice. It is a reminder that we should always be alert to being drawn into accepting a viewpoint without remembering that viewpoints can run away from us. Unquestioned, they slip into the background, influencing our ideas and our behaviour.

In the previous chapters we have been talking about how an elephant can get launched away from you. This chapter is not about how it can happen, but what you can do when it does happen. How can you get the elephant back, off the roller skates, and gradually shape-shift it into something more manageable?

In one sense, the answer to this question is easy – it is about thinking and reflection. Elephants start pulling us along because we are not taking time out to think about what is going on, reflecting on what is happening, and taking action to reel in the elephants that are affecting our lives. This should be a short chapter – all you have to do is remember to take time out to learn, to think and to reflect, and all will be well. So, is it that easy?

It wasn't for me. I was nearly 40 years old when I realised that I had just about lost the ability to think and to reflect. I was sitting in the evening light in a log cabin, just close to the Chesapeake Bay, in the middle of the Wye Woods. This is the winter home of The Aspen Institute, when winter in Aspen means the ski season, and any space for seminars and deep discussion has just about disappeared under a carpet of snow, skis and après-ski parties. I was reading, concentrating on a thick folder of readings, having just spent some hours around a table with a group of fellow participants in a seminar. We had spent some time – most of that day – reading and debating a section of Plato's Republic, a passage that is often called 'The city of pigs'.

I had read the piece before we went in the seminar room: well, I am using the word 'read' rather casually. The first thing that happened was that the moderator asked one of us to read out one early part of the extract. I can still remember to this day how that simple act made me look so much more carefully at the paragraph that had been chosen. Then the moderator turned to me and asked me what the passage meant. I bumbled my way through a half-decent summary of the text. Very kindly, he asked me more questions about the extract, and in so doing revealed some of the nuances and subtleties of this seemingly simple passage. Of course, I had hardly grasped it at all. I was used to superficial reading, reading every word, getting the gist of what was meant, picking out some important 'bits', and then moving on.

That evening I began to read more carefully and think about the passages that had been selected for us. I still have my folder of readings from that seminar, heavily underlined, highlighted and annotated. It was an intense, revealing and rewarding fortnight. I had not realised that Plato's stories, Machiavelli's observations, or Tawney's strictures had so much depth in them. There was a world beyond superficial "understanding", a world of thinking and reflection that I had left behind soon after I had finished my university education. Whatever remnants of truly critical thinking there had been were quickly being dissipated in dealing with the demands of business and later in running an organisation: being busy had pushed all that aside.

I have never looked back from that moment. I began to run moderated discussion groups based on the same approach. I started up a group of older people, meeting just once a month, where we took apart readings – some "ancient" and, in time, some more contemporary. I developed a university course, part of an MBA program, called Great Thinkers, where we sat around a table and used the same approach, reading and exploring the ideas of great writers. In various groups I have drawn on the works of people from 2,500 years ago – Plato, Aristotle, Confucius and Lao Tzu – right through to such contemporary writers as Peter Singer and Francis Fukuyama.

Almost without fail, every time I have sat down at the table to read extracts from great writers and thinkers with a group of other people, we have all learnt something new, and quite often something important. More to the point, despite my familiarity with the texts we discuss, I have almost always gained from hearing the unanticipated perspective of another participant, developed insights that I had never considered before. If I am a better person now, and possibly a better teacher, it all started with that session in the Wye Woods. Without that, all the extraordinary education I received as an undergraduate would have certainly withered away, wasted and unused.

What was it I learnt? I had (re-)learned to think and reflect. They are far from easy things to do. I can sit here today, enjoying the solitude and far from day-to-day demands in the Tuscan hills, and I can think and reflect – it is an ideal environment, quiet, leisurely, peaceful. I am lucky in where I am living in the United States, as it has the same attributes. However, when I am there I have friends who call round or invite my wife and me to dinner; I have a course to plan and teach for the local university; I have projects I am working on with clients in a variety of companies; and, much to my enjoyment, I have a camera and birds in the garden I want to photograph. My wife and I have many other things we want to do, children and grandchildren to keep in touch with, and all the busy life of semi-retirement. I *can* think and reflect at home, but I have to work hard to create the space to do it.

If all this is difficult for me, how much harder is it when you are working full time, when your children are growing up, when there are holidays to plan, places to go, films to see, and all the other activities that fill up our daily lives. Thinking and reflecting can seem like luxuries, something to indulge in occasionally, perhaps when you and your partner have a little time to talk together and explore what has been happening. Without the "luxury" of thinking and reflection, we are likely to be pulled hither and thither by elephants on roller skates – ideas, concerns and issues that tug at our activities and plans, largely unseen. Unseen because we don't have the time to stand back and ask ourselves – 'what are we doing?" Thinking and reflecting aren't luxuries, but necessities!

The theme of this chapter is creating space to think and reflect, a topic we might describe as 'letting go and losing control'! It sounds like a recipe for disaster, a recipe for and approach to living in a world where it sounds like you have given up. It is actually a path to greater understanding and an enhanced ability to grow and take charge of your life.

When I think of letting go, I think about priorities. I went through a major phase of letting go about twenty years ago. When I talk about it now, I present it as if it was a well-considered set of decisions: in reality, I think it was more adventitious and intuitive. What happened was that I realised I did not have all the time I needed to do my job well in running an organisation, to spend time with my wife (I had recently remarried), and to pay attention to the things I cared about. So, I got rid of the only television we had, abandoned my aspiration to be a novelist, set aside my camera, and started to read and think a great deal more selectively.

I made some mistakes, and some were big ones. My older children will tell you that I spent even less time with them than ever before (my track record as a parent leaves a lot to be desired, and it was only the unexpected birth of a daughter at about this time that kept me in touch with my children: my youngest daughter wanted to know her siblings!). I probably invested less time in my marriage than I should have done: my wife and I were happy, but I wonder if that was just happy enough? In fact, I think you could say I let go of too much of the emotional side of my life (and it is only now, married again after my wife died a few years ago, that I feel I have all that in a better perspective).

Setting aside my camera was giving away something that I had not even realised. In doing that I had given a huge priority to the rational, logical side of my life. I didn't lose my intuitive sense, but I pushed it into a corner. I can still remember sitting on an interview panel assessing candidates, and debating the facts we had gleaned. At the time, one candidate stood out on the objective measures, and so I set aside the other concerns I had, less easy to articulate, and argued we should go for the best person who had presented. Had I listened to what my intuition was telling me, I would have avoided a disaster! I did learn to listen to myself more carefully as I became a wiser chief executive, but I could have done so earlier and been far more effective.

The camera was important because photography took me into the world of art, not science, the exploration of composition, aesthetic issues and feelings. By putting it into a cupboard, I had put part of myself there, preferring to lead the controlled and rational life that my school studies in science had supported. In saying that I let go of too much of the emotional side of my life, I also abandoned the insights and understandings that come from lived experience, rather than rules and measures. Today, slowly, photography is helping me access and feel comfortable with the person I am, rather than the logical perfectionist I strove to be.

Letting go is about accepting that you cannot do everything, and trying to make decision about those things that you will abandon, or set aside for a while, so that you do have time left to think and reflect about how you are living your life. If it is important to lead an examined life, then it must be also important to make sure you have time to undertake regular examination! It is also important to consider carefully what you will let go. I abandoned my aspirations to be a novelist, and set aside my passion for photography: they were not good choices, and I could have left room for some of that "right brain" stuff, and spent less time on some of the more task-oriented activities to which I gave priority.

If I am advocating letting go some activities, it is because I see so many people around me who are so busy being busy they are letting their lives slip past them. A busy life is not a good life, it is simply full. It is easy to fill up time, it is much harder to identify those things that really are worth giving attention, and make sure you are giving them the time they deserve. If you let some things go, things that keep you busy without offering you much real value, you will have time to think and reflect. If you have time to think and reflect, you will be able to reduce the risk of being pulled in one direction or another by an elephant you have ceased to acknowledge.

Many of us are uncomfortable about deciding what to pursue, and what to set aside. In part this reflects a degree of fear, that in abandoning something we will be regarded as less successful or even be seen as a failure. This is so clear when you work inside an organisation, and imagine all the expectations that sit around you: being busy shows commitment and perseverance. In part the task is also asking that we reexamine ourselves, allocating priority to those elements of our lives that will define who we are. It is easy to choose to invest most of our time in work because work identifies us ("what do you do? I am a marketing manager with XYZ corporation." No wonder so many people still cling on to the position they held when asked what they do after they have retired!). That trite old question "Do you work to live, or live to work?" is still worth asking.

A person is not a position, a job is not a way of life. Work can be fulfilling and enjoyable, but it is unlikely to touch more than part of our capabilities and aspirations: leave room for some things that matter to you, and give away some things that are less important. Cabinet making as a hobby is far more fulfilling than endless after-work socialising: the former offers real opportunity to do more than make things, it creates the space to think; the latter fills up time, and crowds out the opportunity to reflect.

There is another element in letting go, and this has to do with "forgetting". I don't mean forgetting in the sense of forgetfulness, which seems to be an increasing problem as I get older! In this case, I am referring to the task of setting aside some of the frameworks you have developed in making sense of the world around you, and being willing to explore new ways. I have sometimes referred to this as being willing to "stand in another person's shoes". When I used to ask my students to do this, I was struck by hard it is for many people to take on an alternative perspective[91]. To let go or forget a framework is to allow yourself to adopt a new perspective. One way to do this, which I often recommend to managers, is to become a customer of your own business. It is often revealing, and sometimes quite shocking, to experience the organisation from the outside: trying to find out whom to contact, trying to work out how to get the right assistance (it only works, of course, if you do this with people in the company who do not know you!).

Being willing to give some things away is part of what can help us. In an earlier chapter, I told you about an episode that brought home to me the need to become a somewhat better leader in my organisation – exercising the skills of servant leadership rather than being the clever boss who runs things. I wonder if you saw a second theme inside that story, which was that by stepping back from trying to be in control things often appear to work rather more effectively!

When I tried to control my organisation, I was a "micro-manager". I was overworking, and I was ignoring the skills, intelligence and abilities of my staff. Once I was willing to give away some control, I enabled others to step forward to deal with their areas of responsibility. Instead of an organisation run by one person, I had an organisation led by many people – a form of "distributed leadership" if you like. When I was asked about my approach as a leader, I used to say, "If the saying is that 'two heads are better than one', then surely several heads are better than two".

When I was young, the image drummed into my head by my teachers was that leadership was about control. Good teachers have a lasting effect, and I still find there are circumstances where it is hard for me to give up control, and allow others to get on and do things! It is often said there are two types of people, those who are paragons of control and organisation and those who seem to live with a constant muddle all around them. I am sure you will not be surprised to learn that I am close to being one of those "paragons of control and organisation" (after all, just look at the way I described these two types of people!).

I still like being in control. My desk is always neat; topics on which I am working are neatly filed and put in order; my surroundings are always tidy. Before I go away on a trip, everything has been booked, checked, and listed: little is left to chance (and, as my wife reminds me, little has been left to spontaneous choice). I am better than I used to be, now channeling my obsessive tidiness into housework where it least has some benefit, and less risk of cutting into my creative time. Retirement has saved me in the sense I really do have time to do things that are rewarding, so now I write, enjoy photography, and luxuriate in times of solitude and reflection.

Control is a greedy monster, and it can gobble up all your time. Being willing to lose control over things is a way to release the time we should be devoting to rethinking and reflection. Indeed, the value of letting go and being willing to step back from always being in control is not about changing those activities themselves, of course, it is about their consequences. We change the way we live in order to give room to activities that otherwise get crowded out by the business

– perhaps I mean the busy-ness – of life. As I said before, busy does not mean productive, it means 'full'. Our lives can be full, but very non-productive. Nor does productive mean just producing things; you can be doing a lot, but not really thinking about it, acting more like a robot, and less like a human being, being pulled along by unseen elephants on roller skates. To go back to that quote from Socrates, a truly productive and worthwhile life has to be an examined life.

What is an examined life? It means a life where you are willing to take time out from the 'doing' of things to thinking about things. It means asking questions about yourself, what you are seeking to achieve with your life. It means asking questions about your relationships with other people, how you treat them, and what you understand in terms of what they are seeking to do with their lives. It means being willing to take nothing for granted, and making sure to take time out every so often and re-examine what otherwise will sink into the invisible area of embedded taken-for-granted assumptions, ideologies and beliefs (those things I have been calling elephants on roller skates throughout this book).

If we go back to Heidi and the challenges she faced when she found out about some duplicity in her workplace we can see a clear example of trying to live an examined life. I was impressed by Heidi, because she really did take some time out to try to work out what was the right thing to do. She didn't see herself as a paragon of virtue, nor did she see herself as a passive accessory to what had happened. She wanted to take action, and saw that choosing the right action to take was far from easy, and that whatever her choice there might be consequences she would prefer to avoid – at least insofar as she could control or influence them. She had an initial reaction to what she learnt, but was willing to let that go, in order to think more carefully. She was willing to accept that this was a situation in which she could not control the outcomes.

Both letting go and being willing to give away control are techniques to help create space, space to ensure you examine closely the life you are leading, and explore how you have enhanced the value and the richness of what you do both for yourself and for others. Rather than allowing yourself the short-term satisfaction of being busy, they are actions that help you ensure you have to time to reflect and do some things really well, and enjoy the longer-lasting satisfactions of seeing outcomes and achievements that are worthwhile.

It is not just a matter of time. Earlier in this book we looked at the power of ideologies, blinkered perspectives, which can keep running along unquestioned. There our concern was not so much about immediate actions as with the framework within which actions are planned. To act morally is usually far from straightforward: principles abound, they are often contradictory, and the need to be sensitive to circumstances is critical. As we saw when we looked at one moral viewpoint in particular, that of the importance of individual liberty, we realised that to advocate liberty and freedom of thought and action (albeit limited by the impact on others) is easy. To examine our right to liberty and the proper limits that should be put around that right is a very different matter.

Are we able to take on the task of paying attention to some of these issues? Socrates was very interested in human nature, and the way in which this seems to influence many things we do. We examined two elements of this, looking at whether or not it is in our nature to always want more, and whether or not we can really change our nature and our approach to life to achieve a greater alignment with the person we want to be in the future. If it is true that we are constantly looking to understand and do more, so we also saw that the question is not just about what is fundamental to how we behave (questions that we are still trying to address 2,500 years after Socrates), but it is also about how we analyse such issues as "more" and "change". As thinking and reflective beings, we can re-consider what we want to do, and understand that these behaviours can be rethought, and pursued quite differently.

The same challenges exist when we turn our focus to questions about how we pay attention to others and how we can live together. Socrates was concerned with justice, and some of the big questions about how we create a good and decent society. I have chosen to focus on some rather more domestic issues – what we mean by loyalty, tolerance, and a willingness to accept difference.

****

Why do people write books? No, that is not the right question. Why did I write this book? For me writing is a form of exploration, helping me to think through and understand issues that intrigue me. As I look back over this book, I realise it is a work in progress. Some parts are better thought through than others. In some of the earlier chapters I have taken up topics I have examined before, and this time around I think I have developed a more satisfying commentary. Some of the later chapters, on our ability to change and on keeping in touch; well, these certainly are works still in progress: I suspect I will be back worrying away at them again next year! I need time to think again, and I am not sure if I am correct in suggesting that we need to let go and lose some control in order to create the time needed for thinking and reflection. However, what I have said in these still incomplete and untidy attempts at examining issues may be enough to encourage you to explore a little further.

Elephants on roller skates: it seems a rather crazy metaphor. However, it is a metaphor for something very important, which is our tendency to stop thinking carefully, and to allow simple ideas, comfortable ideologies, and even untested assumptions to pull us along in life. We have some very precious skills. These include the ability to think, to reflect, and to examine what we are doing and what we could do. This book is my attempt to suggest that it is worth using these skills to live a life worth living.

Index

There are various short quotations in this book. Many of these are from sources that are no longer in copyright. Others have been included on the basis of "fair use".

Endnotes

[1] F M Cornford, Microcosmographia Academica: being a guide for the young academic politician, Cambridge, Bowes and Bowes, 1908

[2] Both quotes come from the facsimile edition, included in G Johnson, University Politics, Cambridge University press, 1994, page 105

[3] The elephant can conjure many varied associations. For Shakespeare, it was an image of power, limited by inflexibility and stupidity. For many it is the symbol of the Republican Party. For progressive thinkers today, George Lakoff recommends it as something you should *not* be thinking about if you want to reframe political debate.

[4] A good account of Sherron Watkins can be found in 'Sherron Watkins: the Party Crasher', by Jodie Morse and Amanda Bower, Time, 30 December, 2002

[5] See 'Whistle-Blower Awarded $104 m by IRS', by David Kocieniewski, New York Times, September 11, 2012

[6] Kant, I, *Grounding for the Metaphysics of Morals 3rd ed.* translated by James W. Ellington [1785] (1993), New York: Hackett. pp. 30

[7] Although many have developed the ideas of utilitarianism, it is Bentham who is usually seen as the seminal theorist: Bentham, Jeremy (January 2009), *An Introduction to the Principles of Morals and Legislation (Dover Philosophical Classics)*. Dover Publications Inc.. pp. 1

[8] A R Jonsen and S Toulmin, The Abuse of Casuistry, Berkeley: University of California Press, 1988

[9] The complexities of this issue are explored by Stephen Carter, in 'The dissent of the governed', Harvard, 1998: what follows is a great simplification of his important and revealing analysis

[10] See an excellent argument in favour of this approach in Richard Thaler and Cass Sunstein's book, Nudge: Improving Decisions about Health, Wealth and Happiness, 2008, Yale University Press: London and New Haven, especially pages 215-226

[11] www.mittromney.com

[12] The twist in that very clever novel being that no one knew what had made Gatsby successful, but he just appeared that way!

[13] Mill, J S, On Liberty, Chapter 1

[14] What isn't for sale, The Atlantic, April 2012

[15] The Price of Civilization, New York: Random House, 2011, page 46

[16] The Dian Rehm Show, NPR, Thursday 29 November, 2012

[17] Richard Titmuss, The Gift Relationship, London: Allen and Unwin, 1971

[18] This sense of reciprocity was explored in Marcel Mauss' seminal book, The Gift, published in English in 1954, London, Cohen and West

[19] Kenneth Arrow, Book Review; 'Gifts and Exchanges', Philosophy and Public Affairs, 1972

[20] J S Mill, On Liberty, available through Project Gutenberg, 1859, Chapter 1

[21] Viviana A Zelziger, The Purchase of Intimacy, Princeton University press, 2005

[22] Ibid, Chapter 1

[23] K Marx and F Engels, The Communist Manifesto, 1848

[24] Ibid

[25] Mill, Ibid, Chapter 1

[26] M Friedman, Capitalism and Freedom, Chicago: University Press, Revised, 2002, Chapter 1, page 15

[27] Ibid, pp. 34-6

[28] Supreme Court of the United States, Nos. 11-393, 11-198 and 11-400, Judgement of June 28, 2012

[29] See, for example, New York Times, 21 March 2012, 'Please stop apologizing' by Bill Maher

[30] Mill, op cit

[31] Richard H Thaler and Cass R Sunstein, 2008, Nudge: Improving decision about health, wealth and happiness, New haven and London: Yale University Press

[32] Friedman, op cit, page 15

[33] Wikipedia, Principality of Hutt River, as at 5 December, 2012

[34] Thomas Hobbes, Leviathan, Chapter XIII, Of the natural conditions of mankind, 1651

[35] Wikipedia, Amish, as at 26 December 2012

[36] P Singer, How are we to live? East Melbourne: Text, 1993, from pages 179-222

[37] Sherry Turkle, Alone Together, New York: Basic Books, 2012

[38] M L King, "I have a Dream", Speech in Washington, 28 August 1963, The Martin Luther King, Jr. Research and Education Institute

[39] M L King, Letter from Birmingham City Jail, April 16, 1963, reprinted in Why we Can't Wait, New York: Harper and Row, 1964

[40] A Smith, The Wealth of Nations, London: Strahan and Cadell, 1776, Book 4, Chapter 2

[41] "The Enfranchisement of Women," first appeared anonymously in the *Westminster Review* in 1851. These quotes come from the text in John Stuart Mill and Harriet Taylor Mill, *Essays on Sex Equality*. Alice Rossi, editor. Chicago: U of Chicago P, 1970

[42] M L King, Op Cit

[43] J Rawls, A Theory of Justice, Oxford: University Press, 1972

[44] If you want to read more about this, Michael Sandel explores this issue, and the debates it has aroused, in Liberalism and the Limits of Justice, Cambridge: University Press, 1982, especially pages 82-95

[45] J Rawls, Justice as fairness, Cambridge: Belknap, 2001, page 42

[46] Ibid, page 43

[47] Ibid, pages 85-88

[48] J Locke, Second Treatise on Government, Chapter V, 1690

[49] Ibid

[50] S Turkle, op cit

[51] See Chapter 14 of J Diamond, Collapse, New York: Viking, 2005

[52] E F Schumacher, Small is Beautiful, London: Blond and Briggs, 1973, Chapter 2

[53] Ibid

[54] An overview of this is provided in C Anderson, Makers: the new industrial revolution, London: Crown, 2012

[55] Halderman, J. Alex, and Felten, Edward, Lessons from the Sony CD DRM Episode, *Center for Information Technology Policy,* Department of Computer Science, Princeton University, 2006-02-14.

[56] Congressional Record, Volume 144, 1998, H1456-H1483, March 25, 1998

[57] See, for example, the Adelphi Charter put forward by the Royal Society for the Arts in London: 13 October 2005: this was a submission to the UK Government's Gower's Review of copyright, which continues to seek a way to balance public interest against commercial imperatives in this areas

[58] Kyle Jensen and Fiona Murray, "Intellectual Property Landscape of the Human Genome", *Science* (October 14, 2005)

[59] All this has come to a head in a challenge over breast cancer genes. The ACLU position is documented at - http://www.aclu.org/free-speech-womens-rights/aclu-challenges-patents-breast-cancer-genes. As I was writing this, the New York Times of 15 April 2013 reported that "Today the Supreme Court is scheduled to hear argument about that decision in Association for Molecular Pathology v. Myriad Genetics. The petitioners in the case — doctors, scientific researchers and women's health organizations — argue that the isolated genes are not materially different from genes before extraction, and that allowing Myriad a patent on them would allow the patenting of nature itself, at untold cost to scientific research, medical treatment and patients."

[60] Anonymous

[61] N Machiavelli, The Prince, 1532, Section 17: Of Cruelty and Clemency, and Whether It Is Better to Be Loved or Feared, available through the Gutenberg Project

[62] Ibid, Section 16: Of Liberality and Niggardliness

[63] Robert K Greenleaf, Servant Leadership, New York: Paulist Press, 1977

[64] Ken Binmore, Natural Justice, Oxford: University Press, 2005, page 186

[65] C Handy, Beyond Certainty, London: Hutchinson, 1995, Chapter 3, Balancing corporate power: a new federalist paper, page 41

[66] C Handy, Beyond Certainty, London: Hutchinson, 1995, page 63, reprinting 'What is a company for?', the Michael Shanks Memorial Lecture to the Royal Society for the Arts, Commerce and Manufactures, 1990

[67] Op cit, pages 70-72

[68] See a summary of the role of the Centre at http://www.tomorrowscompany.com/about-tomorrows-company-2

[69] 'Prancing On a Volcano', Vanity Fair, Letter from Washington, February 2013

[70] President Abraham Lincoln, annual message to Congress, December 1, 1862. Cited in The Collected Works of Abraham Lincoln, ed. Roy P. Basler, vol. 5, p. 537, Rutgers University Press, 1953

[71] R K Greenleaf, Servant Leadership, op cit

[72] David Simon website, The Audacity of Despair, http://davidsimon.com/dirt-under-the-rug/, 'Dirt under the rug', 18 June 2012

[73] Op cit

[74] A key researcher in this are is Carlota Perez, especially her book Technological Revolutions and Financial Capital, London: Edward Elgar, 2002

[75] The documentary was screened on PBS on 16 April, just three days before the 24th anniversary of the events in reported. Made by Ken Burns, Sarah Burns and David McMahon, the events it covers remain controversial: the police and city government would not contribute to the documentary, and some of Ken Burns long-term sponsors refused to support his making of this film.

[76] This is based on a summary of the events as reported in a New Yorker Daily Comment blog, The Saudi Marathon Man, by Amy Davidson, on 17 April 2013

[77] See, for example, the discussion in M Matravers, Responsibility and Justice, Cambridge: Polity, 2007, pages 71-80

[78] C Lasch, Revolt of the Elites, New York: Norton, 1995, pp. 44-5

[79] Ibid, page 49 - the actual wording reflecting the earlier draft of this article

[80] Putnam, Robert D. (1995), page 67 of 'Bowling Alone: America's Declining Social Capital', *Journal of Democracy* **6** (1): 65–78.

[81] Ibid, page 70

[82] E Becker, The Birth and Death of Meaning, Free Press, 1962, Reprinted by Penguin: London, 1971

[83] Ibid, Penguin edition, page 19

[84] Becker joined the staff at SUNY in 1960, teaching anthropology in the Psychiatry Department. A strong supporter of Thomas Szasz, whose views about the medicalization of illness were unpopular in the 1960's, he was dismissed in 1962, eventually ending up at Simon Fraser University, before his early death in 1974.

[85] New York: Free Press, 2012

[86] Dylan Evans, 'The Mask Falls', Aeon Magazine, 17 January 2013

[87] Anything Goes, Cole Porter lyrics and music, 1934; lyrics © Sony/ATV Music Publishing LLC, Royalty Network, Warner/Chappell Music, Inc., Universal Music Publishing Group

[88] As an example, differences in death rates and illness as a result of an extreme heat wave in Chicago in 1995 were found to relate to the strength of community interaction in different areas, as discussed in Eric Klinenberg, Heat Wave, University of Chicago Press, 2003

[89] These lectures were slightly revised and published in: Stephen L Carter, The Dissent of the Governed, published in 1998, Harvard University Press.

[90] The list comes from Maxwell Anderson's book The Quality Instinct, published by

AAM Press for the American Association of Museums, 2012.

[91] I explored this topic in some detail in an earlier book, in Chapter 9 of How Shall I Live, published by Travelling North in 2012

www.ingramcontent.com/pod-product-compliance
Lightning Source LLC
Chambersburg PA
CBHW022355280326
41935CB00007B/195